IN THE WORLD, YET NOT OF THE WORLD

Orthodox Christianity and Contemporary Thought

Series Editors: George Demacopoulos and Aristotle Papanikolaou

This series consists of books that seek to bring Orthodox Christianity into an engagement with contemporary forms of thought. Its goal is to promote (1) historical studies in Orthodox Christianity that are interdisciplinary, employ a variety of methods, and speak to contemporary issues; and (2) constructive theological arguments in conversation with patristic sources and that focus on contemporary questions ranging from the traditional theological and philosophical themes of God and human identity to cultural, political, economic, and ethical concerns. The books in the series will explore both the relevancy of Orthodox Christianity to contemporary challenges and the impact of contemporary modes of thought on Orthodox self-understandings.

IN THE WORLD, YET NOT OF THE WORLD

Social and Global Initiatives of Ecumenical Patriarch Bartholomew

ECUMENICAL PATRIARCH BARTHOLOMEW

Edited and with an Introduction by
JOHN CHRYSSAVGIS

FORDHAM UNIVERSITY PRESS
New York 2010

Library of Congress Cataloging-in-Publication Data

Bartholomew I, Ecumenical Patriarch of Constantinople, 1940–
[Selections. 2010]
In the world, yet not of the world : social and global initiatives of Ecumenical Patriarch Bartholomew / edited by John Chryssavgis.
p. cm.— (Orthodox Christianity and contemporary thought)
Includes bibliographical references and index.
ISBN 978–0-8232–3171–3 (cloth : alk. paper)
1. Orthodox Eastern Church. I. Chryssavgis, John. II. Title.
BX395.B37A25 2010
281.9—dc22

2009025831

Printed in the United States of America

12 11 10 5 4 3 2 1

First edition

Contents

Foreword

It gives me great pleasure to welcome, introduce, and recommend this book by His All Holiness Ecumenical Patriarch Bartholomew.

It has been a personal privilege for me to become acquainted with the ministry and initiatives of the Ecumenical Patriarch over the past few years, during which period we have both had occasion to exchange formal and informal visits at the European Commission in Brussels as well as at the Ecumenical Patriarchate in Istanbul.

The book is aptly entitled *In the World, Yet Not of the World* because Patriarch Bartholomew speaks from the depth of the Orthodox Christian tradition dating back to the earliest Apostolic community, while at the same time addressing the breadth of crucial global issues confronting our contemporary world. With his historical background and spiritual heritage, he speaks comfortably and convincingly—at once with authority and humility—about such burning problems as racial discrimination or religious tolerance, religion and politics, terrorism or corruption, human rights and freedom of conscience, as well as ecological protection and world hunger.

For almost two decades the Ecumenical Patriarch has provided extraordinary leadership on raising people's awareness about international peace and the natural environment. He has worked tirelessly for the reconciliation of Christian Churches and greater understanding among the major faith communities of the world. He has used his spiritual position and international profile to decry the global economy and the growing mistrust between East and West.

I know few religious leaders of his ecumenical stature who travel as widely to address such a diversity of audiences—religious and secular, political and social, interchurch or interfaith. This is why it is both a pleasure and a privilege to read these texts and messages, a documentary witness to the Ecumenical Patriarch's remarkable service and extraordinary ministry.

There is nothing either archaic or arcane about the statements of this religious leader. Patriarch Bartholomew knows how to connect seemingly unrelated worlds. It is no wonder he has been called a bridge builder. His words are influential and inspiring. And as such, they deserve the widest circulation and attention.

José Manuel Barroso
President, European Commission

Preface

This volume contains a selection of major addresses and significant messages as well as public statements initiated by His All Holiness Ecumenical Patriarch Bartholomew on a variety of critical social, global, and interfaith issues. The original documents have been edited solely for the sake of structure and consistency, while footnotes have been added to provide readers with the historical context of events or theological explanation of terms. Portions of this book have previously appeared in the Biographical Note and in Chapter 8 ("The Transfiguration of the World") of the Ecumenical Patriarch's *Encountering the Mystery: Understanding Orthodox Christianity Today* (New York: Doubleday, 2008) and appear here with the kind permission of Doubleday.

This book is the first in a projected series of three volumes that will feature a selection of texts by the Ecumenical Patriarch. The second volume will include his ecumenical and theological addresses, while the third volume will assemble his environmental statements.

Meanwhile, readers are encouraged to consult a separate volume, which represents the formal, comprehensive collection of the Ecumenical Patriarch's encyclical letters, addresses, and interviews on issues related to environmental degradation, global warming, and climate change. Topics covered include the ecological symposia and award responses as well as numerous related occasions, such as international conferences, ecclesiastical assemblies, and entries in journals. See John Chryssavgis, editor, *Cosmic Grace—Humble Prayer: Ecological Vision of the Green Patriarch Bartholomew I* (Grand Rapids, Mich.: Eerdmans, 2003; 2nd revised edition, 2009).

The present publication was originally inspired and sponsored through the Orthodox Christian Studies Program at Fordham University, which provides a venue for the academic study of Eastern Orthodox Christianity that is enriching for not only students and faculty but also the Orthodox and non-Orthodox communities in New York and throughout the United States. Dr. Aristotle Papanikolaou and Dr. George Demacopoulos serve as the co–founding directors of this program at Fordham University. I am deeply grateful to both of them for their gracious encouragement and support of this volume. Finally, I am indebted to the efficient editorial team at Fordham University Press for their cooperation in producing this book in a timely fashion: Fredric W. Nachbaur, Director; Eric Newman, Managing Editor; Loomis Mayer, Production and Design Director; Katie Sweeney, Publishing Assistant; Nicholas Frankovich, copy editor; and Johnna VanHoose Dinse, indexer.

J.C.

IN THE WORLD,
YET NOT OF THE WORLD

Introduction: Ecumenical Patriarch Bartholomew

Rev. Dr. John Chryssavgis

How can an ancient Christian faith, dating its liturgical existence and doctrinal expression to the earliest apostolic period, speak to a contemporary world? How can the "first among equals," the spiritual leader of 300 million Orthodox Christians throughout the world, address issues of critical concern from a tradition that spans twenty centuries? How can the Ecumenical Patriarch, living in historical Constantinople (modern-day Istanbul), assume a *leadership role on broader social and global matters*, even though the Ecumenical Patriarchate is a spiritual and not a political institution? How can a Church leader speak *in and to the world* from a perspective that is *yet neither of nor from the world?*

As readers consider the breadth of issues addressed by Ecumenical Patriarch Bartholomew, they will appreciate the unique theological and spiritual perspective that defines his worldview and determines his position on critical issues of our time. Indeed, the response to such crucial questions as social justice, peaceful coexistence, and religious tolerance is neither political nor secular. Rather, it is derived from a rich spiritual legacy informed by the heavenly kingdom. It is not easy sometimes to comprehend how the age-to-come can inform the affairs of this world. Yet, Orthodox theology draws its ultimate word from the "last times," from what—in theological terminology—is called "eschatology," or the study of the last events (*eschata*).

Most of us assume that "the last times" and "the last things" imply an apocalyptic or escapist attitude toward the world. It took a long time for theologians to realize that eschatology is not the last, perhaps unnecessary chapter in some systematic manual of dogmatics. Eschatology is not the teaching about what *follows* everything else in this world and in these times, but in fact the teaching about *our relationship to* those last things and last times. In essence, it is about the last-ness and the lasting-ness of all things of this world and age. It is the Omega that gives meaning to the Alpha; this world is always interpreted in light of the age-to-come.

Thus, as readers follow the thought of the Ecumenical Patriarch in his formal statements and pronouncements, they would do well to remember that he is always speaking as if he were living *in the world, yet not of the world.* It is this high-priestly vision that defines his responsibility toward and response to the world, and from which all his words and phrases ultimately assume their shape and form. However, in order to understand how this is possible, it will be helpful first to sketch his biographical outline.

Early Years and Education

The current Ecumenical Patriarch, Bartholomew, was born and baptized Dimitrios Archondonis on February 29, 1940, on the small island of Imvros (today known as Gokceada) off the coast of Turkey. On the day of his election, October 22, 1991, he became 270th Archbishop of the 2,000-year-old Church founded by St. Andrew, serving as Ecumenical Patriarch and Archbishop of Constantinople, New Rome. Since then, His All Holiness Bartholomew presides among all Orthodox Primates as the spiritual leader of 300 million faithful. From his childhood years through his ecclesiastical tenure, Patriarch Bartholomew has inherited a combination of authority and vulnerability alike.

The son of the local café proprietor (who sometimes also served as a barber) Christos Archondonis, the young Dimitrios grew up in the humble village of Saints Theodores on the small mountainous Aegean island.[1] Christos and Merope had four children: the eldest was a girl; Dimitrios

1. Theodore Teron (or the "recruit") and Theodore Stratelates (or the "general") were both military saints of the early Church. They are often closely associated in the Orthodox Church.

was the second of three boys. His father was strict; his mother was gentle. Dimitrios worked in the café during his summer vacations, acquiring social skills in the village center where people gathered to chat, drink coffee, and click their worry-beads as they discussed politics and the destiny of the world.

At the time, some 8,000 Orthodox Christians lived on Imvros. Today, although life has become peaceful once again, few inhabitants remain; much of its land has been confiscated; Greek schools have been closed; Saints Theodores is now called "Village of the Olive Trees." The village chapel of St. George has been restored at the initiative of the present Patriarch, while the priest currently serving the chapel is the son of the Patriarch's former parish priest, Fr. Asterios. Dimitrios' family used to own some property with a small chapel dedicated to St. Marina. To this day, an icon of the Saint in his bedroom reminds Patriarch Bartholomew of his childhood years; he also preserves some soil taken from that chapel, which his family would tend.

He was blessed with a spiritual father, the village pastor, Fr. Asterios, who called on the young Dimitrios to assist in the altar both in the village at the central church dedicated to St. George and whenever he traveled to the numerous remote, tiny white chapels that adorn the island's countryside. Fr. Asterios would walk for miles along narrow paths, through snow and rain, accompanied by a donkey carrying the young Dimitrios and the sacred vessels for the services. Although no one was present but the two of them, Fr. Asterios would look at his pocket watch and ring the bell when it was time to start the service with Dimitrios. Fr. Asterios was a faithful, elderly man with no formal education beyond the primary level; he would repeatedly make basic errors in reading the prayers and psalms. Yet, Dimitrios was early on inspired by the liturgy and ritual of the Orthodox Church as well as its spiritual practices and traditions. Fr. Asterios gave Dimitrios the fabric for his first vestment as a deacon. His son, Fr. George, serves to this day as the village priest.

The then–church head of Imvros and Tenedos was Metropolitan Meliton (1913–89),[2] a highly gifted and influential bishop in the hierarchy of Constantinople, who would surely have succeeded Patriarch Athenagoras (1886–1972) to the Ecumenical Throne had his name not been removed

2. Later Metropolitan of Chalcedon.

from the list of eligible candidates by Turkish authorities. Recognizing early on the diverse talents of the future Patriarch, Meliton took Dimitrios under his wing, supporting and directing him throughout his primary, secondary, and tertiary education, often at his own expense.

The Theological School of Halki

After completing elementary studies in his native village of Saints Theodores, Dimitrios traveled to the city of Constantinople, where he attended the junior high school of the Zographeion Lyceum. He returned to Imvros to attend the first years of his secondary education, walking daily a distance of five kilometers each way to the closest town, Panagia. Some of his early essays and favorite poems, preserved in the original manuscript exercise-books, have been recently published in Greece.[3] His senior secondary education and seminary formation took place at the prestigious Patriarchal Theological School of Halki, an island with two pine-covered hills among the "islands of the princes" on the Sea of Marmara.[4] In close proximity to Istanbul, which offers regular ferry service, Halki is a quaint island with no cars; people travel on foot or by carriage. There, numerous leaders of the (especially, but not only) Greek-speaking Orthodox world have been trained. There, also, aristocratic Greek families from Istanbul vacationed. The function of Halki has been diminished both as a secondary school and a graduate seminary since the late 1950s, and it was officially closed by Turkish authorities in the early 1970s. The magnificent nineteenth-century building contains a library of 40,000 books and historical manuscripts, as well as classrooms filled with old wooden desks, and spacious reception and dormitory rooms. It is Patriarch Bartholomew's dream and desire to reopen the Theological School. He persistently underlines the 1923 Treaty of Lausanne and Turkey's obligation to recognize the legal status of the Patriarchate as being ecumenical in scope and nature as well as to respect its right to educate its clergy and leaders.[5]

3. See, for example, *When I Was a Child* (Athens: Kastanioti Publications, 2003 [in Greek]).

4. In Byzantine times, disgraced princes would be exiled to this island.

5. The Ecumenical Patriarchate is recognized simply—legally—as a Turkish institution, while Turkish law from 1936 to this day places all Orthodox Christian property

Postgraduate Studies and Travels

After completing his undergraduate studies at the Theological School of Halki in 1961, Bartholomew served as a reserve officer in the Turkish military in Gallipoli from 1961 to 1963. During the same period, he was ordained to the diaconate in 1961, later to be ordained to the priesthood in 1969. It was at the time of his ordination to the diaconate that Dimitrios received the monastic name Bartholomew, in honor of an Imvrian monk who had lived on Mount Athos and edited liturgical texts. Patriarch Bartholomew still recalls his ordination as the fulfillment of all his dreams. The ordination to the diaconate was held at the Cathedral of Imvros.

Between ordinations, however, he pursued graduate studies at the Pontifical Oriental Institute, which is attached to the Gregorian University in Rome. The Institute was founded in 1917 by Benedict XV in the hope that Roman Catholic and Orthodox students would study together. In Rome, Bartholomew mastered Italian, Latin, and French. He was also exposed to the theology of Jean Daniélou (1905–74), Henri de Lubac (1896–1991), and Yves Congar (1904–95). Moreover, Bartholomew was in Rome during the sessions of the Second Vatican General Council (1962–65), the first time in centuries that any Orthodox representative was present at a Council of such magnitude. In Rome, Bartholomew completed his doctoral dissertation, "The Codification of the Holy Canons and the Canonical Constitution of the Orthodox Church," subsequently published in 1970 by the Patriarchal Institute of Patristic Studies in Thessaloniki (Greece). Bartholomew later became a founding member of the Society of Canon Law of the Oriental Churches, serving also as its vice president for multiple terms.

After his studies in Rome, Bartholomew was sent on scholarship by Patriarch Athenagoras to the Ecumenical Institute in Bossey (Switzerland), an academic center affiliated with the World Council of Churches and directed at the time by the progressive Greek Orthodox theologian

under the General Directorate of Foundations, which has the authority to dismiss foundations and seize property. Moreover, according to a 1974 ruling of the Turkish Supreme Court, the Turkish government forbids the purchase or sale of property by minority groups after 1936. For more information about the Ecumenical Patriarch's mission to reopen the Theological School of Halki, see the interview by G. Gilson, "Vartholomeos Demands Equal Rights," in *Athens News*, February 22, 2002, p. 3.

Prof. Nikos Nissiotis (1925–86), who was also Professor of the Philosophy and Psychology of Religion at the University of Athens. Under Nissiotis, Bartholomew was introduced to the contemporary philosophy of existentialism and personalism as well as to the understanding of theology in light of the mystery of the Holy Spirit. Finally, at the University of Munich, Bartholomew learned German and was initiated into the writings of such theologians as Karl Rahner (1904–84) and the current pope, Joseph Ratzinger (now Benedict XVI).

Return to Constantinople

During this period of his life, Bartholomew became well acquainted and worked closely with Patriarch Athenagoras, the renowned and charismatic leader of the Orthodox Church at the time, who later promoted Bartholomew to the rank of Archimandrite. Upon completion of his studies, Bartholomew returned to Constantinople in 1968, where he served as assistant dean at Halki Theological School from 1968 to 1972. Patriarch Athenagoras died in 1972, whereupon Bartholomew served as personal secretary to his successor, Patriarch Dimitrios (1972–90), whose side he never left. Bartholomew was elected Metropolitan of Philadelphia on Christmas Day 1973, while retaining his position as director of the private Patriarchal Office until 1990.

As personal and administrative assistant to the Ecumenical Patriarch, Bartholomew was largely responsible for many of the initiatives undertaken by the late Patriarch Dimitrios. These included a commitment to ecumenical relations through bilateral dialogues, such as the Theological Dialogue between the Roman Catholic and the Orthodox Churches, which officially opened in 1980. This "dialogue of truth" complemented and completed the "dialogue of love" previously initiated by Patriarch Athenagoras together with Popes John XXIII (1881–1963) and Paul VI (1897–1978). To date, this dialogue has produced three significant statements on the sacramental understanding of the Church (1982); on faith, sacraments, and the unity of the Church (1987); and on the ordained ministry (1988). It also attempted to deal with the thorny problem of Uniatism (1993). After a hiatus, the dialogue resumed its commitment and work in 2006.

Moreover, through the inspiration and collaboration of Bartholomew, Patriarch Dimitrios continued preparations for a forthcoming Great and Holy Council by convening three significant Pan-Orthodox Conferences at the Orthodox Center of the Ecumenical Patriarchate in Chambésy, Switzerland. Finally, in 1989, the Ecumenical Patriarchate initiated its worldwide efforts for the protection of the natural environment with the publication of an Encyclical Letter to all Orthodox Churches, establishing September 1—being the first day of the ecclesiastical calendar—as a day of prayer for God's creation.

In 1990, Bartholomew (then metropolitan of Philadelphia) was elected Metropolitan of Chalcedon, serving at a young age as the senior metropolitan on the Holy Synod and representing the Ecumenical Patriarchate on the highest levels at various commissions of interchurch and interreligious relations, accompanying Patriarch Dimitrios on numerous visits to Orthodox Churches and nations, while also effecting official visits to the pope, the archbishop of Canterbury, and the World Council of Churches; in the latter, Bartholomew served as a member of the Faith and Order Commission and as an elected member of the Executive and Central Committees.

Ecumenical Patriarch Bartholomew

When Patriarch Dimitrios died in 1991, Bartholomew was unanimously elected and enthusiastically received as the Ecumenical Patriarch, at the tender age of 51. He was solemnly enthroned on November 2, 1991. From the outset, Patriarch Bartholomew has been profoundly conscious of his commitment to the ancient see that he has inherited as its Primate, as well as of the vision that shapes and directs his ministry. For he serves at once as a son and a father of the Church, obligated simultaneously to adhere to and to advance its living tradition.

His tenure has been characterized by inter-Orthodox cooperation and inter-Christian and interreligious dialogue as well as by formal trips to other Orthodox countries seldom previously visited. He has exchanged official visitations with and accepted numerous invitations from ecclesiastical and state dignitaries. In his home city of Constantinople, Patriarch

Bartholomew has restored all of the existing churches, monasteries, pilgrim sites, and charitable centers that had formerly been either dilapidated or abandoned.

At the same time, the Ecumenical Patriarch has traveled more widely than any other Orthodox Patriarch in history; he has also conducted liturgical services in historically significant places in Asia Minor, such as Cappadocia and Pergamon, where acts of worship would have been unthinkable even twenty-five years ago. He has also received sympathetic, albeit sometimes controversial, attention in the Turkish media and been invited to offer public lectures in Turkish on Christian–Muslim relations.

Ecumenical Mission

His personal experience endows him, as a citizen of Turkey, with a unique perspective on religious tolerance and interfaith dialogue. The Ecumenical Patriarch Bartholomew has worked for reconciliation among Christian churches (through the World Council of Churches[6] and significant bilateral dialogues)[7] and has acquired an international reputation for environmental awareness and protection. He has worked to advance reconciliation among Catholic, Muslim, and Orthodox communities, such as in the former Yugoslavia, and is supportive of peace-building measures to defuse global conflict in the Balkans and ecclesiastical politics in the Ukraine. He has also presided over the restoration of the autocephalous Church of Albania and the autonomous Church of Estonia, proving a constant source of spiritual and moral support to those traditionally

6. He has served on the WCC Executive Committee and the Faith and Order Commission as well as attended general assemblies in New Delhi (1961), Uppsala (1968), Nairobi (1975), Vancouver (1983), and Canberra (1991).

7. He formally accepted the 1989 official statement of proposed unity between the Eastern Orthodox and Oriental Orthodox Churches and recently restored the official Theological Dialogue between the Orthodox and Roman Catholic Churches, which was established in 1980 but suspended its deliberations in 1998. The Dialogue resumed in September 2006. He has also revived the bilateral dialogue with the Anglican Communion and laid the foundations for discussions with other churches, such as the World Methodist Council.

Orthodox countries emerging from decades of wide-scale religious persecution behind the Iron Curtain.

The Ecumenical Patriarch's roles as the primary spiritual leader of the Orthodox Christian world and a transnational figure of global significance continue to become more vital each day. Patriarch Bartholomew has cosponsored international peace conferences as well as meetings on the subjects of racism and fundamentalism, bringing together Christians, Muslims, and Jews for the purpose of generating greater cooperation and mutual understanding. He has been invited to address the European Parliament, UNESCO, and the World Economic Forum as well as numerous national parliaments. His efforts to promote religious freedom and human rights and his initiatives to advance religious tolerance and mutual respect among the world's religions, together with his work toward international peace and environmental protection, earned him the Congressional Gold Medal of the United States Congress in 1997.

His initiatives for reconciliation include his efforts to raise environmental awareness throughout the world. He has organized annual educational seminars and institutes on the Island of Halki (1994–98), which were cosponsored by His Royal Highness Prince Philip, Duke of Edinburgh, as well as biennial international, interreligious, and interdisciplinary symposia (1995 to date) on the Mediterranean Sea, the Black Sea, the Danube River, the Adriatic Sea, the Baltic Sea, and, most recently, the Amazon River. Plans for a symposium on the Caspian have been postponed indefinitely, but it was planned to go to the Arctic in 2007.[8] These endeavors have earned Patriarch Bartholomew the title "Green Patriarch" and the award of several significant environmental prizes.

Ecumenical Patriarch Bartholomew holds numerous honorary doctorates, from institutions such as Athens and Thessaloniki (in Greece), Georgetown and Yale (in the United States), Flinders and Manila (in Australasia), and London, Edinburgh, and Leuven as well as Moscow and Bucharest (in Europe). Besides his native Greek and Turkish, he is fluent in English, Italian, German, French, English, classical Greek, and Latin.

---

8. Plans for a symposium in the Caspian (2007) were posptoned indefinitely, but a symposium was held in Greenland (2007) and another is currently planned for the Mississippi (2009).

The Patriarch as Bridgebuilder

"To build a bridge between the East and West has long been a major concern for His All-Holiness," noted Dr. Joël Delobel of the Catholic University of Leuven, Belgium, in conferring an honorary doctorate on Patriarch Bartholomew in 1996. "The Patriarch's entire life has been one of preparation for the task of bridge builder."

> The first of these bridges is one that reaches out to the various Orthodox churches. . . . The second bridge is one which reaches out to Europe, a bridge which has been created from the Patriarch's vigorous pleas for the extension of the European Union to the East and the Southeast of Europe. In the midst of current hesitation concerning the future of the Union, his unremitting plea for a complete Union and his concern for the protection of the environment are guiding lights for both East and West. The third bridge is one that will facilitate the dialogue between all the Christian churches.
>
> It is all the more important, then, that a church leader such as Patriarch Bartholomew travel all over the world to encourage mutual understanding, to face the problems and create solutions. There is no other way. Such bridge-builders are desperately needed.

As early as 1993, Patriarch Bartholomew intensified his wide-ranging outreach to the non-Orthodox world by traveling to Brussels in order to meet with the president of the Commission of the European Union, HE Jacques Delors, making such a powerful and positive impression that he was invited to address a plenary session of the European Parliament the following year. In 1994 and 2005, Patriarch Bartholomew also joined with the Appeal to Conscience Foundation to organize the International Conference on Peace and Tolerance held in Istanbul. The conference assembled Christians, Jews, and Muslims in an effort to reduce the friction between the various faiths and diminish the hostility that often results.

In 1995, during a visit to the Holy Land, Patriarch Bartholomew met not only with the Orthodox Patriarch of Jerusalem but also with Israeli Prime Minister Yitzhak Rabin and the PLO chairman Yasser Arafat. Later that same year, in addition to formal visits throughout the world in order to meet leaders and faithful in his own pastoral jurisdiction, he traveled to Norway, to celebrate the one thousandth anniversary of Christianity in that country; to Paris, to meet with President Jacques Chirac; and to

Lourdes, to address a conference of Roman Catholic prelates, as well as to Japan and England to attend international summit conferences on the environment. These visits not only indicate the busy schedule of the Ecumenical Patriarch but reflect the inner soul of an open-minded leader.

In 1997, Patriarch Bartholomew made his first official visit to the United States and the second ever by a Patriarch. During this visit he was awarded the highest honor bestowed by the United States Congress—namely, the Congressional Gold Medal of Honor—being praised by President Bill Clinton, at a dinner hosted at the White House, "as a great world leader who can inspire every American." In 2001, only weeks after the tragedy of September 11, Patriarch Bartholomew initiated a major interfaith conference in Brussels, cosponsored by the President of the European Commission, HE Romano Prodi. The Patriarch played a key role there in forging the Brussels Declaration, which affirmed, echoing the Berne Declaration of 1992, that "war in the name of religion is war against religion."[9]

In 2003, the Patriarch continued his program of visits to Orthodox communities around the globe and held the fifth of a series of meetings as part of a dialogue he helped initiate several years earlier between Jews and Orthodox Christians. The following year, he made a bold effort to build a bridge to a corner of the world most hostile to religion, namely, Cuba. Fidel Castro, whose government rebuilt a church belonging to the island's small Orthodox community as a gesture of respect for the Patriarch, personally welcomed the religious leader and praised him for his efforts to promote international understanding and environmental protection.

In early 2006, the Ecumenical Patriarch again visited the United States, where, after celebrating the Feast of the Epiphany (January 6) with Orthodox Christians, he flew to New Orleans to view the destruction of Hurricane Katrina and comfort victims of the natural disaster. A photograph on the front page of the *New York Times* pictured him walking through the wreckage of the city.

Throughout his ministry, Patriarch Bartholomew has focused on the people most in need and on the most difficult issues facing humanity. His tireless efforts on behalf of religious freedom, human rights, and protection of the natural environment have justly earned him a special place among the world's global leaders and foremost apostles of love, peace, and reconciliation.

---

9. For the full text, see Chapter 6, "Major Declarations: Public Proclamations."

The Patriarch as Peacemaker

As mentioned, one of his favorite phrases has been "War in the name of religion is war against religion."[10] The Patriarch knows what it is like to be under siege. His see, established in the fourth century and once possessing holdings as vast as the Vatican, has been reduced to a small, besieged enclave in a decaying corner of Istanbul called the Phanar ("lighthouse"). Almost all of its property has been seized by successive Turkish governments. Its schools have been closed, and its prelates are taunted by extremists who demonstrate almost daily outside the Patriarchate, calling for its ouster from Turkey.

The Patriarch himself is often jeered at and threatened when he ventures outside this enclave. His effigy is periodically burned by Turkish extremists and Muslim fanatics. Petty bureaucrats take pleasure in harassing him, summoning him to their offices to question him about irrelevant issues, blocking his efforts to make repairs in the few buildings still under his control, and issuing veiled threats about what he says and does when he travels abroad. The Turkish government as a whole follows a policy that deliberately belittles him, refusing to recognize his ecumenical status as the spiritual leader of a major religious faith but only as the head of the small Greek Orthodox community of Istanbul.

Yet none of the abuse Bartholomew has either experienced or witnessed has lessened his compassion and support for the Turkish people and his determination to serve as a bridge between Turkey and Europe. Despite his difficulties with the government, he has supported all international efforts to strengthen Turkey's economy and democracy, often inviting severe criticism from Greek conservatives. He has been a fervent advocate of Turkey's efforts to join the European Union, traveling widely throughout Europe to speak out in favor of its admission. "The incorporation of Turkey into the European Union," he told Europeans in several capitals, "may well provide a powerful symbol of mutually beneficial cooperation between the Western and Islamic worlds and put an end to the talk of a

---

10. This section draws on comments by Prof. John Silber, president emeritus of Boston University. See his article entitled "Patriarch Bartholomew—a Passion for Peace," at www.patriarchate.org.

'clash of civilizations.'" The unqualified support of such an eminent Christian leader has helped blunt the opposition both of the European Union, which opened negotiations with Turkey at the end of 2004, and of many skeptics in Europe who doubt the wisdom of admitting a predominantly Muslim country of 70 million.

At a time when hostility and misunderstanding between the Christian West and the Muslim world have reached a deadly standoff, Patriarch Bartholomew is making a deliberate effort to reach out to Muslims throughout the Middle East. "It is our strong belief that Orthodox Christians have a special responsibility to assist East–West rapprochement," he affirms. "For, like the Turkish Republic, we have a foot in both worlds."

Pointing out that Orthodox Christians have a 550-year history of coexistence with Muslims in the Middle East, he has initiated a series of meetings with Muslim leaders throughout the region in what he calls "a dialogue of loving truth." In order to strengthen that dialogue, he has traveled to Libya, Syria, Egypt, Iran, Jordan, Azerbaijan, Qatar, Kazakhstan, and Bahrain and met political and religious figures in those countries whom no other Christian hierarch has ever visited. As a result, the Patriarch has earned greater credibility and achieved more opportunity to create bridges between Christianity and Islam than any other prominent Christian leader.

Patriarch Bartholomew has used the international respect he enjoys both in the West and in the Muslim world to create a strong front among religious leaders against the use of violence. During the conference that he organized in Brussels in the aftermath of September 11,[11] he addressed strong words about religious extremists and terrorists, noting to *Time* magazine that "they may be the most wicked false prophets of all. When they bomb, shoot and destroy, they steal more than life itself; they undermine faith, and faith is the only way to break the cycle of hatred and retribution."

Ecumenical Patriarch Bartholomew feels that he is a servant of the Church, while at the same time being defined by his mission; in the words of St. Barsanuphius the Great (d. 543), he is "but . . . a servant on

11. For the full text, see Chapter 6, "Major Declarations: Public Proclamations."

a mission."[12] Over the past eighteen years, Ecumenical Patriarch Bartholomew's inclination and intention has been to address the most difficult issues facing the world—the deep and ever increasing mistrust between East and West, the decay and ever widening destruction of the natural environment, and the sharp divisions among the various Christian confessions and diverse faith communities—whether on religious, racial, or cultural levels. He regards it as a primary obligation of his spiritual ministry to be a servant of reconciliation—no matter how extensive the cost, no matter how little the reward, and no matter how numerous the individual tasks at hand. For the Ecumenical Patriarch, the material and spiritual, the liturgical and the pastoral, the global and the local are intimately and inextricably interconnected.

Indeed, Patriarch Bartholomew is *as comfortable preaching about the spiritual legacy of the Orthodox Church as he is promoting sociopolitical issues of his immediate cultural environment and praying for respect toward Islam or for global peace.* It is almost impossible to fathom the intensity of his daily routine or imagine the breadth of the tasks that he balances. These could quite easily involve a scheduled appearance or address at an international or local conference, a presentation or open forum at a political meeting or parliament, or indeed an official visit to a sister Church or foreign nation. What is perhaps most impressive is not so much the ordinary business or daily schedule, which in itself is surely exceptional and extraordinary. Rather, it is the personal encounter with numerous individuals and the pastoral engagement with diverse groups that keep the Patriarch grounded in reality and even humility.

The difficulty of the issues he grapples with as he ventures out in the world does not daunt him any more than the abuse he must endure every day at home in Turkey. He knows that reconstructing bridges can happen only stone by stone, that reestablishing peace and understanding can only take place gradually and humbly, and that rebuilding openness and trust can occur only with sensitivity and authenticity. Yet, he is determined to persevere. He wants to make a difference. And it is abundantly clear to those who have witnessed his struggle—both in the past two decades during his tenure as Ecumenical Patriarch and, before that, as a senior hierarch at the Phanar—that his effort is already bearing fruit.

---

12. *Letter* 139. See J. Chryssavgis, *Letters from the Desert: A Selection from the Letters of Barsanuphius and John* (Crestwood, N.Y.: St. Vladimir's Seminary Press, 2003).

1

The Ecumenical Patriarchate: Visionary Ministry

Mapping the Future: Enthronement Address

In the Church of St. George at the Phanar, Istanbul, November 2, 1991. Bartholomew was elected archbishop of Constantinople, New Rome, and Ecumenical Patriarch on October 22, 1991.

Venerating the Holy, Consubstantial, Life-giving and Undivided Trinity, obedient to the will of the One Lord as expressed by the Church through the unanimous canonical ballot of the holy Brotherhood, and professing the holy Orthodox Christian faith, we assume from the hands of the blessed Dimitrios I, great among Patriarchs, the Cross of Andrew the First-called[1] in order to continue the ascent to the Place of the Skull, to be co-crucified with our Lord and His co-crucified Church, to perpetuate the light of the Resurrection.

Only by interpreting in this manner the canonical ballot of the most respected hierarchy of this venerable Ecumenical Throne and "being in a wondrous state" by the events that surround us these days (see Lk. 24.18) have we accepted the sacred responsibilities of piloting this spiritual ship, the Church of Constantinople, which "was established out of piety and has shown forth shepherds equal to the apostles—as their successor, I, the unworthy, have come—and which the Chief and First-called among the

1. The Church of Constantinople is traditionally regarded as being founded by St. Andrew. Its first bishop of Byzantium was Stachys (38–54), a disciple of the Apostle Andrew. The patronal feast, or "feast of the throne," is celebrated on November 30.

apostles had as a foundation," as we might say with Symeon of Thessaloniki.[2]

Already, being conscious of our unworthiness and humbleness, and looking ahead to the insupportable cross, which we have borne, we seek refuge in the mercy of the Lord and we invoke His grace in order that He might enable us to perfect His power in our infirmity (2 Cor. 12.9).

Indeed, the tremendous concerns which the Patriarch of New Rome assumes and the various temptations and adverse influences which he must battle demand that he be experienced in the task of piloting the great ship. Thus, in self-emptiness, we approach at this moment the burning and unconsumed bush of the Ecumenical Patriarchy—by which we are called to see God—in the service of the mystery of unbroken apostolicity, in *diakonia*[3] and witness of Orthodoxy, and to the edification of Christian unity.

Speaking for the first time from this Holy See, we say before all else, along with our predecessor among the saints, John Chrysostom,[4] "glory to God for all things."

Ministry in Conciliarity

Then, turning in deep respect and sincere love to the august college of Hierarchs of the Throne, to those here and everywhere in the *oikoumene*,[5] to those who have cast their ballot willingly, we offer wholeheartedly our thanks for their indeed moving vote of confidence, which they have placed in our humble person. We affirm again along with the holy shepherd of the Thessalonians: "You, therefore, brothers, have accepted me hospitably and have honored me greatly, you have displayed much love"

2. Archbishop of Thessaloniki (1416–29), Symeon is the author of influential liturgical commentaries. See the forthcoming book by Stephen Hawkes-Teeples, *St. Symeon of Thessalonika: The Liturgical Commentaries* (Rome: Pontifical Institute of Mediaeval Studies Publications, 2009).

3. Greek for *service* or *ministry.*

4. John Chrysostom (347–407) was archbishop of Constantinople. See J. N. D. Kelly, *Golden Mouth: The Story of John Chrysostom—Ascetic, Preacher, Bishop* (Grand Rapids, Mich.: Baker, 1998).

5. Greek for *universe* or *world,* a term originally used in Greco-Roman times to refer to the inhabited world. The term also implies a united Christendom or civilization.

and, as Paul said, "you have accepted me as a messenger of God, as Jesus Christ. You have given yourselves to the Lord first and then to me through the will of God, for which I have offered favor to God and am forever thankful."

Hence, we state from the outset that not only shall we follow the canonical order of our Orthodox Church and respect in particular the venerated tradition and praxis of the Great Church of Christ but, moreover, being firmly convinced by sacred experience of the indispensable value of conciliarity[6] through which the Holy Spirit speaks to the Church, we shall walk the road of the *diakonia* of the Church only under her light, within her framework and in her canonical function, in harmony with our most respected brothers and co-celebrants in Christ. In saying this, by no means do we restrict our conviction and intention on this capital subject to those things that concern only our Most Holy Church of Constantinople, but we extend this sacred confession and declaration also to all that concerns the whole Orthodox Church worldwide.

On this auspicious occasion, on which before God and man we accept the responsibilities of this ecumenical watchtower, we should like to state that we assume our responsibilities under the protection of the constitution and the laws of the Republic of Turkey. Continuing the age-old tradition of the Patriarchs after the Fall, we shall remain a faithful and law-abiding citizen of our country, as are our spiritual children of the Church here, ministering to God and following the command of the Lord by giving honestly and sincerely, rendering unto Caesar what is Caesar's (Mt. 22.21). On this point, we deem it our responsible obligation to state clearly that the Ecumenical Patriarchate shall remain a purely spiritual institution, a symbol of reconciliation and an unarmed force. Exercising the components of our holy Orthodox faith, safeguarding and conducting itself with regard to pan-Orthodox jurisdictions, the Ecumenical Patriarchate is detached from all politics, keeping itself far from "the smoky hubris of secular authority." Besides, human power alone, as well as everything else that is human, is nothing else but vanity and delusion of power.

6. The Orthodox Church attaches fundamental ecclesiological importance to the synodical, or conciliar, system of governance. Together with the concept of primacy, synodality, or conciliarity, constitutes the backbone of the Church's government and organization. This interdependence between synodality and primacy runs through all the levels of the Church's life: local, regional, and universal.

We express our fervent thanks to the honorable Greek government readily represented on this auspicious occasion by its head, his Excellency Constantine Mitsotakis, followed by his chosen collaborators. From the height of this Throne we bless the pious Greek Orthodox people in whose behalf an official parliamentary delegation is here present.

We also reiterate from this position the thanks of the Ecumenical Patriarchate and the personal thanks of our Humble Selves to His Excellency the President of the United States of America, who desired to send an official delegation of the White House to our Enthronement.

Now, with all our love and affection, we address our flock here with whom at this moment we draw up a testament in the Lord. Unhesitatingly, we state that we shall be a shepherd, ready to sacrifice his soul for his sheep. But we also make the same promise—to the entire *pleroma*[7] of the Holy and Great Church of Christ, in Crete and the Dodecanese, in Epirus and Macedonia, in Thrace and the Islands, in the so-called New Regions which live aggregately, in North and South America, in Australia

7. Greek for *fullness* or *plenitude*, signifying the breadth of the immediate jurisdiction of the Ecumenical Patriarchate worldwide, including the Archdiocese of Constantinople, together with the four metropolitan sees in Asia Minor, namely Chalcedon, Derkon, Imvros (with Tenedos), and the Prince's Islands; the thirty-six metropolitanates of the "New Lands" in Northern Greece; the semiautonomous Archdiocese of Crete; the five metropolitanates of the Dodecanese Islands; the Archdiocese of (North) America; the Archdiocese of Australia; the Archdiocese of Thyateira and Great Britain (with Western Europe, Malta, and Ireland); the Metropolitanates of France, Germany (and central Europe), Austria (with Hungary and Mid-Europe), Sweden and all Scandinavia, Belgium, New Zealand (and Japan), Switzerland, Italy (and Southern Europe), Toronto (and Canada); the Ukrainian Diocese of Canada; the Metropolitanates of Buenos Aires (Argentina and South America), Panama (and Central America), Hong Kong (with India, the Philippine Islands, Singapore, and Indonesia), Spain and Portugal, and Korea; the Exarchate of the Russian Orthodox Parishes in Western Europe; a number of Patriarchal and Stavropegic institutions, such as the monastery of St. John the Evangelist on the island of Patmos, the monastic republic of twenty communities and numerous hermitages on Mount Athos, the historical monasteries of Vlatades and St. Anastasia in Thessaloniki, and others; a number of international Patriarchal Institutes, such as the Patristic Institute in Thessaloniki, the Orthodox Center in Chambésy, the Orthodox Academy in Crete, and others; and a number of organizations worldwide, such as the Permanent Representative Office in the World Council of Churches, the Orthodox Liaison Office in the European Union, the Patriarchal Representative Office in Athens.

and Europe—that we shall be vigilant in all things and that in no way shall we be paternally negligent in serving them from here.

Therefore, to Their Eminences, the archbishops and metropolitans, and Their Graces, the bishops who have been entrusted directly with the shepherding of this most beloved worldwide *pleroma* of the Mother Church, we extend our embrace of love and peace in Christ and the assurance of our close and fraternal collaboration with them, both for the good of the flock but also in the broader sacred interest of the Throne. We shall convoke gatherings of the entire venerable hierarchy of the Ecumenical Patriarchate in this see as often as possible, for the mutual exchange of information, support, and common projection of the Orthodox faith. . . .

Proceeding beyond our immediate canonical jurisdiction, we direct our thoughts to the messengers "of the Orthodox churches which are constituted and illuminated by the one Spirit of Christ" [the heads of autocephalous Orthodox churches] . . ..[8] United in this common faith, in the common Chalice and in love that activates faith, we extend our hand of communion to our venerable colleagues, the primates, and we promise that in collective responsibility with them we shall give witness in the midst of a divided world that desires unity and reconciliation as perhaps never before in history.

This witness of Orthodoxy is much more necessary and imperative today, as Divine Providence has reserved us to behold the indeed rapid world-changing evolutions and developments in the life of the people of the world—evolutions and changes that bring to contemporary man the hope of a better future, a future of peace, freedom, and respect of human dignity. These rapid rearrangements have taken place and are still taking place, mostly in countries and among peoples who are, by tradition, Orthodox, and therefore it is mainly the Orthodox churches that are more influenced by them. It is therefore natural, particularly for the Orthodox churches, to be called to vigilance, collaboration, and service, so that these

8. Autocephalous Churches include the ancient patriarchates of Alexandria, Antioch, and Jerusalem (together with the ancient Archdiocese of Mt. Sinai), the patriarchates of Russia, Serbia, Romania, Bulgaria, and Georgia, as well as the Churches of Cyprus, Greece, Poland, Albania, and the Church of the Czech Lands and Slovakia. Autonomous Churches include those of Finland and of Estonia.

developments might indeed result in what will benefit man, who has suffered greatly in our century.

Orthodoxy has much, much more to offer to the world of today. In Orthodoxy, one can find not only the correct faith in the true God but also the correct perception of man as the image of God, of the world, and of creation.

An Ecumenical Ministry

We extend the kiss of peace and love to the venerable primates of the Armenian, Coptic, Ethiopian, and Syrian—in Damascus and in Malabar—churches.[9] Their closeness to us in the Orthodox faith leads us today to the active quest, with possibly early results, for the common confession of faith and expression in the common Chalice.

From this sacred courtyard, we also greet His Holiness the Pope of the Elder Rome, John Paul II, with whom we are in "a communion of love."[10] We assure him that a most serious concern for us shall be the realization of the sacred vision of our late predecessors, Athenagoras and Dimitrios, so that the way of the Lord will be fulfilled on earth for his holy Church in the reunion of all who believe in Him through "the dialogue of truth."[11] We shall do everything in our power to move in this direction, in fear of God, sincerity, honesty, and prudence. We are convinced that our brother in the West will exhaust all the many possibilities at his disposal and cooperate with us toward this sacred and holy objective.

Out of deep esteem we embrace in the Lord the venerable primate of the Church of England, the archbishop of Canterbury George Carey, and

---

9. See John Meyendorff, *Imperial Unity and Christian Divisions: The Church 450–680* AD (Crestwood, N.Y.: St. Vladimir's Seminary Press, 1989).

10. The dialogue of love was a journey of mutual embrace established by Ecumenical Patriarch Athenagoras and Popes John XXIII and Paul VI.

11. The official theological dialogue between the Roman Catholic and Orthodox Churches commenced in 1980 with the establishment of the Joint International Commission by Ecumenical Patriarch Dimitrios and Pope John Paul II. To date, the Commission has met in Patmos and Rhodes (1980), Munich (1982), Crete (1984), Bari (1987), Valamo (1988), Freising (1990), Balamand (1993), Baltimore (2000), Belgrade (2006), and Ravenna (2007).

the entire Anglican Communion. Manifesting our intention to continue with faithfulness the long tradition of fraternal relations with the Anglican Church, we express our desire to promote our theological dialogue until we achieve the unity of faith.

In the same spirit we greet and embrace the Old Catholic Church throughout the world in the person of its venerable primate, Archbishop Anthony of Utrecht, expressing the sincere wish that the dialogue with his Church will lead us to the glory of Christ.

With feelings of peace and love, we embrace with the kiss of Christ all the other Christian churches and confessions—the Lutheran and the Reformed, with whom we are also in theological dialogue; the Methodists, with whom we are in the preparatory stages of dialogue; and the Christian communities one and all throughout the world, as many as believe and preach, according to the scriptures, the crucified Christ and bear the good spirit, that they may partake of the common banquet of the faith in the unity of the apostolic-patristic tradition.

From this sacred see, we extend a most special greeting in Christ to the World Council of Churches, to the president of the Central Committee who is among us, to the general secretary, his inestimable staff, and to all the member churches. We were fortunate for many years and in various capacities to cooperate and struggle along with the Christians of the Council and to share each other's anxieties in the quest for and the edification of Christian unity and also the Christian position and witness on the contemporary problems of humankind. We recognize this Council as an important expression of the ecumenical movement and the schematic function of the ecumenical spirit. The Ecumenical Patriarchate, being one of the founding members of this Council, will not diminish its concern for the good and correct orientation of the Council and its concern that there not be a departure from its first and principal mission, which is the service of Christian unity. This is the position of all churches in the East before the World Council of Churches, as our common action on the issues at hand both in Canberra, Australia, and Chambésy, Geneva, has proven.

Furthermore, we greet here present among us the honorable secretary general of the Council of European Churches, of which the Ecumenical Patriarchate is a member. Through him we extend our greeting in Christ to all its member churches.

We shall not be idle in promoting good relations with the major non-Christian religions, with the aim of cooperating on the practical level for the safeguard and preservation of the great spiritual and moral values of true civilization and for the rejection of every negative and catastrophic force to the human person.

If necessary, we shall not refuse to dialogue even with those who ignore, reject, and even insult God. Rather, we shall transmit to them—indeed, to them—the witness of the love of Christ, who left the ninety-nine in search of the one, because Christ was crucified also for it (Mt. 18.12).

The Great Church of Christ, called from above and from the beginning to be a church of evangelization, cannot deny herself. She cannot but evangelize and be continually re-evangelized. "And woe to me if I do not proclaim the Gospel" (1 Cor. 9.16).

We extend our special paternal greetings and heartfelt Patriarchal blessing to the youth, who constitute not only our future but also our dynamic present, since there is no future without the present. From the Mother Church, we express her and our boundless and sincere empathy with regard to the problems of contemporary youth throughout the world and consider these problems to be ours. . . .

Pray for us, all of you, who have come "from the West and the North, by sea and the East" in order to install us on this sacred cathedra of the Apostle Stachys as yet another in the long line of his successors. Pray that, faithfully and favorably to God, we may serve the Lord, this most holy church, and Orthodoxy under the heavens. Pray that we may sustain our people and maintain the privileges and the rights of this most venerable Throne, which "we sign with great pleasure," as our predecessor to the Throne of Chalcedon, Eleutherios, affirmed at the Fourth Ecumenical Synod. Pray that we are at all times a tool of the will of God in the service of all of humanity. Pray that our tenure will be unharmed, bountiful, hopeful, unhindered, according to the names and through the intercessions of the martyrs from Persia whom the Church commemorates today. Pray that the Lord will sustain the Church, strengthen the faith, and bring peace to the world. . . .

Again and many times over, "glory to God for all things."

"God is love" (1 John 4.16).

A Beacon of Hope: The Ecumenical Patriarchate

At the conferral of an honorary doctorate at the Fletcher School of Law and Diplomacy, Tufts University, Massachusetts, October 29, 1997.

We are deeply grateful for the honor you bestow on us today. We accept this honor not as an individual but on behalf of the Holy Orthodox Church's more than 300 million communicants, whom we humbly serve as Ecumenical Patriarch. Receipt of this honorary degree, a doctorate of International Laws from Tufts University, encourages our reflection as well as gratitude. We are heartened by the message of hope, optimism, and willingness to serve, reflected in the conferral of this honor. Likewise, we are sobered by the challenges and the yet unrealized potential that this degree brings to mind.

It is only appropriate that an institution such as Tufts University, with a long and successful history of combining intellectual creativity with constructive activism, should make the decision to confer this degree on our Modesty and, in so doing, on the Mother Church of Constantinople. Your university's history demonstrates recognition of the importance of moving beyond arid intellectualism, which results in excesses of rationalism and unidimensional secularism.

Tufts is an authentic model of the university as lived from antiquity until the high Middle Ages. Tufts University has remained loyal to the classical ideal of the university as an environment in which the noble pursuit of truth imposes no boundaries on the human intellect and spirit. This is evidenced by the diversity of your institution's programs in disciplines and professional domains. These include veterinary sciences, medicine, engineering, international relations, physics, religion and philosophy, and the arts. In short, we understand your conferral of this honorary degree on our Modesty as a shining example of your university's self-perception as an icon, a door and a threshold, which invites students to pass into a place where their pursuit of truth takes them on an adventure of inquiry into things both secular and sacred.

Our presence here today reflects Tufts's commitment to education as a voyage of discovery into truths reflected in the universe of both spiritual and temporal realities. We are also encouraged by the lived expressions of your commitment to education as a mission of service and activism.

Again, in their willingness to serve, the faculty, students, and alumni of Tufts University have demonstrated an extraordinary awareness of the spiritual aspects of our humanity. More specifically, you recognize religion as a profound and powerful force for peace and reconciliation in the world.

Indeed, one of your university's flagship schools, the Fletcher School of Law and Diplomacy, is a brilliant exemplar of the view that the path to global peace involves, rather demands, visionary leadership and daring policy initiatives. In this respect, the Fletcher School of Law and Diplomacy represents the holistic philosophy of education, which characterizes Tufts University as a whole. Your university stands at the forefront of scholarship and policymaking in international affairs, precisely because of the recognition that the world's great religions offer incredible resources. Whether through individual leaders, communities, or ideas, these resources must be incorporated in the efforts to secure the ideals of the late twentieth century.

The Potential of Orthodoxy

Dear friends, we accept today's honorary degree with full awareness of the responsibility which accompany a doctorate in International Laws from a university such as Tufts. By the same token, we offer up the Holy Catholic and Apostolic Orthodox Church as uniquely endowed with worldwide and historical experiences and exceptionally suited to meeting the challenges of global peace on the eve of the new millennium.

However, in humbly offering ourselves to this service, we also exhort you to help create the possibilities for Orthodox Christianity to contribute to this process of building peace. Sadly enough, Orthodox Christianity—despite its more than 300 million communicants in countries as far-flung as the United States, Panama, Israel, Kenya, Greece, Turkey, Russia, Ukraine, Korea, Australia, Japan, and many others, despite its unbroken continuity of tradition with the Church of Christ, and despite its survival of systematic persecution in former communist countries over the better part of this century—remains largely unknown to scholars well versed in the Western Christian churches as well as in the four world religions of Judaism, Islam, Hinduism, and Buddhism.

Equally discouraging is that, despite the richness of Orthodox Christian theology and the reemergence of the institutional Orthodox Church in Eastern Europe, policymakers involved in traditional diplomacy, and nongovernmental organizations involved in efforts at conflict resolution, have failed to engage the community-building and reconciliation potential of the Orthodox Church.

Clearly, our presence here today indicates that Orthodox Christianity is not terra incognita for the scholars and practitioners who make up the Tufts University family. However, our optimism about your recognition is necessarily tempered by the realities just mentioned. We are aware of the challenges associated with introducing Orthodoxy into rich scholarly debates begun in the intellectual tradition of Max Weber. We are cognizant of the even greater challenges related to educating policymakers about the democracy-building and peacemaking potential of Orthodox churches across the globe.

However, above all, as believers in the God-given possibility for the salvific transfiguration of each and every member of humankind, we are confident in the unique contributions, which the theory and praxis[12] of the Orthodox Christian Church can make toward peace in our time and our common future.

As the Ecumenical Patriarch, the "first among equals" of all the Orthodox churches, we would like to take a few moments to share with you some of the most crucial, yet not fully known, and, likewise, not fully accessed, strengths of the Orthodox Church. We have much to contribute to the efforts of teachers, researchers, and policymakers inasmuch as we are committed to making religion a force for the prevention and resolution of conflicts that continue to undermine the security of human beings in societies.

Three Principles of Orthodoxy

We suggest to you three particular strengths of Orthodox Christianity,[13] which our Church can bring to bear in cooperation with these efforts. We

12. Greek for *practice* or *application.*

13. See Timothy Ware, *The Orthodox Church*, 2nd ed. (London and New York: Penguin, 1993).

accept the reality of the nation-state, but we categorically reject systems of repression and oppression that are premised on parochial nationalism, fragmenting communalism, and aggressive expansionism.

We begin with the first strength, which is Orthodox Christianity's conception of the human being as person, such that personhood is an ontological category of being. This theological thinking is deeply rooted in our tradition, which understands God as a Trinity—a community, if you will, of Persons.[14] The human being, as an existential reality, can be a person only when he lives in freedom. Only in a condition that reflects the whole range of possibility open to us through conscious choice are we able to transform ourselves and our temporal reality into the image of the Divine Kingdom. Our humanity is realized through the free act of relationship with others. Personhood is a free act of communion that makes heterogeneity and uniqueness fundamental aspects of our humanity.

In addition to its conception of personhood, Orthodox Christianity brings a second strength to efforts at international peacemaking and reconciliation. Specifically, Orthodox Christianity is a way of life wherein there is a profound and direct relationship between dogma and praxis, faith and life.[15] This unity of faith and life means that the reality of the eternal truths lies in their experiential power rather than in their codification into a set of ideological constructs. Furthermore, the equal importance of creed and experience points to an understanding of Holy Tradition as the living continuity of the personal encounter of man with God.

Third and finally, Orthodox Christianity understands the inherent character of all creation—both humankind and the physical, or natural, environment—in terms of its original and potential integrity.[16] Because the inherent character of all creation lies in its whole, unified integrity, an integrity that has been disrupted by the disintegrating actions of mankind,

14. See John Zizioulas, *Being as Communion: Studies in Personhood and the Church* (Crestwood, N.Y.: St. Vladimir's Seminary Press, 1985).

15. See Vladimir Lossky, *The Mystical Theology of the Eastern Church* (Crestwood, N.Y.: St. Vladimir's Seminary Press, 1976).

16. For a full bibliography, see John Chryssavgis, *Cosmic Grace—Humble Prayer: Ecological Vision of the Green Patriarch Bartholomew I* (Grand Rapids, Mich.: Eerdmans, 2003).

the salvation of all creation can come only through the restoration of the innate harmony expressed in the Divine Kingdom.

Global Significance of Orthodox Principles

You may wonder what relevance these three concepts—first, personhood; second, way of life; and third, integration—have for peace in the international system. You may argue that these three concepts are nothing more than theological abstractions divorced from the hard realities of a world marred by abominations committed in the name of religion. You may consider these concepts hypocritical meandering in the face of the economic blight, political charlatanism, cultural discrimination, military savagery, and environmental toxification that destroy individuals, villages, cities, nations, and regions with near inconceivable regularity. Indeed, we may wonder why it is that we have presented these three concepts as the potential strengths that the Orthodox Christian Church brings to the processes dedicated to encouraging order, providing meaning, and promoting justice in the international arena.

Yet, we would submit that each of the three concepts suggests common points of solidarity between the Orthodox world and the increasingly transnational community of peacemakers. Specifically, the principles of freedom and relationality with respect to individual human rights make Orthodoxy's conception of personhood fully compatible with democratic norms. Moreover, the heterogeneity and dynamism of personhood reinforce secular principles encouraging toleration of differences within society rather than defensive reaction against otherness. Debates over multiculturalism within the context of the United States, as well as efforts to craft new constitutions in the multiethnic societies in southeastern Europe, would be enriched by attention to Orthodoxy's vision of the person.

Likewise, Orthodox Christianity's definition of religion as a way of life opens up an entirely new role for tradition in our late modern, postmodern world, a role whereby tradition provides for fluid changes rather than destabilizing rupture in societies undergoing all forms of modernization. Equally important, the unity of doctrine and praxis means that Holy Tradition is a continual, reiterative experience of truths that are inwardly changeless even while constantly assuming new forms.

Orthodox believers can experience their faith in a variety of local, national, and regional contexts rather than reacting defensively against homogenizing global tendencies of liberalizing, pluralist changes. The seamless quality of the Orthodox unity of belief and practice also means that each person experiences his or her faith in both the public and the private spheres, in a myriad of cultural contexts, through all types of activity, rather than through the narrow mechanisms of political power.

From the Orthodox perspective, religion as a way of life eschews political institutional power and, in fact, the Mother Orthodox Church of Constantinople is a signatory, on behalf of all Orthodox Churches around the world, to the Bosphorus Declaration of 1994, an interfaith document that condemns, as a crime against religion, all crimes in the name of religions.[17]

Finally, the holistic character that marks the Orthodox conception of the sanctity of creation is strikingly consistent with the international community's emphasis on reconciliation. Social scientists and government policymakers, scholars, and practitioners—all those individuals and groups concerned with describing, analyzing, and managing our current system of international relations—would do well to look to Orthodox Christianity's theology of creation. It is a model for how human beings can accept responsibility to participate as "co-creators" with the Creator, reconcile humanity with itself, and end the alienation of humanity from the natural environment.

The Pledge of Orthodoxy

Members of the policy, academic, and media communities who are genuinely interested in redefining the tools, constructs, and perceptual landscape that currently affect conflict resolution and peacemaking would do well to look to the Orthodox theologian, the late Nikos Nissiotis,[18] for an insightful formulation of peace as the restoration of the original integrity

17. For the full text, see Chapter 6, "Major Declarations: Public Proclamations."

18. Nikos Nissiotis (1925–86) was a Greek theologian who taught philosophy and psychology of religion at the University of Athens. A pioneer in translating Orthodox Christianity to the West, he was deeply involved in the World Council of Churches, emphasizing the theology of the Holy Spirit and of God's glory.

of the cosmos. For Nissiotis, peace is principally a hard process of reconciliation in and with one's self and with the whole of creation.

Thus, dear friends, we close with a pledge. The Ecumenical Patriarchate will do all that is within our power to live up to the responsibilities that accompany the honor that you have bestowed on us today. To this end, and in keeping with the venerable tradition of this university's contributions to international law and diplomacy, we humbly pledge to "pursue what makes for peace" (Rom. 14.19).

We also pledge that the Orthodox Church will undertake all its works for global peace and international reconciliation through the "perfect love which casts out fear" (1 Cor. 16.13–14; 1 Jn. 4.18). Moreover, within the context of Tufts University as an institution committed to knowledge as the quest for truth, we pledge to enliven the truth-seeking journey of the scholars, students, and alumni of the Tufts community with the beliefs and public works of the Orthodox Church.

We match our closing pledge, dear friends, with an entreaty to you. In the name of the rigorous standards of international law and the codification of human rights, of which the Fletcher School has become a standard-bearer, we entreat you to renew your pledges on behalf of global peace, reconciliation, democracy, and freedom. Your pledge demands that you endeavor to bring the rich intellectual tradition of Orthodox Christian thought, long hidden behind the curtains of captivity, into today's academy and into its scholarship and research in international relations, conflict resolution, and security studies.

The painful and joyful experiences of the Ecumenical Patriarchate of Constantinople seal our pledge to uphold the principles of the honorary doctorate that you have conferred on us today. By the same token, we ask that you work to alleviate the suffering of the Orthodox Church and all other individuals and groups persecuted because of their quest for truth. We exhort you to enliven your knowledge through a life of service to the peaceful reconciliation of all creation.

2

Orthodoxy in America: Local Paradigms

The Light of Christ Shines on All

Ecumenical Doxology at the Washington National Cathedral, Washington, D.C., October 20, 1997. The address was part of the first official visit of Ecumenical Patriarch Bartholomew to the United States. The first Ecumenical Patriarch to visit the United States was Ecumenical Patriarch Dimitrios (1914–91). The official visit of Ecumenical Patriarch Bartholomew in 2009 marks his sixth journey to the United States.

At this hour, when the orb of the sun descends out of view, leaving us only the remains of its light, we have gathered in this magnificent edifice to give thanks and praise to God. We express and extend our deepest and abiding thanks to this gracious invitation and likewise grace-filled welcome to this cathedral of the American people. Like the many fragments pieced together in the stained-glass windows that adorn this house of prayer, and that are suffused with every color and hue under heaven, the American people constitute such a radiant image of humanity.

Indeed, the yearning of Americans for freedom to worship according to the dictates of their conscience seems in particular to resemble the West Rose window, which, as we understand it, is formed from prisms of glass in order to intensify the waning light of the setting sun. So also it is this intense love for freedom, especially as it relates to religion and the free choice of worship, expressed in the faces of all of you, that fills this place, through your very diversity, with the plenitude of the American religious experience.

Your aspirations are the very embodiment of this cathedral. For it was the gift of light, the science of light, that inspired the master builders and craftsmen of bygone centuries to stretch and reach for the divine, for God, through Gothic architecture. Their guiding principle was the True Light, who came into this world in order to enlighten every human person, in order to shed on the whole of creation the uncreated light of His uncreated Godhead. The Orthodox faith and liturgy celebrates this light of Christ in a special way every evening as it chants at Vespers:

> O Joyous Light, of the holy glory, of the immortal heavenly Father, the Holy, the Blessed One. O Jesus Christ, now that we have come to the setting of the sun, we praise Father, Son and Holy Spirit, God.

The light that inspired the builders of the great cathedrals, among which this National Cathedral most certainly ranks, is the inner light that seeks expression in the outer world of human experience. Too often in the contemporary human condition, this light is placed under a bushel or, even worse, extinguished through coercion and persecution. The failure of political expediency, the vanity of purely material gain, the alienation of individuals from society and of whole societies from the individual—all testify to the eclipse of our natural and God-given powers as living icons, created in the image and according to the likeness of God. Especially in the Western world, where technology has advanced by leaps and bounds, to the extent that wisdom is now chasing after science, the verities of human experience have come into question in ways that a generation ago could not have been imagined.

The Illumined Heart

Yet our message to you today is a simple one. God is light and in Him there is no darkness at all, as the theologian of love remarks. Through this light we see those things visible to the eye, and, if we are enlightened in the spiritual mind, we shall become conscious of what is invisible. On yet another level, we distinguish what is good from what is evil. We come to know things in and of themselves, and, in this way, are guided to "faith as the evidence of things not seen" (Heb. 11.1).

A heart that is enlightened by the light of virtue will accomplish great deeds of goodness, of a higher ethical stature.[1] To speak of these things in every country is necessary and useful—for the perfection of virtue is always exceeded by ever reaching beyond perfection, which truly has neither limit nor end. Consequently, our movement toward likeness with Him is limitless and full of joy and astonishment, never lacking in wonders.

But beyond the light of knowledge and the light of conscience, there is the divine and uncreated light. Divine energy descends on the pure in heart and makes us sufficient to see with immediacy the operations of His divinity (Mt. 4.3, 1 Jn. 3.2), but not the God Whom no one has ever seen (Jn. 1.18, 1 Jn. 4.12). With respect to this light we are all impoverished. And if we would consider what is truly salutary for this life, we would labor with all our might to acquire this light of knowledge. And if we would consider what is good, we would strive to acquire this light of virtue, by which we are made worthy vessels for the descent of the heavenly light, the light that demolishes the wall of death and opens wide the door of life everlasting.

In whatever form God's light enters into our hearts, there is a way it must be welcomed to transform our lives and those around us. No one lights a lamp and places it under a bushel but on a lampstand, that it may give light unto all who are in the house (Mt. 5.15). The city on the hill cannot be hidden.

And so it is here on Mount Saint Alban this evening. This wonderful National Cathedral speaks, with resplendent eloquence, of the aspirations of the American people to achieve a society in which the light of conscience is raised high as a torch of freedom.

Throughout the world, where our Modesty has had the privilege as Ecumenical Patriarch to travel, Americans are known as much for their dedication and devotion to freedom as for their material prosperity. That we can come together this evening, in a spirit of mutual respect and understanding—a spirit not only of tolerance but of goodwill, even a spirit of esteem and admiration—this reflects the achievement of the American vision of religious liberty.

---

1. See Elizabeth Behr-Sigel, *The Place of the Heart: An Introduction to Orthodox Spirituality* (Torrance, Calif.: Oakwood Publications, 1992).

As Ecumenical Patriarch occupying the First Throne of Orthodoxy, the Holy Mother Church, the Great Church of Christ, and bearing the responsibility of spiritual hegemony among the world's three hundred million Orthodox Christians, we affirm that religious liberty is a necessary condition for authentic faith. The lamp of faith must never be shielded by prejudice, fear, or hate.

Beloved friends and children in the Lord, we have come to your home from our home, bearing in our heart the light that shines on at the Phanar, the "lighthouse" of the Church of Constantinople.[2] We see that, in the honor you have shown to our ever memorable predecessor in the Ecumenical Throne, Patriarch Athenagoras,[3] by enshrining his image among the stained-glass commemorations of this cathedral, you truly desire that light. We give you our assurance that, just as you receive our light, we shall always welcome yours. Our fervent hope and prayer is that this gathering with all of you will be only the first of many such occasions to share with one another this blessed light and to illumine the world with love, peace, and hope.

Faith and Freedom

Homily at Saints Constantine and Helen Church, Washington D.C., October 19, 1997.

To God do we ascribe glory and thanksgiving; for He has granted our Modesty to visit this great country, the United States of America. The purpose of our visit is to participate in the festivities and celebration of the seventy-fifth anniversary of the founding of the Greek Orthodox Archdiocese of America and to become even more familiar with all of her pious faithful.[4] We come to you from the sacred seat of the Ecumenical

2. *Phanar,* meaning "lighthouse" in Greek, refers to the old lighthouse quarter of Istanbul, and it is also the main quarter for Greeks. The name is also seen as coterminous with the Ecumenical Patriarchate because the residence, administrative offices, and cathedral church of the Ecumenical Patriarch are there.

3. Athenagoras (1886–1972) was archbishop of America (1930–48) and elected Ecumenical Patriarch on November 1, 1948.

4. The Greek Orthodox Archdiocese of America has a unique relationship with the Ecumenical Patriarchate. The late Ecumenical Patriarch Athenagoras (1886–1972) was

Patriarchate in the Phanar, bringing to all of you the heartfelt salutation of the Mother Church, the great Church of Christ, and our own personal greetings.

And now that we see you face to face, we are deeply moved and filled with great joy. Here in this holy church, which honors the names of Saints Constantine and Helen, we tangibly feel the unbreakable sacred bonds that bind us together. Constantine the Great, the founder of Constantinople and the first emperor of the Eastern Roman Empire, which developed into the Greco-Byzantine Empire, was also a political visionary, dedicated to tolerance. He, together with his mother, St. Helen, a holy woman and equal to the Apostles, put an end to the persecution of Christians by recognizing and permitting the free practice of their worship.

We have received the fruits of this tolerance in this country, in the United States of America, where freedom of the individual constitutes the fundamental axis of social and civic life. In a concrete way, America teaches the nations of the world the kind of foundation necessary for their own progress.[5]

Ecumenicity and Tolerance

The Eastern Orthodox Church as a whole is known as the Greek Orthodox Church in the reality of the *oikoumene*—that is, the whole world. It welcomes every person of goodwill—of whatever nationality, race, or language—and offers them the truth. The Church serves all our fellow humans with the utmost respect for the individuality of each. The Ecumenical Patriarchate seeks to fortify the faithful in the Orthodox Church and at the same time preserve their unique ethnic and linguistic qualities. The Ecumenical Patriarchate has never deviated from this line. Our joy is to behold our Lord Jesus Christ worshipped in the right way—that is, in

---

archbishop of North and South America from 1930 to 1948, when he was elected Patriarch. As archbishop, he was a great pioneer, founding the seminary of Holy Cross School of Theology and the orphanage of St. Basil's Academy. As Ecumenical Patriarch, he was a great visionary, establishing connections with other churches and—together with then Pope Paul VI—removing the anathemas (excommunications) from the Great Schism, of 1054, between the Eastern and Western Churches.

5. The Greek Orthodox Archdiocese of North and South America was incorporated in 1921. Before the establishment of an archdiocese in the Western Hemisphere, there

the Orthodox way, by Greeks as Greeks, by Slavs as Slavs, by Americans as Americans, and so on. Our faith is based totally on the freedom of individual choice. And our respect for this freedom is also total. Consequently, we rightly rejoice, for we find ourselves in a country that proceeds with this belief and respect.

We rejoice, with great gladness, also because we find ourselves with our most beloved and Christ-loving people. The ecumenical character of the Ecumenical Patriarchate, the ecumenicity of the Eastern Orthodox, the Great Mother Church, does not preclude a special love for her own people. A mother of many children does not love her many children less than one who has only one. Love is a tree that, the more it bears fruit, the more its branches grow and spread.

The encounter of the son who was not the prodigal, in our Lord's well-known parable of the prodigal son (see Lk. 15)—the son who witnessed the fatherly love for his prodigal brother is not the encounter with Orthodoxy. It has no place in this country, and it is certainly not welcome in the Orthodox Church. The Orthodox Christian rejoices at the return and salvation of his brother. He never fumes with anger. He never burns with jealousy. He never sees the embrace of the Mother Church as a threat to his own position, because her embrace encompasses the whole world.

Overcoming Racism in the United States

Address to religious and civic leaders in Atlanta, Georgia, October 31, 1997.

By the grace and mercy of God, we bring to all of you here assembled the greetings and blessings of the Ecumenical Patriarchate of Constantinople. We express our thanks to you for your warm welcome and legendary Southern hospitality. We feel both joy and spiritual satisfaction at the sight of such a diverse gathering of religious and civic leaders sharing in a

were numerous communities of Greek Orthodox Christians. The first Greek Orthodox community in the Americas was founded in New Orleans by a small colony of Greek merchants. History also records that on June 26, 1768, the first Greek colonists landed at St. Augustine, Florida, the oldest city in America.

common meal that is filled with hope and love. It is truly a sign of the success that the people of Atlanta rightly celebrate.

This success cannot be measured only by the material prosperity symbolized by the magnificent skyline of the American South's premier city. In the city where moral, spiritual, and ethical leadership are personified by the figures of Martin Luther King Jr. and President Jimmy Carter, we see that Atlanta's success must be perceived in relation to the Divine.

For those with eyes to see and ears to hear, and with hearts to understand, there is a profound mystery in the conjunction of their legacies and their presence in Atlanta. One man was completely powerless, at least by the world's standards—a preacher and the son of a preacher. The other was the most politically powerful person on the face of the earth. Yet, Martin Luther King Jr. changed the course of this nation's understanding of social justice, by his death as much as by his life. And Jimmy Carter, a person very dear to our Modesty and the Ecumenical Patriarchate, has become a powerful spiritual force for peace and reconciliation, and this in the years after his term as president of this great nation.

So it is that we find ourselves with leaders of religious institutions and governmental agencies this morning, in a spirit of mutual interdependence and appreciation. As Ecumenical Patriarch, we recognize the preeminent position of the American vision of religious tolerance and freedom of expression. This is the key to understanding how Athens and Jerusalem, if you will, meet in a coincidence that enriches our culture. Only in a society that values the free expression of conscience, the primacy of choice with respect to religious belief, can ethical and spiritual values retain their proper place in the public arena. The very opportunity for diversity is the guarantee that the *agora* of civic life will have the benefit of godliness. Here in the United States of America, and in Atlanta, we can say with the Psalmist that "mercy and truth have met together, righteousness and peace have kissed each other" (Ps. 84.11).

We congratulate you on your efforts to achieve such a common and shared wealth of human and divine values, for in the end we know that, because the divine has already become human, the human has the full potential of the divine. Truth really can spring up from the earth, because the Son of Righteousness shines down on us from the heavens (Ps. 84:12, Mal. 4:2). May His grace and infinite mercy be with you all.

A Visit to the Inner City of Los Angeles: Faith in Every Footstep

At the Berendo School in Los Angeles, California, November 7, 1997.

It is a great joy to be in your midst this afternoon and to reach out a hand of peace and friendship to all, especially the children and young people. The Ecumenical Patriarchate of Constantinople, the "elder brother" of world Orthodoxy, embraces you today with all our love and blessings.

As we look on one another, we see so many similarities in our journey of life. Our own Orthodox Christian forefathers and mothers came to this blessed new land not so long ago. They fled war, persecution, prejudice, and the tyranny of economic deprivation. Many of you are immigrants and children of immigrants who rejected conditions in your own home country, which demeaned and defiled your basic humanity.

The local community gathered to greet us today here at the Berendo School is a dramatic witness to the fact that our lives have been characterized as one, where faith has moved our every footstep. Since we share so many traditions and similarities, we can develop a common agenda of renewal in a part of this city where God has planted us.

The reality and holiness of the Kingdom of God must begin here on earth, with each and every one of us. We can no longer create or maintain artificial barriers that separate us from the reality of our shared life. Here in the great inner city of Los Angeles, the City of Angels, we have much to accomplish to merit this angelic designation.

Mutual Respect and Tolerance

Our common agenda must be reflected by mutual respect of each other's traditions and an appreciation of each other's hopes and aspirations. With God's help and our own commitment, we must address the issues of human and civil rights and the responsibilities of all. We must support every effort to secure a quality education for all our children.

For all who struggle to make their daily bread in the context of free and legitimate enterprise, we must work to expand economic opportunities that can enrich lives with the nobility of labor. The curse of crime, drugs, and inner-city decay must be confronted head on and without compromise. And we must expand our sights to include concern for a healthy environment, not only in our neighborhoods but also for the entire planet.

To this end, our Orthodox Church, parish by parish, here in America and especially in Los Angeles, will partner with all who wish to till the soil of human potential and development. If we are truly committed to a positive future, we must transcend narrow self-interests and explore the meaning of duty and opportunity for the good of all.

Our own St. Sophia Cathedral, which is privileged to share in the multiethnic and multicultural interaction of the area, has been working and praying for a number of years now with an active local citizenry. Churches, public agencies, and friends whose basic roots are from Central America, Mexico, and beyond are working together to renew and revitalize this part of the inner city. We bless and celebrate this exciting partnership and hard work in what has been officially designated by the city as the Byzantine-Latino Quarter of Los Angeles. This is a unique and historic concept, joining Hellenic ideals and Latin American traditions, fused into a vibrant synergy of brotherhood and love.

We recognize the power at work here, a power so great that the dreams it nourishes can be limited only by the measure of our inner faith and the boundaries of our imagination. It is our spiritual foundation that defines us and our love that moves us. So, as we work with one another, let us pray for one another. Our Lord Jesus Christ taught that "man does not live by bread alone" (Deut. 8.3; Mt. 4.4). Thus, in our desire to solve our daily problems and to improve the conditions of our social and material existence, we must be ever mindful of those who are crying out for spiritual nourishment.

This visit to the United States has been a journey of faith for us. From the eastern shores to the western coast of America, faith has marked our every footstep. Faith has brought us here today, and it is our prayer that those footsteps of faith will bless the labors of each and every one of you.

With all that you seek to accomplish, you are indeed beacons of light for your community. With your inner will and power of determination you can accomplish anything. "That which is impossible for man is possible with God" (Mt. 19.26). There is a touching and wise saying that points us in the right direction: "We are, each of us, angels with only one wing. And we can fly only by embracing each other."

Dear friends, we thank you for embracing us today with your presence and your love in this, the City of Angels. Your enthusiasm and hospitality will live long in our memories. It can be a living example to the entire world of what can happen when brothers and sisters work with a common vision toward a common goal, with peace and harmony and in service to humanity.

Enduring Common Traditions

Address before the United States Congress on the occasion of being awarded the U.S. Congressional Gold Medal, October 21, 1997.

In the name of love, peace, and hope, we convey our warmest greetings, greetings from the 270th successor to the See of St. Andrew the Apostle, to the 105th Congress of the United States of America. We are truly humbled to receive so great a tribute from so great a nation.

This is a moment rich with layers of meaning. Consider, for example, the graceful dome that arches over our ceremonies and protects us, the way America itself has protected the world from adversity throughout this century. That dome is a link with Greco-Roman civilization, which, together with both the Old and the New Testaments, forms the wellspring of Orthodoxy and was so admired by America's founders. Yet it represents an even closer link between us: how many of us realize that an Orthodox Church was used as a model for this dome? It was the famous Cathedral of St. Isaac, on the banks of the Neva River in St. Petersburg, that inspired the architect who designed and built the final dome for the Capitol. Thomas U. Walter actually obtained a drawing of St. Isaac's and closely replicated its dimensions.

So we feel quite at home here today, for many reasons. We have come from one of the most ancient civilizations on earth to one of the most modern. However, both the United States Congress and the Orthodox Church represent great traditions that have endured. We can learn much from each other.

Diversity and Liberty

You represent about 270 million Americans; we represent about 300 million Orthodox Christians, five million of whom live in the United States. And if you look beyond our robes and your business suits, there are many other things we have in common. Like the United States, Orthodoxy is composed of many different peoples, not just Greeks but also Native Americans, Russians, Germans, Albanians, Romanians, French, Serbs, Bulgarians, English, Ukrainians, Palestinians, Chinese, Nigerians, Egyptians, and many, many more.

Like the United States, these diverse peoples are united by certain principles held in common—in your case, the Constitution; in our case, the Nicene Creed. It is indeed fitting that the very first article in our Creed, the words "I believe," is the very first guarantee in the Constitution's Bill of Rights, which recognizes the inalienable right of all human persons to freely choose and practice their religious beliefs.

This commitment to the ideals of religious liberty is the cornerstone of American democracy and the genius of American diversity. It is no wonder that Orthodox Christian peoples from the world over have found a welcome reception and secure haven in these United States, especially when you consider the persecution endured in this century.

For, as a church, the Orthodox Church (independent of the behavior of her members) may be opposed, but opposes no one; may be persecuted, but does not persecute; is fettered, but chains no one; is deprived of her freedom, but does not trample on the freedom of others.

Together, this nation and our Church share principles of receptivity, diversity, and tolerance. This orientation brings the capacity for another kind of freedom. It is the freedom of the individual from within.

Openness and Tolerance

As you have opened your arms to us, so we open them to you. The Orthodox faith is for all people, and is always offered with respect for difference and freedom, never with coercion or threat. This is the fundamental meaning of *catholic*—"for all people."[6] And this is the message of

6. See John Meyendorff, *Catholicity and the Church* (Crestwood, N.Y.: St. Vladimir's Seminary Press, 1983).

the United States, a society that is free and open, respectful and tolerant of difference. We bless this nation, for this land has been in the past and continues to be a great refuge and hope for all humankind.

Indeed, the greatest lesson about America lies under this magnificent dome. Although American armed forces are heroic in every sense of the word, for they have given their lives time and again to save the world from catastrophe, if one had to choose a building that represents what is great about America it would be not the Pentagon but the Capitol.

The Pentagon embodies might, but the Capitol embodies right. In these halls, different points of view meet and are reconciled. In these halls, narrow interests are compromised for the greater good. And, most important for the Orthodox Church during many dark decades, in these halls human rights are preserved and human dignity is enhanced.

We Orthodox will never forget the horrors of those years. Out of 70,000 churches in Russia before the Bolshevik revolution, only 6,500 remained by 1986. The very same Saint Isaac's Cathedral that served as a model for this Capitol was turned into a "Museum of Atheism" from 1924 until 1991. Its religious functions have since been restored, and in 1993 our Modesty was deeply moved to celebrate the Divine Liturgy under that dome.

We thank you, the American people, for helping preserve the Orthodox faith under communism. Indeed, it is you who should be receiving this medal, not we. We pledge to continue to work with you to bring peace and democracy to the world and to ensure that human rights and religious freedom prevail around the globe. In helping to restore worldwide Orthodoxy, we have seen the fruits of our labors. The Orthodox Church in Albania has been re-established.[7] Moreover, a viable pan-Orthodox solution in Estonia was achieved.[8]

As Ecumenical Patriarch, we have the fraternal care of upholding not only the Orthodox churches but, by the preaching of the love of God, to

---

7. One of the youngest among the autocephalous churches, the Church of Albania, established in 1937, suffered gravely during communist rule, especially after 1967; Ecumenical Patriarch Bartholomew appointed Archbishop Anastasios as exarch to Albania in 1992.

8. After being recognized as an independent Orthodox church by Moscow (1920) and subsequently by Constantinople (1923), the Church of Estonia was subordinated to a diocese within the Church of Russia in 1945. The autonomy of the church was formally reinstated by the Ecumenical Patriarchate in 1996, receiving its first permanent resident hierarch, Stephanos, in 1999.

work for the reconciliation of all humankind, the propagation of peaceful coexistence, and the preservation of the natural environment. With those ends in view, we have been happily informed that the academic dialogue between Orthodox Christians and Muslims, whose most recent meeting was June 3 of this year in our city, has found a corresponding group in the United States. We also recently sponsored an international conference on how to save the Black Sea from ecological disaster.[9]

Lessons Learned

It is clear that the Orthodox Church can learn much from America; but there are also a few things America can learn from the Orthodox Church. We come before you today as spiritual leader of a Church that is not merely revived but growing rapidly, and not just in our ancestral lands of Europe, Asia, and Africa but also in the United States. Indeed, Orthodoxy was recently cited as one of this nation's fastest growing religions. Why is this? How is it that this ancient Church, which prides itself on maintaining an unbroken tradition of faith from the day of Pentecost, is today thriving in the most modern country in the world?

There is a great hunger for spirituality, and there is a thirst for transcendent meaning. We believe that, as we enter the next millennium, religious values, religious feeling, and religious faith are undergoing a massive revival.

Since the Enlightenment, the spiritual bedrock of Western civilization has been eroded and undermined. Intelligent, well-intentioned people sincerely believed that the wonders of science could replace the miracles of faith. But these great minds missed one vital truth—namely, that faith is not a garment, to be slipped on and off; it is a quality of the human spirit, from which it is inseparable. The modern era has not eliminated faith; one could no more eliminate faith than love. Even atheists believe in atheism. The modern era has simply replaced spiritual faith in God with secular faith in man.

Today, three centuries after the birth of Voltaire, the pendulum is swinging back. The twentieth century showed our enormous capacity for

9. On the Black Sea symposium, see Sarah Hobson and Laurence David Mee, eds., *The Black Sea in Crisis* (Singapore: World Scientific, 1998).

creativity, but it also demonstrated our boundless capacity for destruction. We saw 75 million human beings killed between 1914 and 1945 alone. In its own fearsome power, humanity recognized its own appalling fallibility. Thus began our return to faith.

The urge that brings us here is not a complicated one: We want some meaning to our lives; we want to care about our neighbors and we want them to care about us; we want a decent life for ourselves and our families. Mother Teresa, of blessed memory and with whom we share this honor, once said that the greatest disease in America is loneliness.

And so it is no longer considered unfashionable or backward to believe. A generation that worshipped many false idols, from drugs and cults to power and wealth, now seeks an authentic tradition for its own children. Many of them are drawn to our Church and its simple, unadorned faith, which is untainted by vain attempts to explain what cannot be explained, a religion that is unstained and, we hope, unpretentious.

Therein lie the lessons of Orthodoxy for America—that, paradoxically, faith can endure without freedom, but freedom cannot long abide without faith. And while God has led us to reason, reason alone can never lead us back to God. Only faith can do that.

We accept this medal on behalf of the Greek Orthodox Archdiocese of America, which is celebrating its seventy-fifth anniversary, and on behalf of Orthodox Christians everywhere, especially those who were martyred for the faith. We note with great spiritual satisfaction that this medal was first awarded on March 25, 1776, to the Father of the American nation, George Washington. For Orthodox Christians everywhere as well as for our fellow Christians led by our brother, His Holiness Pope John Paul II, March 25 marks the celebration of the Annunciation of the Virgin Mary by the Archangel Gabriel.

It is a day on which we celebrate not only the love of God, incarnate for us in Christ, but the free, open, and receptive response of a human person, the Virgin Mary, to the will of God. It is in this spirit of freedom that we pledge to redouble our efforts as peacemakers among different peoples and faiths. And we will continue our work as a religious and spiritual institution, teaching, edifying, serving humanitarian ideals, civilizing, and preaching love in every direction.

Dear friends, God is love, and, although we stand at the end of a century filled with strife, we know that this love can lead to a new millennium of peace. The Orthodox Christian Church will do everything in her power to help fulfill this mission. May we all become apostles of love, hope, and peace. This medal is further proof that there is more that unites the community of man than divides us. And so we say to you: "Glory to God in the highest, and on earth, peace and goodwill toward all people."

The New Cultural Divide

Reception of the Los Angeles World Affairs Council, November 7, 1997.

We come to you from the ancient Christian East. As Ecumenical Patriarch of Constantinople, we serve the 300 million Orthodox Christians the world over, as the "elder brother" among the heads of all the independent, local, and national churches. We say "independent," but this should not be construed to mean there is a difference among us. We are united by a common faith, a shared tradition, and bonds of Christian love that have held us together for two thousand years.

Our present theme this morning is "the new cultural divide," an exploration of the emerging world culture. From our vantage point at the Phanar, which rests on the cusp of Europe and Asia, we have a perspective that may prove helpful in this consideration. There has been an increasing tendency in political discourse to speak of a "clash of civilizations,"[10] as the frontiers between the Muslim and Christian worlds begin to dissolve before political and economic forces on a global scale. The fall of the Iron Curtain and the rise of peoples seeking self-determination have energized the religious sensibilities of whole peoples. Nationalist ideals converge with religious zeal and cultural pride, creating unexpected geopolitical tides that seem to have a power all their own.

The experience of the Ecumenical Patriarchate has been one of continuity and stability through centuries of global change. At one time, our Patriarchate was coterminous with the boundaries of the Roman Empire. Today, as the 270th successor to the First-called disciple, Saint Andrew, our domain is a ministry of spiritual leadership, but our center is situated in the same location we have known from the Apostolic Age. Our mission embraces Orthodox Christians on every continent. From our vantage

10. See Samuel Huntington, *The Clash of Civilizations and the Remaking of World Order* (New York: Simon and Schuster, 1996).

point, we see as many possibilities for cooperation and shared goals as we do dangers of division.

Interreligious and Ecological Vocation

We see our vocation to be one of discovering common ground in the lands in which we live, move, and have our being. This means finding constructive means for bringing divergent opinions together. To this end, we have sponsored international conferences promoting understanding between Muslims, Christians, and Jews.

We consider a lively dialogue between these three faith traditions to be essential to softening the sharp edge of the cultural divide. Knowledge and mutual appreciation of legitimate differences between cultures leads to the enhancement of civilization, not further alienation. For Orthodox Christians, peace is not merely the cessation of hostilities. There is an ontological basis for peace, and that is love. Love of God, love of neighbor, love of the stranger—indeed, love of one's enemy—has existential impact in the phenomenal world. Anywhere and everywhere we are able, as a religious leader, to advance the fundamental principles of faith traditions, principles that they hold in common, we increase the possibilities for love. These potentialities manifest themselves as tolerance, respect, and even admiration. We are committed to not allowing the tides of history, often scarred by acts of unimaginable human evil, to sweep away the past, present, and future glories of human endeavor.

Recognizing the power of religious faith to contribute to the positive encounter of different cultures will go far toward bridging this new cultural divide. When we proclaim, as we did in the Bosphorus Declaration, that "a crime in the name of religion is a crime against all religion,"[11] we have begun to set in place the girders of the bridges that build unity out of diversity. Religious faith must be seen by temporal powers to be an advocate of reconciliation and an instrument for peace.

In addition to mustering our spiritual forces in the cause of mutual understanding, the Ecumenical Patriarchate has been in the forefront of promoting another means of spanning cultural division—namely, a shared concern for the environment. Here too, the Orthodox Church

---

11. For the full text, see Chapter 6, "Major Declarations: Public Proclamations."

unites theology and ontology, for we see more continuity between natural and supernatural spheres than discontinuity.

In the teaching of our Church, nature is perceived as being full of the glory of God, even though it groans with the rest of creation, awaiting the revelation of our redemption (see Rom. 8.22,23). Humankind is seen as the nexus of creation, the point of convergence that mediates the cosmos, which was created as "very good" (Gen. 1.26), for the glory of God. Humanity has a meditative and, indeed, eucharistic role in exercising dominion over the earth. This is a far cry from the domination and exploitation that have characterized the technologically capable, post-industrialist era.

As Ecumenical Patriarch, and in cooperation with the various international organizations and multinational federations, we have sponsored regular symposia on the ecological crisis of our time.[12] Most recently, we set sail across the Black Sea, an ecosystem whose shores extend across the cultural divide, in order to heighten awareness to the imminent threats posed by pollution, not only to the sea itself but to the indigenous peoples who surround it.

As a result of our efforts, we have received the epithet "the Green Patriarch."[13] And if this appellation signifies our abiding concern for bringing about in the global community responsibility for our shared resources, then we accept it gladly. We have found that people of diverse cultures, religions, and national interests can come together in a common effort to meet the challenges of environmental responsibility coupled with the economic needs of people.

We hope that these two examples of our efforts, to close the gap in the new cultural divide, will be a cause for hope in the power of religious faith to be a meditative and transformative force for peace in the world.

---

12. For further information on these ecological symposia, organized by the Religious and Scientific Committee, established by Ecumenical Patriarch Bartholomew in 1994, see the website of Religion, Science and the Environment, at www.rsesymposia.org. The committee is chaired by His Eminence Metropolitan John of Pergamon and is facilitated by Maria Becket.

13. An appellation originally ascribed to the Ecumenical Patriarch publicly by *Time* magazine (May 1997) and formally in the White House (October 1997) by Al Gore, former Vice President of the United States and 2007 recipient of the Nobel Prize for Peace.

As Ecumenical Patriarch, we reiterate our pledge to work for reconciliation and understanding between peoples of all cultures. We are all the children of God, and we believe that it is ultimately through the love of God that we shall be able to bring about a better world and to be deserving of it.

The Missing Link

Address to the Conference of the Chief Executive Officers Organization, Istanbul, June 10, 2005. Originally remarks to the Young Presidents Organization, Istanbul, May 9, 2003. The same remarks were later variously presented at the NATO Parliamentary Assembly of the Twelfth Mediterranean Dialogue Seminar, entitled "The Middle East at a Crossroads," held in Istanbul, May 3, 2006.

Greetings and welcome to Istanbul, the seat of the Ecumenical Throne of the Orthodox Christian Church—spiritual home of 300 million Orthodox Christians worldwide. Here, not only the continents meet, but people from all over the world gather to enjoy the mystery, majesty, and history of the Queen City.[14] We are deeply honored to receive so distinguished a group of global corporate leaders.

We must admit that we were a little confused when we were invited to speak to a group searching for "missing links." We are clearly a kind of *link* between East and West; however, we do not normally think of ourselves as *missing*.

But indeed, as we considered it, for too many people in the West we *are* missing—missing from the history lessons they learn in grade school, missing from their understanding of Christianity, and missing from their idea of their cultural inheritance. In fact, the legacy of the Eastern Roman Empire—also known as the Byzantine Empire—may be the best-kept secret in the West.[15]

Byzantium preserved the works of classical civilization and Roman law and made them available to the West in time for the Renaissance. Byzantium Christianized the Slavs—and protected Europe from countless invasions. From the forks we eat with, to the hospitals we are healed in,

---

14. That is, Constantinople, or modern-day Istanbul.

15. See *The Oxford Dictionary of Byzantium*, ed. Alexander P. Kazhdan et al. (New York: Oxford University Press, 1991).

to the universities in which we pursue advanced studies—the legacy of Byzantium is everywhere.

Yet, so few know what Byzantium is—or are aware of the immeasurable contribution that it made, through Orthodoxy, to world Christianity. In fact, you could be forgiven, after speaking to the average person, for thinking that the history of Christianity starts with Jesus Christ, moves on with St. Paul at Corinth and Ephesus, continues with the archbishop of Rome, and climaxes with the Protestant Reformation.

The history and life-giving legacy of Byzantium and the Orthodox Christian faith are too often ignored. How many of us realize, for example, that all seven ecumenical councils of undivided Christianity were held not in Greece or Rome but in the East, in what was then Asia Minor and is now Turkey?

In 476, the West was overrun by barbarians and entered the Dark Ages, while the Eastern part of the empire radiated forth as the center of civilization for a thousand more years—and preserved a spirituality that we now carry into its third millennium.

We are here as the representative not of that empire but of its spiritual legacy. The West has never truly acknowledged its debt to Byzantium. Our Western civilization could never fully appropriate the mysticism of the East, which felt the presence of our Lord Christ, the Theotokos, the myriad angels and thousands of saints.

Many of the most famous monuments of Byzantium can be found here in Istanbul, and later today you will see them. But when you do, please remember—Byzantium is not merely some museum piece, a civilization that died and has been dug up by archaeologists. Its spirit lives on today. The spirit of Byzantium is alive here in Istanbul, the seat of the Ecumenical Patriarchate. The spirit of Byzantium is also alive in Eastern Europe and the Middle East, where Orthodoxy is an unbroken tradition for two thousand years.

You are searching for missing links. The best place to find them is in the frontiers between societies. The last great frontier was Eastern Europe, where free enterprise has taken root—many of those nations are now either members of or on track to become part of the European Union. But the next great frontier is the Islamic world, and the path to that world begins in Turkey, which itself is also approaching admission into the European Union.

Historical and Cultural Crossroads

We stand today at a crossroads, in every sense of the word.

Literally, we are at the crossroads between continents—that is, between Asia and Europe. Istanbul is the only city in the world that straddles two continents.

Figuratively, we are also at the crossroads between two sometimes antagonistic civilizations—that is, between East and West.

And metaphorically, we are at a crossroads in human history, a moment in time when we face a choice eloquently described by the American martyr Dr. Martin Luther King Jr.: "To learn to live together as brothers or to perish together as fools."

There is no salvation through war. There can never be a "war to end all wars" here on earth. The tragic train of events, from September 11, 2001, in New York City to the wars in Afghanistan and today in Iraq, will not save humanity from future struggles—indeed, strife and conflict are constants of human history. Imperfect beings lead an imperfect existence.

Only God in heaven is free of war, of strife, of hatred. Only God offers us the possibility of perfect love and brotherhood. And only by struggling to emulate that perfection ourselves is it possible to lend dignity to our flawed existence.

By reaching out to our fellow human beings, across real or imagined boundaries, we are reaching out for God, in whose image we were made. By coming to Istanbul at a time of conflict between East and West, you are serving the cause of peace. Some have pointed to a modern "clash of civilizations" as inevitable. We who live at the crossroads disagree—indeed, we are living proof that different cultures and different faiths can coexist in peace.

Distinguished guests, we believe the world has suffered a centuries-long crisis of faith from which it is only now emerging. There is a great hunger for spirituality; there is a thirst for transcendent meaning. We believe that, as we enter a new millennium, religious values, religious feeling, and religious faith are undergoing a massive revival.

Since the Enlightenment, the spiritual bedrock of Western civilization has been eroded and undermined. Intelligent, well-intentioned people sincerely believed that the wonders of science could replace the miracles of faith. But these great minds missed one vital truth—namely, that faith is not a garment, to be slipped on and off; it is a quality of the human spirit, from which it is inseparable. The modern era has not eliminated faith—you could no more eliminate faith than love. The modern era has simply replaced spiritual faith in God with secular faith in man.

Religious Leadership and Religious Extremism

There has never been a greater need for spiritual leaders to engage themselves in the affairs of this world. We must take a visible place on the stage, especially because too many crimes today are committed in the name of faith. "Beware of false prophets, which come to you in sheep's clothing, but inwardly they are ravening wolves" (Mt. 7.15). Although those words come from the Christian tradition, their truth is transcendent.

Religious extremists and terrorists may be the most wicked false prophets of all, for not only do they commit horrible crimes against humanity; they do so in the name of a lie. When they bomb, and shoot, and destroy, they steal more than life itself; they also undermine faith, which is the only way to break the cycle of hatred and retribution.

International spiritual leaders must play an active role in discrediting false prophets and in healing the wounds of our people. For, as Rabbi Hillel asked: "If not us, then who? If not now, then when?"[16] Almost a decade ago, in Istanbul, a group of religious leaders signed the Bosphorus Declaration. We proclaimed that "a crime committed in the name of religion is a crime committed against religion."[17]

Our Church has had its own experience with such crimes. Today in Turkey, the Patriarchate has earned much popular support, from important national figures down to the average man or woman on the street. Turkish citizens reach out to the Patriarchate regularly to tell us how proud they are to have the First Throne of Orthodoxy on their nation's soil.

If the Church faces a threat in Turkey today, it comes not from the state, or even from the Muslim mainstream, but from the handful of

16. Pirkei Avot 1.14. Rabbi Hillel (110 B.C.–A.D. 10) was one of the most renowned Jewish scholars and influential rabbis.

17. For the full text, see Chapter 6, "Major Declarations: Public Proclamations."

fundamentalists who have appeared on the scene in recent years. We have seen our graveyards and monuments desecrated; we have seen bombs planted in holy places. Fundamentalism is a threat, not only to the Ecumenical Patriarchate but to the Turkish state itself. And fundamentalism is a danger not just in Turkey but in New York City and Madrid as well as throughout the world.

The rise of fundamentalism has given greater urgency to the cause of East–West unity. To return to the point we made earlier: that cause would be served in important ways if Turkey were admitted to the European Union. It would help defuse East–West tensions, bring about greater global understanding, and undermine the cause of fundamentalists and racists on both sides.

Working Toward Peace

There are other events that could also make a difference. Continued progress in opening the Greek–Turkish border on Cyprus could prove yet another breakthrough for East–West unity. In each of these instances, international business has profound interests and will play a critical role.

If Turkey is integrated into the world economy, the gate is opened wider not only to the Islamic world but also to the former Soviet republics with strong historic links to Turkey—Azerbaijan, Kazakhstan, Uzbekistan, Turkmenistan, and Kyrgyzstan. These Central Asian republics are in need of Western capital and entrepreneurial expertise. The Turks know the situation there better than most and can help mediate their development.

Many other interests would be served by the integration of Turkey into the European Union. It would have a powerful, positive, and stabilizing effect on all of this country's institutions—including, of course, the Ecumenical Patriarchate.

We must put behind us the divisions and feuds of the past. Once, only conquest united Europe and Asia; today, commerce can achieve the same result. The modern way to bring about unity and peace is to open our borders to one another and let people, capital, ideas, and products flow.

Much has already been achieved in the political world. But neither politicians nor businessmen alone can heal the rifts in our society today.

As we said earlier, religious leaders have a central and inspirational role to play; it is we who must help bring the spiritual principles of ecumenism, brotherhood, and tolerance to the forefront. It is our strong belief at the Ecumenical Patriarchate that Orthodox Christians have a special responsibility to assist in East–West rapprochement. For, like the Turkish Republic, we too have a foot in both worlds.

We have always lived at the crossroads between East and West; we have witnessed great suffering on both sides, as we see again today in Baghdad; but we have also witnessed the most extraordinary acts of tolerance, such as the welcoming of the expelled Sephardic Jews in 1492 by a Muslim sultan. We have lived side by side with Muslims and Jews, and we have developed close, trusting relationships with both. In the years ahead, you will see us continue to work to establish and enhance a dialogue between the faiths.

The Church of Peace serves the Prince of Peace, and will do everything in its power to bring about the blessed community. To quote Dr. Martin Luther King Jr.: "Love is the only force capable of transforming an enemy into a friend." But we will succeed only if we are united with our fellow spiritual leaders in the spirit of the one God, "Creator of all things visible and invisible." Catholic and Orthodox, Protestant and Jew, Muslim and Hindu, Buddhist and Confucian: it is time not only for rapprochement, but even for alliance and teamwork to help lead our world away from the bloody abyss of extreme nationalism, fundamentalism, and intolerance.

We, at the Ecumenical Patriarchate, will continue our efforts to be peacemakers and to light the lamp of the human spirit. We, as the Bride of the Resurrected Bridegroom, wish only to remain a church—a church, however, that is free and respected by all. We wish to continue as a religious and spiritual institution, teaching, edifying, serving global ideals, civilizing, and preaching love in every direction. We will always work in the spirit of divine love. The Ecumenical Patriarchate is the Church that was founded by the God of love, whose peace "surpasses all understanding" (Phil. 4.7). We "pursue what makes for peace" (Rom. 14.19). We believe that "God is love" (1 Jn. 4.16), which is why we are not afraid to extend our hand in friendship and our heart in love, as we proclaim that "perfect love casts out fear" (1 Jn. 4.18).

Dear friends, we are convinced that there is more that unites the community of man than divides us. We have within our grasp the vision of the Psalmist: "Behold, how good and how pleasant it is for brethren to dwell together in unity!" (Ps. 133.1). We pledge to you today that the Orthodox Christian Church will do everything in her power to fulfill that vision. "Glory to God in the highest, and on earth, peace and goodwill toward men."

3

Religion and Society: Social Insights

"For the Peace from Above"

Remarks before the U.S. Secretary of State, the Hon. Madeleine Albright, State Department, Washington, D.C., October 22, 1997.

We rise to express our gratitude and profound sense of appreciation to you, Madame Secretary, for your hospitality to our Modesty and this tribute to the Ecumenical Patriarchate. We rise to address you not as another dignitary among many but as a fellow laborer in the vineyard of peace who honors your commitment to the work of reconciliation and the greater scope of dignity and justice for the whole human family.

We are making this pastoral visit to America in observance of the seventy-fifth year of our beloved Greek Orthodox Archdiocese. Part of our mission is to reach out beyond the borders of our faith tradition, as many of you here reach out beyond the borders of your countries, in order to preach and to teach peace to those who are afar and those who are near (see Eph. 2.17).

Tonight we bring to you a message of hope for the world—that God is our peace and that, through love, we can break down the walls that separate us and can abolish enmity and bring forth peace (see Eph. 2.14–15). We affirm, in the strongest terms, that this spiritual perspective is much more than a comforting sentiment in time of trouble. For without vision, nations, peoples, civilizations perish (Prov. 29.18). One vision can transform the world. One idea can achieve the lasting peace that has for so long eluded the human family. It becomes a call, a summons to action, based not on an exclusive hold on truth but on the shared hope of humanity.

The Marshall Plan: A Model

Fifty years ago, amidst the ashes of the Second World War, America rose up to meet a seemingly insurmountable challenge: the rebuilding of postwar Europe. Secretary of State George C. Marshall called on the American people to "comprehend the plight and consequent reactions of the long-suffering peoples" of Europe, and he set out to establish what became known as the Marshall Plan. This one visionary idea is what Arnold Toynbee termed "the signal achievement of our age."[1] The jubilee of the Marshall Plan should give us all pause to consider how we might rebuild Eastern Europe and begin building bridges to our Muslim sisters and brothers. In confronting the complexities of peacemaking in the post-communist era, we must call on the lessons of history to discover a new vision to guide us on our quest for peace.

Madame Secretary, you yourself have posed the question "How can we best live up to the spirit of the Marshall Plan?" May we, beseeching the illumination of God's Holy Spirit, humbly offer to you and to this esteemed assembly a meditation by way of response.

As Ecumenical Patriarch, we have the responsibility of spiritual seniority among the family of independent Orthodox churches worldwide. As did our beloved and ever memorable predecessor on the Ecumenical Throne, Patriarch Dimitrios, we have traveled extensively through the lands that were barred and held fast behind the Iron Curtain. We rejoice that these "gates of hell" have not prevailed. The bars have been shattered and liberation has come to long-suffering peoples. We are witnessing firsthand their struggle to come to terms with fragmentation and reintegration. The Orthodox churches of these nations represent hundreds of

1. Arnold Toynbee (1889–1975) was the author of an analytical study of world history, including the rise and fall of civilizations. See *A Study of History*, 12 vols. (London: Oxford University Press, 1934–61).

millions of souls, human beings, whose needs range from day-to-day necessities to spiritual renewal. The solution to this complex phenomenon requires a unique perspective.

The genius of the Marshall Plan was that it understood the nature of the problem it confronted: "hunger, poverty, desperation, and chaos." Against prevailing notions of national self-interest, the economic recovery and future of Europe was envisioned as the historical responsibility of the American people. And the benefits of that genius in the cause of world peace and stability are undisputed to this day.

Not by Bread Alone (Deut. 8.3; Mt. 4.4)

What is the nature of the problem today in Eastern Europe? Are the solutions to be found in narrow economic and political categories formulated in the West? Does "man live by bread alone"? As Ecumenical Patriarch, we ask that you consider that working economies are only partial solutions. You, better than we, understand the onerous task of revitalizing economic infrastructures emaciated by failed social policies. But what of decimated cultures? What of religious institutions abused by secular powers for generations? How are we to rebuild the soul of a nation?

The Ecumenical Patriarchate, as a transnational and spiritual force, has sought to assist in the reconstruction of the moral, ethical, religious, and social fabric that was torn asunder by decades of atheistic totalitarian regimes. In Albania, we have nurtured the revitalization of the Albanian Orthodox Church, which was thoroughly destroyed by the communist government. We have advocated for the inclusion of newly freed countries, mostly Orthodox Christian nations, in the emerging political and economic matrix of Europe.

We have assumed a proactive role in the dialogue of understanding between the Muslim and Christian worlds. The Ecumenical Patriarchate is poised on the frontier between these two religions. Our unique position in history and geography affords us a panoramic view of risks and possibilities. Our experience has taught us that "all things work together for good to them that love God and are called according to His purpose" (Rom. 8:28). If the world is to be culturally and spiritually rebuilt, then this must happen with a spirit of love, and not with a demon of fear; it will occur by means of a spirit of understanding and appreciation of the qualities of "otherness," and not by ignorance.

Our fervent hope is that our pilgrimage to America, our presence in your distinguished company this evening, will be cause for an awakening of the historical, religious, and cultural significance of the civilizations of the East. During this time of transition, we seek to promote absolute values of freedom and tolerance. We must not accept the imposition of cultural norms alien to peoples whose roots are, in many cases, hundreds, even thousands of years deeper than those who seek to re-create them in their own image.

Throughout Eastern Europe, Orthodox Christianity is more than a religion; it is a way of life, rooted in the experience of thousands of years of history. Whatever damage was incurred during the atheistic governments of the recent past does not and cannot invalidate that history. Let us not give in to easy solutions or to the desire to remake the world in our image.

Madame Secretary, your worthy predecessor marshaled America to action by asking: "What are the sufferings? What is needed? What can best be done? What must done?" We must recognize that the spiritual needs of people are of equal importance to their material needs. What is needed is not the love of power but the love of a powerful nation. What can best be done is to lead by loving example. What must be done is to embrace the sanctity of each and every nation: their people, their history, their faith, their civilization.

The Ecumenical Patriarchate stands ready to travel any distance, not only of land and sea but also of knowledge and idea. We are here to preach love, peace, and hope, to those afar and to those who are near (Eph. 2.17).

Spirituality and the Spirit of This Age

Address at the Basilica of the Assumption of the Blessed Mary, Baltimore, October 23, 1997.

We bring you the greeting, the blessing, and the love of the Mother Church of worldwide Orthodoxy, the Apostolic Throne of the First-called Andrew, the Ecumenical Patriarchate of Constantinople. We have come to America and to this wonderful city of Baltimore to celebrate the seventy-fifth anniversary of the founding of the Greek Orthodox Archdiocese of America.

Earlier today our Modesty was pleased to celebrate a doxology of thanksgiving in the Greek Orthodox Cathedral of the Annunciation. Now we are pleased to find ourselves in the Mother Church of Roman Catholicism in America, the beautifully adorned Basilica of the Assumption of the All-Holy Theotokos and Ever-Virgin Mary. We have come to you that we may share in spiritual fellowship as brethren, all of us bearing the name of our Lord Jesus Christ. We want that our words may resound not only in the voice that the ears can hear but in a fellowship of spirit speaking to spirit and of heart to heart. For true fellowship is spiritual only if it becomes a communion of the innermost reality of human persons, even to the point where our blood runs in one vein.

Before we open our heart, we must open our minds to a mystery and understand that our present spiritual situation is not as yet perfected in a common faith. Our desire for unity reveals that there is a great hunger for spirituality in our world today. People have an urgent and God-given desire for transcendent meaning, a God-given thirst for authenticity and wholeness.

As we approach the close of this century, we are confronted both by the legacy of our past and by the promise of the future, a new opportunity for spiritual growth. As we enter the third millennium of Christianity, the shadows of secular materialism shroud the landscape of faith. The allure of surfaces, illusions, and appearances (see Jn 7.24) obscures the truth of the profound mystery of the human person. There are many today who take the surface for the truth and worship mere images. Such images are never spiritually satisfying and are easily exhausted.

The Context of Spirituality

The word *spirituality* is in fact unknown in the language of scripture and tradition.[2] It has become a vague term of mere convenience. It is now used to separate the faithful from those outside the Church. It has become

2. Orthodox theology prefers to use the term in adjectival form, speaking of "spiritual life" and directly relating the word to the Spirit of God.

confused with the proliferation of secular therapies in the jargon of popular psychology.

While recognizing the value and insights of secular psychology and the contemporary culture of therapy, we affirm that these disciplines are nonetheless incomplete, reductive, and in some cases antithetical to the healing traditions of the Church. While recognizing the aspirations for truth that are in many religious traditions, we reject the modern tendency toward religious syncretism. A lack of discernment relativizes faith and compromises the uniqueness and originality of Orthodox spirituality and of Jesus Christ himself, through whom alone we have genuine access to the Father (Jn 14.6).

Orthodox spirituality does not exist in a vacuum. It presupposes Orthodox doctrine and Orthodox ecclesiology and the variety within her many ethnic traditions. It is intimately bound up with the sacramental and liturgical life of the Church. Any attempt to practice it apart from active participation in that life is to cut it off from its living and life-giving roots.

Orthodox spirituality is liturgical, sacramental, and eucharistic.[3] Outside the experience of the Liturgy, it is impossible to understand the spirituality of the Orthodox Church. Holy men and women are those persons who have discovered the meaning of their life as liturgical beings, as ecclesial persons.

It must also be stressed that Orthodox spirituality is by nature ascetic and monastic. Dying to the world, the monastic person lives for Christ and for others. Unless we become dead to the world, and to the things in the world (1 Jn. 2.15), how shall we live the "life that is hidden in Christ" (Col. 3.3)? Have we not been buried with him through baptism and do we not die daily for the sake of God? It is difficult to accept that one must "lose one's life in order to save it" (Mt. 10.39). We must die to this world so that we may live in God, as St. Symeon the New Theologian[4] says: "If you do not want to die, that means you are already dead."

---

3. See Archimandrite Vasileios, *Hymn of Entry: Liturgy and Life in the Orthodox Church* (Crestwood, N.Y.: St. Vladimir's Seminary Press, 1984).

4. A Byzantine monk and mystic, Symeon (949–1022) is one of only three saints given the title "theologian" by the Orthodox Church, the others being St. John the Evangelist and St. Gregory Nazianzus. See Basil Krivochéine, *In the Light of Christ: Saint Symeon the New Theologian (949–1022), Life, Spirituality, Doctrine* (Crestwood, N.Y.: St. Vladimir's Seminary Press, 1986).

If we fully embrace the true spiritual life, out of love for the Lord, we will be full of joy and gladness. As a hymn of our Church says: "For those in the desert, life is blessed, they take flight with wings by their divine love."

Orthodox spiritual praxis seeks to bring the fallen image of man back to its glorious prototype, to interiorize the life of Christ to the point that we can attain "the measure of the stature of the fullness of Christ" (Eph. 4.13). Only then may we proclaim together with the Apostle, "It is no longer I who live, but Christ who lives in me" (Gal. 2.20). This transformation in Christ certainly includes the notion of a moral and ethical *imitatio Christi*,[5] but it goes beyond the external to the ontological, it is a change in the whole human being: heart, mind, body, soul, and spirit. It is the mystery of the resurrection, which enters deep into the darkness of our dead nature and raises us up from within, breaking down the gates of hell.

Genuine spirituality, an honest spiritual life, a life in the Holy Spirit, ought to be lived by everyone—clergy, laypeople, monastics.[6] And if we progress in it, we will find ourselves raised higher and higher. Should the Lord find us transformed by the performance of his commandments, at the moment when we depart for Jerusalem on high, he will surely grant to the workers of his vineyard the wages of their labors. For the Lord abundantly rewards the laborers of the eleventh hour, as abundantly as he does the disciples of the first rank.

As you know, many people who seek after spirituality are ultimately deceived and led astray, even into perilous situations. All Christians have a responsibility to their brothers and sisters. We who strive to live a spiritual life, a life in the Holy Spirit, must reach out to all our brethren and lead them by the hand. We must lead them back to the wellsprings of spirituality.

"Behold, now is the acceptable time, behold, now is the day of salvation" (1 Cor. 6.2). The Lord knocks at the door of our soul and waits for our answer. Let us open up to him, that he may enter in and partake of the banquet of faith with us, and abide in us. He is our most beloved

5. Latin for "imitation of Christ."

6. See Kallistos Ware, *The Orthodox Way* (Crestwood, N.Y: St. Vladimir's Seminary Press, 1995).

friend. Life with him is the perfection of the human person. For with him, the Holy Spirit is always present and the Father ever existent. The life in Christ, by the Holy Spirit, is life within the grace of the Holy Trinity, eternal blessedness unto the ages.

Spirituality and Human Rights

At the conferral of an honorary doctorate, Southern Methodist University, Dallas, November 3, 1997.

We thank you for your warm hospitality and for the high honor of this degree. We feel as though you have conferred it not on us but on the entire Orthodox Christian Church, which we lead as Ecumenical Patriarch. As the Ecumenical Patriarch, we have the sacred responsibility of guiding the faithful of the Greek Orthodox Archdiocese of America in their spiritual growth and development. This blessed archdiocese is celebrating seventy-five years of growth and progress this year. We are proud of the accomplishments that our faithful have made in America.

As the Ecumenical Patriarch, we also have the privilege of being elder brother among the leaders of the worldwide Orthodox Church. The origin of our position as Ecumenical Patriarch reaches back to the very beginning of Christianity. We are the 270th successor to the Apostle Andrew, the First-called disciple of Jesus Christ. By the mercy of God, this spiritual authority and ministry has been entrusted to us. It is the authority of Jesus Christ passed on in an unbroken continuity from the time of his earthly sojourn to the present. This authority is at the heart of Apostolic succession. It is the pearl of great price that we are called by God to guard and, at its heart, is the great commandment of Christ to love one another. Our relationship as a community of believers is founded on this commandment of love.

Spirituality and Secularism

The Christian message of love has been marginalized by the rise of modernity in the post-Enlightenment world. Often, the message of love is seen as simplistic, too naïve to matter in a complex secular society. The hallmark of modernity is that social empowerment is centered on the individual's self-conscious understanding of his place in the world. Human rights are seen as an outgrowth of individual rights, rights that have been described in increasingly secular terms since the Enlightenment.

Contemporary society is puzzled by, and often in conflict with, an interpretation of human rights that is centered on a religious understanding. American culture is bifurcated into two broad camps that are separated by differing religious sensibilities. Doctrinaire religious extremism limits human rights to narrow categories of judgmental norms that are mediated by human interpretation of divine will. Such extremism is the dangerous prelude to religious fanaticism and persecution. We reiterate our deeply held belief that violence in the name of religion is violence against all religion.

Secular American culture allows that human rights are God-given, but the relationship between God and man is always seen as personal, private, without any visible or public sign. Such a relationship is enshrined in the American Constitution and the Bill of Rights. These are indeed noble documents, and they are fundamental to the world's understanding of democratic principles. But as noble and necessary as these documents are in the global culture's vision of individual and human rights, they are rationalist constructs. They point to a human relationship with the divine by suggesting that basic rights are divinely ordained. However, they do not aspire to manifest within individual lives the complex spiritual relationship that we believe is the ontological reality of human existence. They prefer a mechanistic sense of order rather than an experience of the divine. The mystery of faith is fundamental to the human spirit, for it allows individuals to perceive their inner life as something more than the temporary conjunction of biology and electrical impulses.

A Seamless Garment

Our faith seeks to understand the entire cosmos and everything in it, as a seamless garment of God's vast creation. The individual exists not separate from the rest of creation and his fellow human beings but in constant relationship to the ontological plenitude. It is this constancy of relationship that informs an individual's understanding of his existence as being grounded in the created order. With this grounding, he is able to value himself in the context of the cosmos. His validation rests on God's love for the creation and not on the vagaries of mere human guarantees. It is in the context of this relationality that a just society may be founded and sustained. We believe that a just society is proof of God's will at work in mankind.

God's will is made manifest through those who conform their will to God. For Orthodox Christians, Jesus Christ is the perfect model of humanity acting in perfect concord with God's will. We believe that Jesus Christ is both perfect God and perfect man. He is the guide and the ultimate end result of the perfect union of the divine with the human. Through Christ's example—suffering, death, and resurrection—the entire creation has been transformed and is being transformed.[7] Since it was God's love that gave us his Son, the preexistent Word of God incarnate, we believe that the world and mankind are being transfigured by God's love.

As we receive the message of Christ's commandment to love one another, we become the agents of change in the world. We become transformed, moving from glory to glory in a process of divinization (or *theosis*).[8] Orthodox spirituality understands this process as one that is not merely individual but corporate. Society becomes transformed as well. We affect all whom we touch, by example and through our actions in the world.

The free will to choose to center our actions, our hearts, our minds on God is the image of God at work in our lives. We are created in his image, and our free will to choose between good and evil is the proof of that truth. The image of God within us is freedom. Since all human beings are created in the image and likeness of God, freedom is an inalienable right. It is inalienable from human being. It is an ontological reality.

Faith in God, faith in his iconic presence within humanity, is the source and guarantee of freedom. There can be no true freedom without faith in God, for, without God, freedom has no ontological reality. When freedom and human rights are threatened, even curtailed by the evil that human beings might perpetrate, faith in freedom is still possible.

---

7. See Archbishop Demetrios Trakatellis, *Authority and Passion: Christological Aspects of the Gospel of Mark* (Brookline, Mass.: Holy Cross Orthodox Press, 1987).

8. On the doctrine of deification, see Norman Russell, *The Doctrine of Deification in the Greek Patristic Tradition* (Oxford; New York: Oxford University Press, 2004).

Orthodox spirituality assures us that Orthodox Christians will always respect the human rights of others. If they do not respect those rights, then they have desecrated the image of God that is inherent in all human beings. It is the responsibility of religion to guide persons toward God, that they might seek justice in the love of one another. We see spirituality, the relationship of the individual to God, as being fundamental to the realization of freedom—the freedom of individuals to express their personhood as well as the faith that is necessary to affirm the personhood of others.

The seamless garment of God's creation places the human person at the nexus of the Creator's union with his creation. Divine and human coincide in every human being. The individual is the window of God's will in the creation. Our faith is the guarantee of our spiritual freedom, and that freedom guarantees our physical freedom in the world. Freedom is the key to the transformation of the world, the key to guaranteeing human rights as fundamental to humanity's existence. Faith assures us that freedom is more than government policy. Faith assures us that the denial of freedom is contrary to a higher authority whose largesse is always benevolent, for his commandment is to love one another.

It is our prayer to Almighty God that the fullest measure of freedom will be enjoyed by all human beings. We affirm that their rights are an inherent element of Orthodox spirituality, a dogmatic truth of the relationship between Christ and man. We pray that the Lord will grant peace and enlightenment to all who seek God in their hearts and minds, that they might keep the commandment in faith to love one another.

Economy and Ecology: I

Message to the Eleventh Eurasian Economic Summit, Istanbul, May 3, 2008.

It is with great pleasure that we have accepted to attend this meeting in order to address and greet the esteemed delegates of the Eleventh Eurasian Economic Summit hosted annually by the Marmara Group Foundation in association with the Social Research Foundation, which have once again admirably gathered an array at the highest level of world leaders in the financial and political sphere, together with representatives from academia and business as well as all influential walks of life.

The topics of your deliberations are undoubtedly at the forefront of global concern—namely, the rightful use of the planet's energy resources, the fair distribution of material goods to overcome poverty worldwide, and the development of authentic dialogue in the pursuit of peace throughout the world. Moreover, the intercultural and intercontinental dimension of the same issues is reflected in the very venue of this summit, which marks the unique historical privilege of our generation to make decisions that will not only resolve current problems but also confront them in an honest and definitive way for the benefit of generations to come.

For this nation—and, indeed, this city—stands at the frontier between Europe and Asia, reminding us that any appropriate response to and resolution of such critical issues can be anticipated only when people of all disciplines and backgrounds, above and beyond racial or religious boundaries, meet in the earnest hope of working together for a better world. It is the courage to hope for a world where there is enough for all people and where the world's resources are used respectfully and selflessly.

Religious Respect and Mutual Tolerance

We refer to the transcending even of religious boundaries precisely because the foremost purpose of the faith communities is surely the reflection and expression of the goodness of God in the reality and experience of our world. Those who believe in a living God are therefore called to interpret their convictions in a way that both suggests and manifests the divine wish for all people to enjoy the fruits of the earth in an equitable manner, without hurting one another and without abusing the resources of our planet. It is at once inconceivable and incorrect that religious adherents cannot appreciate how the way we pray in churches, mosques, and temples is a direct reflection of the way we live as citizens in our respective professions. And, by analogy, the way we treat other people and the natural environment on this earth is the clearest sign of just how authentically we pray to God in heaven.

During the middle of the sixth century, a renowned monk and mystic living in Palestine, Barsanuphius the Great,[9] remarked, "Not wounding

9. A monk living near Gaza during the sixth century, St. Barsanuphius received numerous visitors for spiritual counsel. While none of them would actually meet him in person, they related to him by means of correspondence.

my neighbor—that is the way of God!" We can think of no better definition of religious belief and moral practice for those of us who strive to inspire our faithful in accordance with godly precepts. At the same time, however, the timely words of St. Barsanuphius, also known as "the great old man," are formative for those who hold positions of leadership and responsibility and who strive to motivate international and interdisciplinary action in response to pressing global problems.

In this way, it becomes evident that religion plays not only a pivotal role in people's personal lives throughout the world but also a critical role as a force of social and institutional mobilization on a variety of levels. While the theological language of religion and spirituality may differ from the technical vocabulary of economics and politics, nevertheless the barriers that at first glance appear to separate religious concerns (such as salvation and spirituality) from pragmatic interests (such as commerce and trade) are not impenetrable. Indeed, such barriers appear to crumble before the manifold challenges of social justice and globalization. Whether we are dealing with environment or peace, poverty or hunger, education or healthcare, there is today a heightened sense of common concern and common responsibility, which is felt with particular acuteness by people of faith as well as by those whose outlook is expressly secular.

Our engagement with such issues does not of course in any way undermine or abolish the differences between the various disciplines or the disagreements that arise between those who look at the world in different ways. Yet the growing signs of a common commitment to work together for the well-being of humanity and the life of the world are encouraging. It is an encounter of individuals and institutions that bodes well for our world. And it is an involvement that highlights the supreme purpose and calling of humanity to transcend political or religious differences in order to transform the entire world for the glory of God.

Economy and Ecology: II

Message to the Twelfth Eurasian Economic Summit, Istanbul, May 6, 2009.

It is an honor to be invited to address this auspicious gathering of the Twelfth Eurasian Economic Summit, organized by the Marmara Foundation here in Istanbul in order for high-level dignitaries, policymakers, and relevant authorities to consider, among other critical issues, the relationship between international economy and global ecology.

Whether we are speaking about economy or ecology, from the perspective of the Ecumenical Patriarchate it is important to recognize that this world is our "home"—which is precisely what the Greek root *oikos*, or the prefix *eco-*, implies. This world is the home of everyone and of all creation. Indeed, the terms *ecology* and *economy* share the same etymological root. *Oiko-nomia* ("care and management of our household"), *oiko-logia* ("appreciation, or study, of our household"), and *oikou-mene* ("way of inhabiting the world as our home") are all derived from the root word *oikos*.

This means that the way we respond to issues related to the economy or to ecology will inevitably determine our worldview and our policy for the future of our planet. In very simple terms, it means that the way we treat basic natural resources, such as air and water, is crucial for the lifestyle that we choose to lead and the politics we choose to practice. The kind of priorities and programs that we establish with regard to consumption and recycling, eradicating biological and chemical waste, addressing the problem of global warming, and preserving our oceans, rivers, and lakes—all of these reflect the genuine interest that we have for the survival of the world, entrusted to us by our Creator.

Thus it is not by chance that the Ecumenical Patriarchate has focused its attention and ministry on preserving the natural environment. It is unfortunate and selfish, however, that we have restricted the application of the words *ecology* and *economy* to ourselves, as if we were the only inhabitants and proprietors of this world. This planet is indeed our home; yet it is also the home of everyone, as it is the home of every animal creature as well as of every form of life created by God. It is a sign of arrogance to presume that we human beings alone inhabit this world. The truth is that no economic system—no matter how technologically or socially advanced—can survive the collapse of the environmental systems that support it.

Beyond Borders: Global Responsibility

This recognition is surely one of the simplest yet greatest lessons we have all learned about globalization. None of us can any longer pretend to live as if the rest of the world does not exist. We engage with the rest of the world in our many travels, in our everyday conversations, in our morning newspapers every day, and on our television sets every evening. We have an ethical responsibility to consider carefully the way that we inhabit the world and the lifestyles that we choose to adopt. We can no longer live as isolated individuals, disengaged from events in our world. We are created for encounter, and we are judged based on our response to each encounter. We are social beings; we share the world; we live in community.

Moreover, the borders of this community have today been broadened to encompass our entire planet, and beyond. Today, we know all too well the sins associated with cheap labor and economic inequality. We are all able to perceive how assets or investments are transferred from one country to another in a way that leaves ordinary people feeling bewildered and disenfranchised, while at the same time making it impossible for anyone to hold investors accountable for their social and environmental behavior. We can see clearly that in global competition for economic gain there are losers as well as winners, victors as well as victims. And, through our own behavior or consumer choices, as well as our generally unquestioning acquisitiveness, we may also be encouraging bad behavior by the companies that dominate the global economy, instead of using in a positive way whatever influence we may have.

The Orthodox Church recognizes the natural creation as inseparable from the identity and destiny of humanity, because every human action leaves a lasting imprint on the body of the earth. Human attitudes and behavior toward creation directly impact on and reflect human attitudes and behavior toward other people. Our global economy is simply outgrowing the capacity of our planet to support it. At stake is not just our ability to live in a sustainable way but our very survival. Scientists estimate that those most hurt by global warming in years to come will be those who can least afford it. Therefore, the ecological problem of pollution is invariably connected to the social problem of poverty; indeed, all ecological activity is ultimately measured and properly judged by its impact and effect on the poor.

Economy, Ecology, and Poverty

This connection is detailed in a stark manner in the parable of the Last Judgment, where the Lord says, "I was hungry and you gave me food; I was thirsty and you gave me something to drink" (Mt. 25.35). A poor farmer in Asia, in Africa, or in North America will daily face the reality of poverty. For these persons, the misuse of technology or the eradication of trees is not merely harmful to the environment or destructive of nature; rather, it practically and profoundly affects the very survival of their families. Terminology such as *ecology*, *deforestation*, or *overfishing* is entirely absent from their daily conversation or concern. The "developed" world cannot demand from the "developing" poor an intellectual understanding with regard to the protection of the few earthly paradises that remain, especially in light of the fact that less than 10 percent of the world's population consumes more than 90 percent of the earth's natural resources.

Closely related to the problem of poverty is the problem of unemployment, which plagues societies throughout the world. It is abundantly clear that neither the moral counsel of religious leaders nor fragmented measures by socioeconomic strategists or political policymakers could be sufficient to curb this growing tragedy. The problem of unemployment compels us to reexamine the priorities of affluent societies in the West, and especially the unrestricted advance of development, which is considered only in its positive aspect in economic terms.

We appear to be trapped in the tyrannical cycle created by a need for constant productivity rises and increases in the supply of consumer goods. Thus, the economy assumes a life of its own, a vicious cycle that becomes independent of human need or human concern. What is needed is a radical change in politics and economics, one underlining the unique and primary value of the human person, thereby putting a human face on the concepts of employment and productivity. People in Western societies—as well as those who proclaim "Western" principles—ought to assume greater personal responsibility. They should contribute to the solution of the environmental crisis in accordance with their capacity in order not simply to assist the poor but to help wipe out poverty itself.

In our efforts, then, for the preservation of the natural environment, how prepared are we to sacrifice our greedy lifestyles? When will we learn to say, "Enough!"? When will we learn that treating all people, including the poor, in a just manner is more beneficial than charitable acts of goodwill? Will we direct our focus away from what we want to what the world needs? We may offer bread to the hungry—indeed, we may feel a sense of self-gratification in so doing—but when will we work toward a world that has no hunger? Moreover, do we endeavor to leave as light a footprint as possible on this planet for the sake of future generations?

Today, there are no excuses today for our lack of involvement. We have detailed information; the alarming statistics are readily available. We must choose to care. And it is with great personal satisfaction that we applaud the efforts of this summit to do precisely that.

Economy and Ecology: III

Message addressed to the G8 meeting, L'Aquila, Italy, July 2009.

The G8 governments will be gathering near Rome, Italy, during the month of July. Alongside critical issues facing the African continent, climate change will be the focus of urgent attention. This meeting provides a significant occasion for the G8 leaders to reflect on the future of our planet. Let us hope, then, that the opportunity will not be ignored and that the issue will not be dismissed. It is critical that the intimate connection between poverty and ecology be recognized if problems of either are to be addressed.

Climate change affects everyone. While the data may be variously debated, the situation is clearly unsettling. Dramatic increases of greenhouse gases in our atmosphere—largely due to the burning of fossil fuels—are causing global warming and in turn leading to melting ice caps, rising sea levels, the spread of disease, drought and famine. The European heat wave of 2003 could give way to unusually cool temperatures by 2060, while the 150,000 people that the World Health Organization conservatively estimates are already dying annually due to climate change will be but a fraction of the actual number.

It is painfully evident that our response to the scientific testimony has been generally reluctant and gravely inadequate. Unless we take radical and immediate measures to reduce emissions stemming from unsustainable—in fact, unjustifiable, if not simply unjust—excesses in the demands of our lifestyle, the impact will be both alarming and imminent.

Religious Leaders and Climate Change

Religious leaders throughout the world recognize that climate change is much more than an issue of environmental preservation. Insofar as it is human-induced, it is, as we have repeatedly stated in the past, a profoundly moral and spiritual problem. To persist in the current path of ecological destruction is not only folly. It is no less than suicidal, jeopardizing the diversity of the very earth that we inhabit, enjoy, and share. We have, therefore, described this path as a sin against God and creation. After all, the G8 accounts for two-thirds of global GDP and half of all global carbon dioxide emissions.

Ecological degradation also constitutes a matter of social and economic justice. For those who will most directly and severely be affected by climate change will be the poorer and more vulnerable nations (what Christian scriptures refer to as our "neighbor") as well as the younger and future generations (the world of our children, and of our children's children). Those of us living in G8 nations either consume or else corrupt far too much of the earth's resources.

There is a close link between the economy of the poor and the ecology of the planet. Conservation and compassion are intimately connected. The web of life is a sacred gift of God—ever so precious and ever so delicate. We must serve our neighbor and preserve our world with both humility and generosity, in a perspective of frugality and solidarity alike. After the great flood, God pledged never again to destroy the world: "As long as the earth endures, seedtime and harvest, cold and heat, summer and winter, day and night, shall not cease" (Gen. 8.22). How tragic it would be, however, if we were the ones responsible for their destruction. The footprint that we leave on our world must be lighter, much lighter.

Africa is the continent least responsible for global warming, yet it bears the most detrimental consequences while also being the least equipped to cope with the changes. Harvest cycles in Ethiopia and other parts of eastern and southern Africa are shortening, leading to further food insecurity for the world's poorest people. Elevated temperatures create an incalculable increase in the range of vector-borne diseases and lack of clean water. Populations affected by fatal diseases such as malaria, dengue fever, and cholera are rising dramatically. Even a conservative estimate indicates the number of people impacted by flooding could increase from 1 million (in 1990) to 70 million (by 2080).

Faith communities must undoubtedly first put their own houses in order; their adherents must embrace the urgency of the issue. This process has already begun, although it must be intensified. Religions realize the primacy of the need for a change deep within people's hearts. They are also emphasizing the connection between spiritual commitment and moral ecological practice. Faith communities are well placed to take a long-term view of the world as God's creation. In theological terminology, that is called "eschatology."[10] Moreover, we have been taught that we are judged on the choices we make. Our virtue can never be assessed in isolation from others but is always measured in solidarity with the most vulnerable. Yet churches, mosques, synagogues, temples, and other houses of worship consume only a fraction of the energy consumed by manufacturing industries, modern technologies, and commercial companies.

Breaking the Vicious Cycle

Breaking the vicious circle of economic stagnation and ecological degradation is a choice with which we are uniquely endowed at this crucial moment in the history of our planet. The destructive consequences of indifference and inaction are ever more apparent. At the same time, the constructive solutions for mitigating global warming are increasingly merging. Government, businesses, and religious institutions pursue cooperation, converging in commitment and compelling people to act. Only when they work together can a problem of this magnitude be addressed and resolved. The responsibility as well as the response is collective. We know how to prevent such rapid climate change. We now need a powerful network of diverse yet connected leaders committed to empowering individual and commercial action.

The G8 meeting is a golden opportunity for world leaders to issue a decisive signal to the entire world that they recognize their unique role, that they respect the more vulnerable in this situation, and that they are prepared to assume responsibility for an issue of critical significance and global urgency.

May they be inspired by grace and justice, guided by reason and responsibility, and filled with selflessness and compassion.

---

10. The teaching about the "last times"—namely, the kingdom of heaven. From the Greek word *eschata*, meaning "last things."

Racial and Religious Discrimination

Statement to the United Nations Durban World Conference against Racism, Racial Discrimination, Xenophobia and Intolerance, March 17, 2001.

From an Orthodox Christian perspective, the virtues of diversity and tolerance provide the fundamentals for a Christian life, much as sunlight and water nurture a plant. Without either of these virtues, nourishment is lacking and spiritual death is inevitable.

An Orthodox Christian celebrates the diversity of the entirety of God's creation, rejoicing in the infinite multitude of beauty and meaning which only diversity can truly manifest. We recognize that diversity is fundamentally necessary for the achievement and sustenance of unity amongst all the members of the Church in the very same Body of Christ. Whenever human beings fail to recognize the value of diversity, they deeply diminish the glory of God's creation. Following the example of the three persons of the Holy Trinity—the Father, the Son, and the Holy Spirit—all human beings are called to exist relationally to one another, united in the bond of love, as different and unique persons, each endowed with specific talents and characteristics, each created in the image and likeness of God.[11] All human beings—regardless of religion, race, national origin, color, creed, or gender—are living icons of God, innately worthy of such respect and dignity. Whenever human beings fail to treat others with this respect, they insult God, the Creator, as is explained through the teachings of the Christian scriptures.

The Orthodox Experience and Practice

Orthodox Christians throughout the world live side by side with peoples of other religions and Christian confessions. With the rapid rise of advances in communication and mobility, human beings are increasingly liberated from the geographical boundaries that used to separate them. As

11. See Boris Bobrinskoy, *The Mystery of the Trinity: Trinitarian Experience and Vision in the Biblical and Patristic Tradition* (Crestwood, N.Y.: St. Vladimir's Seminary Press, 1999).

a result of recast boundaries, people now find themselves living in a global village amid new neighbors who represent widely differing world perspectives, histories, and cultures. The realities of pluralism challenge each person in the global village to reflect more critically on the teachings of his or her own faith, in light of the multitude of differing perspectives. An Orthodox Christian responds to these challenges with the understanding that we must always be tolerant of the perspectives of others, especially when such perspectives differ on the basis of religious, cultural, or historical ideology.

The Orthodox Church does not seek to convince others of any one particular understanding of truth or revelation, nor does it seek to convert others to a particular mode of thinking. Rather, she calls all persons from all walks of life to feel the heartbeat of the Church, to sense the breath of life inhaling and exhaling from her body—the Body of Christ—and to experience her maternal love and comfort, thereby being at peace while listening openly to the perspective of the other with respect and tolerance.

The opposite of the perspective of respect and tolerance is the perspective of fear and self-righteousness. Whenever human beings react to the perspectives and beliefs of others on the basis of fear and self-righteousness, they violate the God-given right and freedom of others to come to know God and one another in the manner inherent to their identity as peoples. Unfortunately, as a result of sin in the world, the effects of which lead ultimately to spiritual death, human beings are easily predisposed to viewing others on the basis of fear. Such xenophobic tendencies are chiefly the result of being out of communion with God, who calls all members of his creation into his love and eternal presence. We see the first example of such an occurrence in the book of Genesis, when Adam fell prey to the effects of evil in the world, being forced away from the close communion he had enjoyed with God, the Creator of the world. Yet God, out of his love for humankind, continues to call all human beings into perfect communion with him. When human beings are in communion with God, who himself is the very essence of inexhaustible love, xenophobia—the Greek word for "fear of the other"—is not possible, since human beings do not see each other as strangers but rather as brothers and sisters in communion with the loving Lord.

Central, therefore, to the teachings of the Orthodox Church is the fundamental belief that Christianity must play an active role in efforts toward the reconciliation of all peoples. This understanding is based on the teachings of Jesus of Nazareth, the Christ, who preached a message precisely of reconciliation, engaging in dialogue and conversation with peoples from all walks of life, with the simple twofold message to love God with all their hearts and to love their neighbor as they would themselves. The reconciliatory role of Christianity can be initiated and sustained only by and through the voice and ear of genuine tolerance. The virtue of tolerance, together with its twin virtue diversity, reflects the divine attributes of love which God maintains in his essence perfectly, infinitely, indescribably, and inexhaustibly.

The Orthodox Church, which heralds this message of love, the Christian Gospel, categorically condemns racism, xenophobia, and all other forms of related intolerance as destructive to the vision of peace that God desires and that human beings, organizations of goodwill, and, above all, the Church aim to promote. Furthermore, the Orthodox Church commends all organizations of social, international, and political character that are dedicated to the pursuit of justice, believing that the work of such organizations serves to advance the good of society and as such is most pleasing before God.

Religious Tolerance and Discrimination

Address at the OSCE Conference, Brussels, September 13, 2004.

It is with great joy indeed that we participate in this conference, although we do not represent some specific state or national or international organization but rather the Ecumenical Patriarchate, which is accorded a precedence of honor over all Orthodox Christian patriarchates and autocephalous churches. The reason of our joy is that this conference revolves around the topic of tolerance and the fight against racism, xenophobia, and discrimination, a topic to which we are very sensitive.

We say this because the Ecumenical Patriarchate is not a national organization and does not represent any particular national or local church, such as the Greek, or the one in Turkey, the country of its see, but is a supranational ecclesiastical institution, holding within its bosom the faithful of many nationalities and maintaining a benevolent and equitable disposition, being open to all human beings on equal terms. It is an institution that demonstrates religious tolerance as a beautiful reality, for we bear respect toward all our fellow humans, irrespective of their faith. Without any trace of fanaticism or discrimination on account of differences of religion, we coexist peacefully and in a spirit that honors each and every human being.

The Ecumenical Patriarchate: Beyond Nationalism

Furthermore, we stand firmly against any racist ideology. Since 1872, a time when nationalism was rife in Europe and abroad, as propounded in chauvinist theories and a host of pan-Slavist, pan-Germanic, and generally pan-nationalist movements, we had condemned nationalism and racism by a synodal decision. These movements were leading to the establishment of national Christian churches and rendering the unifying message of the Gospel the servant of nationalistic divisions and conflicts.

Many centuries ago, at a time when the latinization of all nations was pursued by authorities in the West, we as Ecumenical Patriarchate did not hesitate to create a special alphabet for the Slavic language, through the efforts of our missionary saints Cyril and Methodius,[12] and to translate our church-service books, promoting the establishment of a new, non-Greek civilization: namely, the civilization of the Slavs.[13] In each country we have always sought, and still do, indigenous leaders for the local churches, and, when they are found and/ or trained, we assign to them the responsibility of governing those churches without any racist considerations or discrimination. History records a multitude of such instances, and the present reality confirms our position, even though nationalist tendencies may still exist among certain ecclesiastical figures, without of course our approval.

In 1976, on the occasion of the Fourth Pan-Orthodox Pre-Conciliar Conference, held in Geneva,[14] we expressed the desire that the Orthodox

---

12. Two brothers, Cyril (827–69) and Methodius (820–84), who brought Eastern Orthodox Christianity to the Slavs of central Europe in the ninth century. These great missionaries have been recognized as "equals to the Apostles"

13. See John Meyendorff, *The Byzantine Legacy in the Orthodox Church* (Crestwood, N.Y.: St. Vladimir's Seminary Press, 1982), and Dimitri Obolensky, *The Byzantine Commonwealth: Eastern Europe, 500–1453*, 2nd ed. (London: Phoenix Press, 2000).

14. See Metrop. Damaskinos of Tranoupolis, "Towards the Great and Holy Council," *Greek Orthodox Theological Review* 24 (1979): 99–116. See also Maximos Aghiorgoussis,

Church contribute to the upholding of the Christian ideals of peace, freedom, brotherhood, and love among peoples and to the elimination of racial discrimination—a development leading to interreligious cooperation and, through it, to the abolishment of fanaticism of every kind, and likewise to the reconciliation of all peoples and to the predominance of the ideals of freedom and peace in the world, for the benefit of modern humanity, regardless of race or religious conviction. This issue has occupied our thoughts, and we have discussed the means by which the Orthodox Church would be able to contribute to the elimination of racism and of the fanaticism that derives from it. For extreme racism undoubtedly breeds, or provokes, religious fanaticism, which in turn leads to the scourge of terrorism, which in our present era delivers its blows on humanity so tragically and extensively.

Embracing Strangers

We are not afraid of strangers: on the contrary, we cherish them. The application of the apostolic words "Be not forgetful to entertain strangers" (Heb. 13.2) is our daily practice and has been so for centuries, without concessions to any form of discrimination. Therefore, we consider the topic of your conference most familiar and dear to us and are pleased that humanity has progressed so far as to put forth such a demand, on behalf of all human beings, for what we have always been preaching, even though many have regarded it as utopian. That demand is put forth by means of the present conference and by numerous other praiseworthy activities of the Organization for Security and Cooperation in Europe and of several other international organizations and agencies.

We have often expressed the view that all humans are equal both in spiritual terms and before the law—a view that is espoused by all sensible people, regardless of religious conviction—and have spoken repeatedly of the necessity that all should welcome the differences of others and of their cultures, with all that such an attitude should entail.

With every given opportunity we emphasize that the religious rights of minorities must be respected and that one of the most substantial of those

---

"Towards the Great and Holy Council: The First Pre-synodal Pan-Orthodox Conference in Geneva," *Greek Orthodox Theological Review* 21 (1976): 423–28.

rights involves the right to educate staff members under the care of specially trained educators, for, if this task is assigned to others, outside the minority, there is the direct and real danger of gradually distorting the content of the minority's religious tradition. That is in fact the reason why all attempts to distort peoples' religions involve the effort to gain access to their educational system and to thereby exert influence.

The overstressing of racial origins, and racism as well as discrimination against weaker minorities on the basis of racial, religious, linguistic or any other reasons, together with xenophobia—these are ideologies and mental attitudes that are entirely opposed to the attitude, the convictions, and the principles espoused by the Ecumenical Patriarchate, who is the main exponent of the Orthodox Church. The term *ecumenical* seeks precisely to denote the acceptance of all people who live on our planet, our *oikoumene*, as equal and equally acceptable.

The Ecumenical Patriarchate and Universality

Thus, from the Ecumenical Patriarchate—which is perhaps the very first institution that has historically been accorded the title *Ecumenical* (fourth century A.D.),[15] denoting its universality, not in any sense of holding dominion over the world, but in the sense of accepting all human beings as equals—we feel profoundly moved as we extend to you our wholehearted greetings and praises for your work.

We realize, of course, that there have been times and places when Christians did not live the Christian brotherhood of humanity and that many times they tried to uphold their self-seeking discrimination against their fellow humans by taking recourse to the holy texts of their faith. However, those were but deviations from the right path, and grievous sins on the part of those who behaved in such a condemnable, racist manner. Surely such censure cannot be leveled against healthy Christianity, which unequivocally condemns racism, discrimination, and xenophobia.

Saint Paul the Apostle himself, while being of Jewish origin with a complete Jewish and Greek education, during the first period of his life, when he had not yet come to know Christ, was deeply intolerant and was persecuting the Church of Christ, under the influence of certain Jewish

---

15. See Introduction.

circles of the time. Once he came to know Christ, he overcame his nationalism and religious intolerance, and, owing to his Hellenistic education, became sensible of the unity of humankind, of the equal love that God bears toward all human beings. From that time on, he declared the equality of all before God, an equality that ought to become also the equality of all before one another. He is worthy of admiration for having conceived and expressed the profoundest tenets of Christianity regarding the brotherhood of humanity through pithy and unforgettable statements such as:

> There is neither Jew nor Greek, there is neither slave nor free, there is neither male nor female: for ye are all one in Christ Jesus. (Gal.3.28)

Just a few simple words overturned all the discriminations between human beings of that time. That was immensely daring for his era, an era that recognized slavery as a lawful and morally correct institution, an era that regarded women as objects (*res*), an era when the prevalent attitude among Jews was that they were God's chosen people who had to keep themselves pure from any mingling with the society of the gentiles, an era also when other peoples strongly experienced a sense of their supremacy over all others, as was the case with the Roman citizens vis-à-vis all other nations.

The present conference is a fruit and an outcome of this declaration that was so revolutionary for its time, upsetting established order as it did. Of course, not all of its participants are adherents of the religion preached by the Apostle Paul, but we all rest assured that the principle he voiced in the words we quoted stands true and indispensable for peaceful coexistence and the progress of humankind.

Unfortunately, nationalism of all types and the racial discrimination based thereon, the oppressive measures often reaching to the extreme of eliminating minorities of various kinds, the discrimination based on religious considerations and oppression, the violations of prohibitions on religious conversion often carrying the death penalty, the extreme disadvantage at which women find themselves in many lands, all kinds of exploitation of children, xenophobia and the atrocities perpetrated wantonly against strangers for the sole reason that they differ from the majority inhabiting a given place—all these are shameful and deplorable dark spots on our civilization: dark and shameful spots that the Organization for Security and Cooperation in Europe, in holding this conference, is commendably seeking to eliminate.

The Irrationality of Nationalism

May it be permitted to us to express the view that racist nationalism is profoundly irrational. The racist view of any nazism absolutely lacks any scientific basis. It is the product of empty egotism, which, instead of seeking—as it should—to reward people on the basis of their good and meritorious works, establishes its domineering views merely on the accident of their racial origin. In other words, no person is worthy of any praise, since no one has engaged in an honorable effort in being born within any given race. Thus those who boast merely over their racial origins deserve our pity rather than our esteem, for they have nothing of their own to contribute and so seek to make much of qualities of theirs that they did not have to take pains to acquire.

On the other hand, xenophobia is the product of a timorous conscience—specifically, of individuals who lack sufficient self-confidence, who do not feel secure in their personal status. Strangers are thus regarded as a threat, as posing a hazard.

It is precisely when we do not feel self-assured and confident that we consider others, especially strangers, as the root cause of our worries and turn against them in the hope that by removing them we remove the danger that ostensibly threatens our being. Nevertheless, the insecurity that breeds xenophobia is internal. Strangers are not the cause of it. It exists before their presence is felt. It simply seeks to set them up, blindly, as the object on which to place the blame for its existence. Proof of the truth of this is found in those great nations and confident peoples who receive strangers favorably and apply their resources to the strangers' progress.

The situation becomes unbearable for indigenous minorities, for those who exist within intolerant societal majorities, for they are deemed alien while being just as indigenous as the majority. In many cases the majorities merely indulge in intense attempts to assimilate the minorities culturally, religiously, nationally, and linguistically. There are other, more painful instances where majorities, looking for scapegoats for their backwardness or for their failure to progress, will find them in the members of the minority, against whom they turn virulently with the aim of destroying them, exterminating the minority as the ostensible cause of their real or imagined woes, even though the minority in question is actually not in the least responsible for what it is being blamed for. And then there are cases where confrontations drive minorities to take desperate measures of a bellicose nature that exacerbate the conflict and drive away any hope of peace.

Regrettably, the societies of our times have yet to reach the necessary level of maturity to become fully accepting of strangers. The clause of the European Treaty with respect to the freedom of taking up residence constitutes a courageous move in the right direction, but certain reasonable reservations are bound to curtail its breadth of application. The reason for this would be that unrestricted freedom of taking up residence, if it oversteps certain boundaries, will certainly spark adverse reactions, because societies have not yet reached the advanced degree of freedom espoused and instituted by the Treaty.

For our part, we pray that society will mature even beyond the limits envisaged by the Treaty so that all of humanity, imbued with the spirit of brotherhood, will coexist in equitability, freedom, and mutual respect. And with such a prayer we come to the close of our brief address and express our gratitude to you for having invited us to this forum, and for the attention with which you have followed our words. We add our prayer that the work of the conference will be crowned with success and that during its course resolutions that will benefit humanity will be achieved.

Religious Tolerance and Interreligious Dialogue

Message to the World Summit of Religious Leaders, Moscow, July 3, 2006.

It is with honor and a sense of responsibility that we address this summit of religious leaders who have gathered here today, in an effort once again to work closely together to appeal to the conscience of our world. We all come from a variety of religious traditions, and we might seem to be different in many ways. Yet we share the same frustrations and hopes for the future. We all have a common vision of peace and prosperity for our world, which is experiencing turmoil, division, and conflicts. For us, all forms of dialogue and cooperation between religions are welcome, and we firmly believe that religion can be a key factor and a solid foundation for peace and dialogue among civilizations.

The Ecumenical Patriarchate, in its efforts to support the creation of such a stable basis for peace and reconciliation among the various religions, so that they may stand strong in the face of today's and tomorrow's challenges that lay ahead, has an ongoing interreligious dialogue with all major religions of the world. This dialogue started almost thirty years ago. In 1977 we officially began our academic dialogue with Judaism. In 1986 we began an official dialogue with Islam as well. Interreligious dialogue is one of the main concerns of the entire Orthodox World, as we stated in the Third Pan-Orthodox Pre-Conciliar Conference in 1986.[16] In 2001, religious leaders came together in Brussels at a very important moment in the history of interreligious dialogue and produced a document that became known as the Brussels Declaration.[17] It states:

> Recognizing that, in the history of humankind, members of religious communities have committed crimes, we express our regret and repentance. We nevertheless affirm that extremists do not reflect the teachings of these religions, and therefore religious beliefs are not responsible for the acts of adherents that are committed either by transgression or by misinterpretation. This is why we reaffirm the statement of the 1992 Berne Declaration and the 1994 Bosphorus Declaration that "a crime committed in the name of religion is a crime against religion."[18]

One of the major roles of religion, then, is to bring the peace of God into the world on a local and global level. It is the responsibility of religious

---

16. Four Pan-Orthodox Pre-Conciliar Conferences have been held to date—the first in Rhodes (1972) and the other three in Chambésy (1982, 1986, and 2009). Moreover, four Pan-Orthodox Conferences have been held to decide the convocation of a "Holy and Great Council." These were convened in Rhodes (1961, 1962, and 1963) and in Chambésy (1968). Finally, Inter-Orthodox Preparatory Commissions have met at Chambésy (1971, 1986, 1990, 1993, and 2009). In addition, two Special Congresses have been held at Chambésy (1977, on the common celebration of Easter; and 1995, a meeting of canon-law specialists to discuss regulations for the operation of episcopal assemblies in the diaspora).

17. For the full text, see Chapter 6, "Major Declarations: Public Proclamations."

18. Ibid.

leaders to prevent religious fervor from being used for purposes that are alien to its role.

Our purpose is to continue our constructive dialogues which benefit the world. They are tools for overcoming our problems. We reassert our unwavering resolve to continue with our constructive interreligious dialogues both to achieve a spirit of mutual understanding and sincere cooperation and to promote such a spirit in the practical affairs of our contemporary multicultural society. Therefore, we give our full support to all interreligious and intercultural initiatives that are guided by such a spirit. It is in this spirit of cooperation that we address you today.

The Human and Historical Role Models

Let us take a close look at the realities of today and at how we can offer our insights in an effort to make this world a better place, not only for ourselves but for the generations to come. Unfortunately, there is an ongoing effort by some to present religion as an outsider in the way that society is shaped. We witness how religion is abused and purposely presented as a means of terrorism. We are saddened to witness the injustice that happens in our time when religions are portrayed as closely linked with terrorist activities. People forget quite easily the nature of religion, which is spiritual; and they overlook that the teachings of religions suggest and shape a discernible *human role model* for the structure of society. How can these individuals claim that religions embrace terrorist notions? Fundamentalism can be found everywhere, even in religion. But this does not allow the labeling of an entire religion as a cradle of terrorism. Through their teachings, all religions influence the relationships between human beings, God, and the world. It is obvious that the various religious traditions, which have always shaped the spiritual map of the world, are not a threat to the peaceful coexistence of the peoples.[19]

It is well known that the mixture of nations and religions grew in the period of the empires (of Alexander the Great, of the Romans, of the Byzantines, and so on). However, despite the great diversity of religious and political traditions, relations among the various religious and political

19. See Anastasios Yannoulatos, "Facing People of Other Faiths," *Greek Orthodox Theological Review* 17, nos. 1–4 (1993).

groups were on the whole polarized and strained, inimical to peaceful coexistence and harmony. This may easily be explained by the fact that the state controlled each of these groups individually, and these groups in turn managed their own affairs internally, without any need to relate or defer to other groups.

Despite the occasional explosions of religious intolerance and fanaticism, the contemporary interreligious dialogue between Christianity and other religions rightly seeks in these historical models the standard criteria for the necessity of the dialogue. It also seeks the foundation of a peaceful coexistence of people and nations in the multicultural society of the contemporary world. The efforts by some to label as religions certain groups that endorse violence and terrorism is therefore not only insubstantial but abhorrent. The example of history is here to remind us, if not to teach us, that peaceful coexistence is not only possible but has been a reality for hundreds of years.

The claim that there is a "clash of civilizations"[20] and cultures on the basis of religious convictions is, in our opinion, a groundless attempt to create more frustration among us and to bring the interreligious dialogue to a halt. While some insist that a "clash of civilizations" is inevitable, the representatives of many civilizations have gathered here today in a spirit of brotherhood and harmony. This proves them wrong once again. May our heavenly Father grant us the strength to maintain that fraternal spirit in years to come. We unanimously reject the assumption that religion contributes to an inevitable clash of civilizations. On the contrary, we affirm the constructive and instructive role of religion in the dialogue among civilizations.

The Role of Religion

It is true that religious sentiments are on the rise and that religion is assuming a more prominent place on the world stage. Maybe this is what creates the tensions. One would not expect that people would easily turn to their religious roots, and so we see the effort to label religion as a force not for stability but for further conflict. However, we do know that this

---

20. See Samuel Huntington, *The Clash of Civilizations and the Remaking of World Order* (New York: Simon and Schuster, 1996).

effort will not be successful, and we prove it once more by our common dialogues and efforts to bring harmony and reconciliation to our people. Sure enough, during the last few decades the collapse of the sovereign totalitarian ideologies, as well as the irreversible rapid enforcement of the idea of globalization, has revived the rejected specter of religious intolerance and fanaticism.

These phenomena were manifested with tragic consequences in the unbalanced threat of terrorism, and they poison the relations of nations and religions in a period of multiple political, religious, social, and spiritual bewilderments. It is our unshakable conviction that these ill phenomena cannot prevail, nor can they be prolonged, for they use religion for purposes foreign and definitely opposite to the mission of religion at large. But it is also our unshakable conviction that these ill phenomena will not disappear by themselves, since they are being fed and maintained by superstitions of the past.

It is our sacred responsibility to inform and educate our own flocks and to teach them through our own actions that we all hold a person's life to be the most important gift of God to humanity. We are not immune to the forces of history; but neither are we helpless before them. We cannot lament paradise lost; but we must find hope in the kingdom at hand. We must answer the fratricide and fragmentation of nationalism with the brotherly love and integration of ecumenism. We must teach our people tolerance, which is ultimately based on respect for the sanctity and rights of individual human beings. Indeed, if there is one place where the spiritual and secular universes converge, it is in the individual, in the human person. And it is through education that we will be able to reach out to the world and solidify our claims that religion is only a means of bringing peace among us.

Yet, those in positions of power tend to forget this reality, and we are called to remind them that there is more at stake when they seem to forget that we are all of the same nature, that we all share the same air, and that the sun rises and shines on us all. We witness how poverty and mass destruction affects our lives on a daily basis. We struggle to make our voices heard, but it is only by uniting our voices, by maintaining a common ground, that all of us together will be able to make a difference. Many times in today's world we feel as if our voice is alone in a desert. We have to unite our voices and become like the prophets of the past, calling out to all those in power to stop their actions and see what they have been doing to this world.

We live in modernity, and we have walked on the moon, yet at the same time the unthinkable is a reality: words like *famine* and *poverty* and *mass destruction* are parts of our everyday reality. Countries all over the world stand by witnessing the death of millions of people because of lack of food, water, shelter, and healthcare. We witness how thousands of people each year suffer from HIV/AIDS and so many more illnesses, and yet we feel that there is nothing to be done. The reality of suffering is so powerful, but we tend to easily forget about it. We have to react and react as one entity. We are gathered here today to show the world that as religious leaders we urge those in power to realize the devastation that occurs on a daily basis and to realize the impact it has on our world.

The Orthodox Christian Church has searched long for a language with which to address the strife and havoc that takes many forms. In 1872 a great synod, held in our Patriarchal Cathedral at the Phanar, in the name of the Prince of Peace, issued an unqualified condemnation of the sin of phyletism,[21] saying,

> We renounce, censure, and condemn racism—that is, racial discrimination, ethnic feuds, hatreds, and dissensions within the Church of Christ.[22]

We must answer with deep and uncompromising ecumenism. That is why we convened an unprecedented Pan-Orthodox Council, or *synaxis*,[23] of the heads of the world's patriarchal and autocephalous Orthodox churches in March of 1992[24]—an unusual display of Christian solidarity, and a return to the ecumenism of centuries past. During this truly historic gathering, the spiritual heads expressed deep sadness over "fratricidal confrontation" and for "all its victims," calling on all religious leaders to offer "particular attention, pastoral responsibility and wisdom from God, in

21. Or racial discrimination.

22. A Pan-Orthodox synod convened in Constantinople in August 1872 in order to respond to the heresy of racism.

23. Greek for "gathering" or "assembly."

24. Ecumenical Patriarch Bartholomew was the first ever to convoke such assemblies of heads of autocephalous churches—in Istanbul (1992, only weeks after his enthronement), on the Island of Patmos (1995), in Jerusalem and Istanbul on the occasion of the new millennium (2000), and most recently in Istanbul (2008).

order that the exploitation of religious sentiment for political and national reasons may be avoided."

Misconceptions about Religion

Nevertheless, as we have already stated, there seem to be superstitions that we tend to harbor, either willingly or unwillingly, and they seem to fuel the misunderstandings among our faithful. Such superstitions originated many times in the reproachful and derogatory approach that religions took in contrast to modern political systems. These systems, from misinformation and lack of knowledge, call on religions to adjust to the political and legal criteria of the political systems of the world and, in a parallel fashion, to detach themselves from the influence of their religious nature. These assumptions, however, undermine and degrade the principles of these religions. This is why the radical contestations and disputes of the political authorities of the world create results opposite to those anticipated. Only through dialogue can there be a trustworthy beginning and a procedure whereby people, nations, and political systems are reconciled.

Another superstition has originated in the nonrational evaluation of the difference between the historical depth and the contemporary reality of religions—a superstition whose influence grows not only through demographic development but also through the continual expansion of its presence on a universal scale. This new reality cannot be overlooked or only partially considered. At least, it cannot be overlooked without any detriment to the planning of the relations of the religions, because then the context of peaceful coexistence of the peoples is not really constructed, but on the contrary there is an aggravation of the conflicting relations, with unpredictable and definitely painful consequences for the common vision of peace.

We must not forget, however, the ideological particularity of modern Western civilization's ignoring or even looking down on the institutional role of religion, not only in the internal function of the state but also in intercultural dialogue. It is in this dialogue that religion would be able to contribute in a decisive way both to the qualitative fullness and to the social effectiveness of any constructive proposals. Although the political system of the Western world desires unofficial dialogue with religious organizations, it systematically avoids making use of the influence of the religious leadership to whom all religious organizations refer their existence. Sure enough, religious leaders make their own initiatives for dialogue, but their cooperation with political authorities would give a more immediate social context to the political declarations for the protection of peace, social justice, and human rights, without any ethnic, racial, religious, social, or other unacceptable discriminations.

Without question, there are many political, religious, economic, and social misconceptions that one culture, civilization, or religion has of another, misconceptions that can easily foster the known tendencies toward provocation and conflict. All of us are aware of such situations, but we are certain that, with our determination and prayers, we will be able to promote our common desire and hopes for a peaceful and ample coexistence of all peoples, nations, and religions of our world. It is a sacred goal, and we must always continue to work together and be an example to people worldwide. We do have differences, but what we have in common is much more valuable and much more important. We carry with us, each and every one of us, our religious traditions, which can be used as lights in the darkness of our modern times. We can help our world and together strive for a future in which our children will be able to glorify God.

It is in this sense that this gathering is extremely important for the realization of our goals. The role of religion in the circumstances of the contemporary world requires the transcendence of all morbid manifestations of religious fanaticism and intolerance of the past, which are alien to the spiritual mission of religion and have heaped many woes on humanity. The role of religion involves as well the full-hearted support of peace, social justice, and human rights, which are called for in the teachings of all religions, to a greater or lesser extent, and constitute a common basis for their constructive dialogue with contemporary political ideology vis-à-vis the relations between human beings and between peoples.

Terrorism

Message for the memorial service of victims of the terrorist attack in Beslan, Northern Ossetia, September 21, 2004.

We are gathered here today to pray for the unjust loss, a few days ago, of our children and brothers in the city of Beslan in Ossetia, as holy scripture commands us "to pray for the dead" (2 Macc. 12.44). Children who were innocent and had no trace of evil in them, young students together with their teachers and parents, were grabbed by death, in a matter of seconds, by unlawful and bloodthirsty men who dared to demand their alleged rights through the blood of unsuspecting souls, oblivious of any responsibility. Dreams and hopes, plans for the future, noble visions and expectations fell apart in ruins. "Look away from me; I will weep bitterly, labor not to comfort me, because of the spoiling" of the sons and daughters of my people (Is. 22.4), says Russia, with a bitter taste in her mouth. And the entire Orthodox Church throughout the whole world participates in this bitter mourning and the heavy bereavement, by shedding tears and beating her breast and observing a great mourning (Sir. 38.16–18) commensurate with the value of the victims.

Therefore, we all sympathize with His Beatitude Patriarch of Moscow and All Russia, beloved brother and concelebrant Alexei, spiritual father of those murdered, and we condole wholeheartedly with His Excellency President Vladimir Putin, who bears the grave burden of the injustice and murder of so many young innocent citizens. We are all members of the one Body of Christ, and our sorrow and pain are common.

The murderous killers and terrorists ignore the Lord's command "Thou shalt not kill" and the even more particular command "The innocent and righteous slay thou not" (Ex. 23.7). They disregard the indirect feeling of mercy and justice. They totally ignore all the anger that all sensible humanity feels for them. For this reason, "their hands are full of blood" (Is. 1.15), blood that is entirely innocent and defenseless, blood that is calling out to God from the earth of Beslan. Who drove them to this cruel murder? The blindness of their souls, their demented fanaticism, and the distortion of the religious values they claim to adhere to. But there is no religion that blesses terrorism, blind violence, crime, the killing of the innocent, and no patriotism or racial interest relieves those who committed these acts of the responsibility for the atrocious crime. Let them answer to the Righteous Judge for this unheard-of villainous deed they have dared to commit.

We, however, who believe in Christ the Righteous, the Master of Life and Resurrection, let us bend our knees in prayer so that the bones of the innocent victims of Ossetia might rise as herbs and their souls might find their place among those poor and innocent who had been slaughtered by the murderous Herod, and among all the holy children-martyrs and martyrs of our faith, both of the old times and the new.[25] Furthermore, we pray that the land of Russia, which has given birth to many saints, will never again experience such a terrorist attack, and that her noble people will not mourn any more innocent victims. We pray that for the entire world as well. We also pray that the Holy Spirit will illuminate the darkened minds of the agitators and evildoers, so that they will dissociate themselves from their cruel and outrageous plans and seek more humane and peaceful ways of fulfilling their demands, if they have a sense of justice.

May the memory of the innocent victims of the slaughter in Beslan—the infants, the children, the adolescents, the parents and the teachers, among whom is the teacher John who heroically sacrificed himself, thereby becoming a new example and role model for every teacher—be eternal.

Remembering the Holocaust

Address during an official visit to the United States Holocaust Museum in Washington, D.C., on October 20, 1997.

May the Lord have mercy on us all. May the memory of those who died in the Holocaust be eternal. We are moved to address you today conscious of our tour of this great museum of human suffering and human triumph. Our Modesty is touched by the extraordinary achievement that this monument represents to the spirit of truth and to the depth of human pain that has plagued this century.

We address you this day with mixed emotions, joyful at being here with you to bask in the fruits of those Jews and Orthodox Christians who have worked so tirelessly for understanding between our houses, that our reasoning together might lead to mutual respect and love for one another. We are also deeply moved, saddened by what we have seen and experienced here today. We have seen the face of evil, an evil that we note with profound sorrow. However, we have today seen this hideous evil

25. For martyrs during the Ottoman period, see Nomikos Michael Vaporis, *Witnesses for Christ: Orthodox Christian Neomartyrs of the Ottoman Period, 1437–1860* (Crestwood, N.Y.: St. Vladimir's Seminary Press, 2000).

transformed, its victims preserved by the power of love and memory. This place resolves us to assure all humankind that the unfathomable, unspeakable terror of genocide will never again enter into the realm of human action.

The images of this place, the terror that we glimpse but for a moment here—all this was suffered in the unspeakable depths of living images of God: men, women, and children. To even attempt to contemplate this depth of human suffering is almost too much to bear. Yet we must try. We must understand that such depravity of human action was caused by a deprivation of human spirit. We cannot help but see in this place that Jews and Christians bear a special responsibility for the hope and for the guarantee that this terrible evil will never again take root within the human psyche.

As Jews and Christians, we have a special responsibility to preserve a common memory of this Holocaust and of others as well, that they might be avoided. Our history together is plagued by too many sad instances of fear and loathing, and yet it is, here and there, rich with numerous examples of the Almighty's love for us as individuals and as peoples. Were it not so, the fratricide we know was our inheritance, whose evil fruits we see here, could not now be transformed into an icon of love and fraternal unity.

Remembering the Stories of History

The story of Yolanda Willis's survival,[26] and the story of our ever memorable brother in the Lord, Bishop Chrysostomos of Zakynthos[27]—who when forced by the Nazi authorities to list the Jews of the island wrote but one name, his own—and of many others in occupied Greece, these are the true lessons of love. They are icons of Christ's truth, spoken with courage to the dark principalities and powers of this world (see Eph. 6.12).

In this sacred memorial to the Holocaust, the singular icon of our century's evils has been transformed into an instrument of spiritual renewal. In repenting of the most terrible crimes of our species, we begin

26. Yolanda Willis survived, concealed by a "humble baker," who pretended that she was his godchild and, therefore, a baptized Orthodox Christian.

27. Metropolitan Chrysostomos of Zakynthos (1890–1958).

to find the road to love for one another, the road that has eluded us for so much of our collective histories. That is the highest achievement of this great museum. In this structure's evocation of the dark nadir of human depravity, this nation has enshrined a memorial to an evil that sadly has echoed in too many times and places of this fading century. In creating this memorial and framing this icon of evil as the antithesis of humanity, the United States Holocaust Memorial Museum has simultaneously created an icon of human hope. The museum has assured the posterity of human memory that it will never forget its darkest moments, so that it might always strive to live out its highest aspirations.

Our humble person is shattered by the experience of this sacred memorial, just as we were shattered when we visited Yad Vashem in Israel. We respect the role of Israel as a guarantor of the Jewish people's existence. Since every person is created in the image and likeness of God (Gen. 1.27)—the evildoers and the good, the perpetrators and the victims—we are left to sort out the difference between obeying the will of God and contradicting the commandments of love that are planted by him in our hearts.

The dreadful indifference of so many peoples as their neighbors were taken away against their will constitutes a thorn in the side of the history of the human race. The thorn in humanity's side is its persistent weakness in its relationship with God. For so many Christians the bitter truth of that terrible time was that they could not connect the message of their faith to their actions in the world. They were unable to show their faith in their deeds (Jm. 2.18).

The Ecumenical Patriarchate has sought to remind her spiritual children and all who profess a love for the divine that there has never been a greater need for religious people to go out into the world and witness the true fruits of the Spirit, among which are love, joy, and peace (see Gal. 5.22).

We boldly proclaim to all, to our own spiritual children and to our brothers and sisters in the entire *oikoumene*, that silence in the face of injustice, silence in the shadows of helpless suffering, silence in the darkness of Auschwitz's bitter night will never again be allowed. The faith of the true Christian ought to be manifest toward every people of faith, any faith. For his obligation is the preservation of human life through any sacrifice, even through the sacrifice of his own life. Many say that this suggests a level of faith that is impossible to achieve. But we are creatures who are possessed of a self-reflexive understanding of ourselves. We have the knowledge of the difference between good and evil. We will know joy in the Lord in our desire to do his will.

The rescuers of Jews and others from the fires of evil on earth overcame the bitter snare of fear and faithlessness, self-interest and hatred. They overcame evil with good (Rom. 12.21). All who died in the Holocaust are martyrs, witnesses who point out for us the way to God's love. May their memory be eternal.

Religion, Society, and International Security

Address at the Second Congress of Leaders of World and Traditional Religions, Astana, Kazakhstan, September 12, 2006.

It is with great joy that we participate in this Second Congress of Leaders of World and Traditional Religions in the city of Astana, in Kazakhstan. Kazakhstan, being the largest country in Central Asia and admirably stable, is an example to many countries around the world, for the people of Kazakhstan embrace diversity and do not allow conflict to divide them. . . .

The Ecumenical Patriarchate is an eager participant in the interfaith dialogue and consultation that strives to foster harmony, solidarity, and understanding between our Lord's warring children. We have organized, as well as participated in, many seminars and conferences with our Jewish and Muslim brethren, and we are advocates for dialogue and for the possibility of the coexistence of peoples who come from different cultural traditions. The Orthodox Church, and especially the Ecumenical Patriarchate, has always been in favor of the peaceful and harmonious coexistence of all people and all nations, irrespective of their language and culture, and irrespective of their religious and political convictions, because all people bear within them the image of God, and we are consubstantial and equal among ourselves. This is especially important if we take into consideration the claims that religion has become a factor in the imbalance of international security, since we all witness how religion has been abused and used as a pretense to justify acts of utter cruelty.

We are grateful that opportunity is given to us once again to repeat in the presence of so many distinguished individuals our unswerving conviction that, if we so desire and if our hearts accept it, we can coexist in peace and profitable cooperation, despite our differences of religion. We all try to infuse the world with the spirit of reconciliation and peaceful coexistence. We all are in dispute with the spirit of enmity and conflict between people and cultures, a dispute that we approach in a peaceful manner.

We are indeed living through turbulent times in which the indomitable human spirit appears irreparably fractured. A multitude of horrors are plaguing the international scene with fear and sorrow. This seems to be sustained by an endless reserve of mutual suspicion and cultural disconnect, which can easily bring to mind the period of the Cold War. The purpose of this conference is to address burning issues that threaten the peace and our coexistence on an international scale. And we, as representatives of religion, through a constructive cooperation, will be able to achieve the appropriate framework to maintain the international order of peace in our postmodern times, despite the difficulties that seem to loom before us.

Religious Conflict and Religious Reconciliation

Tendencies to cast out religion and religious teachings from everyday life have been attempted over and over, and the results have been dreadful. We have witnessed how attempting to exclude religion from society has only led to worse situations; subsequently, we have seen with our own eyes how religion has been used and abused in order to serve as pretense for violence and enmity. However, we have also witnessed how politicians have come to realize what an important impact religion has in bridging peoples and society and thereby fulfilling its purpose of reconciliation, rather than becoming the reason for conflict. Recognizing this has helped to bring religion once again back into the reality of our life, so that its influence can be used to strengthen the ties among individuals and peoples of our multicultural world. It is in this spirit that religion can actually become an aid and a stabilizing force in matters of international security.

Many times throughout history humanity has engaged in what has become known as religious warfare. It is a term that has become a synonym for violence and utter cruelty, and it seemed that it had become an issue of the past, an issue one would encounter only in history books. Unfortunately, this term seems to have found its way back into our everyday vocabulary, as we find it increasingly both in tabloids and in international forums and serious discussions. It seems as if there is not a single place in the world that has remained untouched by it, as tragic situations that involve religious violence or conflict associated with religion seem to be omnipresent.

However, what makes the situation even more problematic is that religious conflicts are harder to solve and demand much more honest work and cooperation from the religious authorities involved in them. The reason for this is that religious values are values that are nonnegotiable; therefore, the situations in which they are involved are more complex. Studies show that, whenever religion is associated with conflict, the level of lethality is much higher than in nonreligious conflicts; in any conflict that has a religious component, the higher this component, the more likely the conflict is to be of longer duration, larger scope, higher intensity, and greater severity. As a result, peace communities and conflict communities have a much harder time trying to find solutions in such situations.

It is a known fact that religious warfare brings out the worst in people. There are people who are ready to die for their faith and there are people ready to kill for their faith: the people in the first category are considered martyrs, whereas the people in the second category are considered fanatics. One can say that this is like a coin with its two sides. Nevertheless, we all believe in a God of love, the Creator who fashioned humanity out of love, and whose compassion is eternal. So there should not be any space for those who are using religion as their excuse to commit horrible crimes. Religious fanaticism is one of the thorniest aspects of the problem, and this is where we should focus our efforts if we want to see the world change, if we desire to see a world in which religious warfare will have no place whatsoever. Respect and reconciliation of our differences is what has to be promoted, what has to be taught in every synagogue, in every mosque, in every church. God is the God of peace in all three Abrahamic religions. He is the Prince of Peace, who brings His love and forgiveness and soothes the shattered hearts and minds of all.

Unfortunately, politicians do not have time to look at such a solution. They try to fight fire with fire, and the results, as we see worldwide, are not the bearing of any fruit but instead an increase in the death tolls and the spilling of even more blood. Economic interests, power, and control add nothing but more fuel to the raging conflicts. Reconciliation is religion practiced at its best, and reconciliation is a core value. We have witnessed how politicians and society at large over the years have blamed religion for all the negative things that have happened in the world instead of remembering and realizing that religion is an instrument for bringing people together, not the means of terrorizing one another.

Religious Freedom and International Stability

People must realize that religious freedom, international security, and global stability go hand in hand. If religious freedom is breached, then trouble lies not very far off. It is here that we should focus next. As we have mentioned before, religious values are nonnegotiable values. Diversity and pluralism are traits of our times, traits that no one can deny. We are called to live with them and learn how to grow in them without loosing our identity, without compromising ourselves. How can we attain that goal? Many faithful worry that this will bring an end to their uniqueness, as syncretism is a reality in our times. However, it is our task to educate and inform our faithful and help them, first, to learn and understand their own faith in as much depth and as well as possible. Only then will they be able to understand enough about their neighbor's faith to respect both the "other faith" and the "other person." We witness how many tend to become theologians and create fanatic tendencies that result in real-time conflict. The lack of education and the need to adhere to a religious representative—whether that be a priest, a rabbi, or an imam—makes people lose their focus and drives them to incoherent actions.

There are many places in our world where people of extreme diversity, both in culture and religion, have lived peacefully for centuries, but the immature abuse of extreme religious teachings—which, by the way, occurs only if we present things out of context—has led them to tragic situations. Selfish people abused the content of our holy scriptures and brought enmity to our faithful. Selfish people disrespected religious symbols and created conflicts that often have gotten out of control. We see that lack of respect exists on every level, not only between different religious groups but also between the secular and the religious worlds.

It would be very easy to just point our fingers and accuse our neighbors of everything that is wrong in our world. It would make us feel justified and righteous. We wonder, though: would that do any of us any good? Would that bring a solution to our problems? We assure you, it would only make things worse. Unless we take on ourselves our mistakes and our shortcomings, we will never be able to rest.

The Concept of Security

Having said that, let us look at the term *security* and try to define it from a Christian perspective, in an effort to help us look at the matter from a theological perspective as well. For a Christian, security is not one-dimensional but multidimensional, since it is all-embracing, encompassing physical, economic, and societal security. However, the most vital form of security for a Christian is the security of the soul, which is nourished by love, compassion, and altruism. It is this spirit that we try to promote and in this sprit that we work with our brothers of different religions, for only the spirit of peace and reconciliation will allow us to coexist. We all feel wronged, we all feel that injustices are ensnaring us from all directions, but let us not forget the words Jesus said on his Cross, words that encompass all this love, compassion, and altruism. He said, "Father, forgive them, for they do not know what they do." This is the epitome of reconciliation for us all.

The new millennium has given us a taste of how a few can tarnish the honorable beliefs of millions. Does this mean that we can generalize, create stereotypes, and so demonize millions of faithful, when only a handful is to be blamed? How can this establish or ensure security? Some people have the tendency to generalize and demonize quickly, making things even worse and widening the gap between the already different cultures and identities. It is our sacred duty to avoid such incidents.

Since the tragic events of September 11, our efforts at the Ecumenical Patriarchate to promote interfaith dialogue between Judaism, Christianity, and Islam have taken on an added urgency. In an effort to help the healing process of those wounds and fissures that followed, we organized a high-profile conference of Jewish, Christian and Muslim religious leaders in Brussels in December 2001. In the declaration adopted by this conference, the religious leaders confirmed among other things the following:

> The will of God is for the peace of heaven to reign on earth. The peace of God is not the mere absence of war, it is the gift of abundant life. There is indeed an immediate and inseparable connection between peace and justice. Thus, we pray constantly for peace to prevail in the world and for the peaceful living together among the faithful of all religions in our modern, multicultural, and multi-ethnic global society.[28]

This declaration, which came to be known as the Brussels Declaration, was one step forward in the process of understanding and building confident and trusting relationships among the faithful of the three monotheistic religions—relationships based on mutual respect and a willingness for reconciliation. Since then, the interfaith dialogue has grown, and we are still working together with our Jewish and Muslim brothers and sisters to achieve a peaceful coexistence, which will ensure the security of our world.

The Reality of the Balkans

The last decade of the past century has been marked by rampant hatred, destruction, unbridled nationalism, and religious intolerance, particularly in the Balkans. All that led to the inexcusable suffering of thousands of people, especially of innocent civilians who were uninvolved in the bloodthirsty vengeance that swept through our world. We also witnessed that, out of the phoenix of this terror, peace and tranquility slowly began to appear, as the people involved have been trying to face themselves and their differences in a spirit of reconciliation, for they realized that they were the only ones who could recover their lost sense of security, and the religious leaders helped them slowly reestablish their lost relationships based on coexistence in a peaceful manner.

In the Vlatadon Monastery[29] in Thessaloniki, Greece, in May 2000, representatives of Orthodoxy and Roman Catholicism and of Muslim and Jewish communities of the Balkans met with representatives of the

---

28. For the full text, see Chapter 6, "Major Declarations: Public Proclamations."

29. Founded on the acropolis of Thessaloniki during the late fourteenth century, during the time of St. Gregory Palamas. Under the immediate jurisdiction of the Ecumenical Patriarchate, the monastery houses the Patriarchal Institute of Patristic Studies (established in 1965) and publishes the journal *Kleronomia*.

European Union, NATO, OSCE, and regional governments to establish a common program to strengthen the pulse of peace, reconciliation, and compromise. Together we declared that "religious communities must play a key role in rebuilding a multi-faith, multi-cultural and multi-ethnic society in South-East Europe" and emphasized that the conflict in the former Yugoslavia was not about religion, although that was how it was typically presented. The Vlatadon Initiative gave opportunity to the people who suffered so much to come together again and rebuild what had been destroyed.

Nobody is saying that this process does not take time or that it is without any difficulty, especially in our world today, which on many levels tries to disassociate humanity from religion. It would be immature to entertain such an idea. Religion, however, offers a solution to the spiritual alienation that has become very dangerous for the individual of our times, as this alienation involves the isolation of the person from salvific communion with God, his fellow human beings, and the world at large. Religion aids the individual who tends to feel more and more alone in a global, multicultural society and unable to overcome the suffocative bounds of spiritual confusion and ideological disabilities, overwhelmed by the mass media and the institutional functions of a faceless society—religion helps this individual to find a way out of the spiritual dead end that the world represents and to learn once again to trust and to desire reconciliation.

The redemptive experience that is offered by religion accentuates the relativity of human existence to God and to the world and connects, indissolubly, natural justice with divine law. This is applicable to not only the Christian world but to a universal perspective, as it is also recognized in the United Nations' Universal Declaration of Human Rights.[30] The sanctity of life is a common factor in all three monotheistic religions, and we must keep that as part of our focus, and we must remind the world that we have more to offer than what many try to imply.

Religious Tolerance and World Peace

Please allow us to state once again that the religious beliefs of the Abrahamic religions have love and respect for creation as their common denominator—love and respect for all living things that God has created;

30. Created in 1948.

love and respect for one another; love and respect for the entire world. It is our common Abrahamic heritage that leads us on our way to peaceful living.

This past November, the Ecumenical Patriarchate organized yet another interreligious conference, Peace and Tolerance II, focusing on these topics. That conference declared, among other things, respect for life (in the proverbial expression "Live and let live"); respect for human rights, especially of minorities; and respect for religious tolerance, an important force for safeguarding security. The conference also condemned terrorism and violence. Furthermore, it pointed out the Christian saying "Blessed are the peacemakers, for they will be called Children of God" as well as the Muslim saying "Allah summoneth to the abode of Peace." We expressed our gratitude to God, for He gave us the opportunity to confirm our decision to cooperate for the increase of peace, justice, and human dignity.

It is therefore necessary that we move in that direction, beyond the disabilities of the past. The impartial and incorruptible reality of history has, of course, registered behavior among faithful of all three monotheistic religions that is incompatible with our holy scriptures; nobody can deny this or claim the opposite. But let us now show that those times have passed. Let us show the world that we have learned from our mistakes and that the time has come to act for God. We will all converge to what the will of God commands for all. Those who have opened their hearts to God feel that the merciful and loving God is not pleased by bloodshed but by peace, which is the ultimate good and divine present. In Judaism, Christianity, and Islam alike, we greet one another using the word—namely, *peace*.

We have to keep in mind that there is more that unites us than divides us, and we have to strive to ensure that religion will cease to be considered a force that brings imbalance in international security. The basis of our cooperation and our dialogues and our efforts to improve life for the world should be our common values. We all confess that God does not want anybody's destruction; this, then, should be the basis of our conversations. It is only by searching for common ground—not, of course, for the sake of achieving the impossible unification of our faiths but for the accommodation of our peaceful coexistence—that we will help our fellow believers and nonbelievers to discover God's goodness and become conscious believers. The interreligious dialogue made it possible to witness that out of despair has arisen the reservoir of peace and tolerance.

However, it would be unwise to think that we have found a permanent and secure solution to the problems that we are faced with on an everyday basis. Religion has always respected and honored the importance and the value of human rights. Nevertheless, it seems as though society forgets about the sensitivities of religious people. The neutralizing and numbing of peoples' feelings for religious symbols has been attempted repeatedly. It is true that this happens on a constant basis in the Christian world, and the usual target is the person of Jesus Christ. If, however, we dare to express any discomfort about it, we are accused of disrespect for the right of expression.

The misuse of freedom of expression, to blaspheme what is holy for believers, is an act that we all condemn. As we have already stated, Christianity has also been the receiver of many such blasphemies under the cover of what has come to be considered freedom of expression, and we therefore understand and suffer with you in this time of distress. All religions, whether Islam, Christianity, or Judaism, hold certain symbols and realities of faith as holy, and believers feel extremely strongly about them. What we want to safeguard is the respect of these feelings as well as of the symbols and realities of faith.

We are not against freedom of expression, but, when that particular freedom conflicts with the freedom of religion and religious expression and offends people worldwide, the people responsible for the offense should think twice before they commit such abhorrent acts of violation and insult. We only want to receive the same respect that we show to others.

Therefore, let us all join our voices in prayer that these acts of violence will not be repeated. Let us all pray that we will not mourn more people because of the disrespect of some. Let us all pray that with our faith and hope in God we will be able to transform our world and create the necessary environment that will foster diversity, respect, and peaceful coexistence among all. Let us all pray that God will restore security in our souls, so that we may be able to work closer together in an effort to ensure security for all.

Finally, let us all pray that the warfare in the Middle East, particularly in Lebanon and Israel, that has broken out and the uncontrollable and indiscriminating violence that has taken an immense toll in lives—the lives of hundreds of innocent victims, mostly civilians of both sides—will cease and come to a final halt. Let us ask of God's infinite mercy and hope that he will show those who are involved in this abhorrent bloodshed the way to peace and tolerance, the way that will allow future generations to grow up in an environment of acceptance and forgiveness and not an environment where enmity and hatred reign freely over the hearts and minds of people.

Against Fanaticism: A Local Example

Homily in the Church of the Virgin Mary at Neochorion on the Bosphorus, Istanbul, September 5, 1993.

We have come today as your archbishop and spiritual leader and we have presided in this holy church of Panagia (or, Virgin Mary) Koumariotissa, and we have prayed together with you for two reasons: today is the annual feast day of this holy Church, at which time we also wished to bless in person, as is customary, the faithful of this parish; and we wished to express—first to them, but also, more broadly, to our entire beloved community here—our paternal sympathy and the moral support of the Mother Church following the recent desecration of the graves of our beloved deceased, who held the faith in common and who repose in the picturesque cemetery of the parish of Neochorion.

Are they reposing, in a manner of speaking? They are reposing only euphemistically, because there are those who dared to disturb the peace even of our dead. Even in their graves they did not leave them in peace. Rather, they smashed the crosses—symbols of our expectation and faith in the Resurrection of the dead—and dug out and profaned their remains.

And the question is raised: Why? For what reason? What fault was it of our dead? To what extent did "we who are alive, who are left" (1 Thess. 4.15) insult them, if, in fact, they did this uncivilized (to use a milder expression) act in order to seek revenge against us?

Are we not, in every way, law-abiding citizens of this country? Do we not perform our obligations to our country to the best of our ability? Do we not honor the name of our country in which we live, honor it with honesty, diligent work, our high degree of civilization, our beautiful customs and traditions, and our rich history? Have we not suffered enough, and are we not at all to blame, except that we are Greek by origin and Orthodox in faith? Because of this—being a minority, that is—we are regarded as a negotiable crowbar in the relations between neighboring and allied countries? Is it not enough that so few of us have remained here because of this last point? Should we be expected to endure more? Indeed, should this be expected of our deceased, who "are asleep" and awaiting the common resurrection?

We are certain that the official state authorities of the country are not in any way involved in this recent sorrowful episode. The government is aware that we never create instances in this land but, on the contrary, are a force for civilization and peace. The government, ultimately, will apply the laws if we give cause, and never will it resort to unacceptable and uncharacteristic acts, such as the one being denounced today.

But those who have contrived and dared such acts must know that they do a disservice to Turkey, that they expose her internationally, that her interests at the highest level are harmed while perhaps their own interests are served, that they expose their own selves. And so we call on them to sober up and come to their senses and at least to leave our dead in peace, our dead who are lying awaiting the Second Coming of the Lord, unable to react and defend themselves. Unfortunately, it is not the first time the dead have suffered such a cowardly assault.

The Abuse of Rights and Freedom

On the other hand, we, as law-abiding citizens, demand that the esteemed government of our country protect all we hold as sacred and holy, our lives and property, and not allow every adventurer or every hateful fanatic to release his frustrations by destroying Orthodox cemeteries. This avenue, this method, leads nowhere, only to impasse and vicious circles.

If fanaticism in general blinds, religious fanaticism degrades man and his dignity and stands against freedom, a divine gift, as well as against democracy. But, taking this opportunity, let us come to the babble written by a part of the press against us personally and against our Ecumenical Patriarchate, which, allegedly, cooperates in an effort to realize a "terrible plan." Indeed, how easy it is for exaggerated and impressive adjectives to be employed! How easy it is for one to be fooled when making assertions totally without basis and totally unable to be proven, especially when speaking on behalf of a nonexistent Church, which took over and unlawfully possesses and reaps the benefits of houses of worship, houses that our fathers founded by the sweat of their brow and hard-earned contributions. For someone to say or write whatever comes from his imagination—not to say out of dishonesty—is very easy and very simple. However, fundamental self-respect and fundamental respect for truth are demanded; and it is the truth that will set us free (Jn. 8.32).

Not only have we not envisioned the Ecumenical Patriarchate as a second Vatican or tried to transform it into such, but, on the contrary, we have stated on numerous occasions that, even if such an idea were proposed to us, we would reject it as being contradictory to the ecclesiology and tradition of the Orthodox Church. The Ecumenical Patriarchate does not wish to become a state. It wishes to remain only a church—a church, however, that is free and respected by everyone—only a religious and spiritual institution, teaching, edifying, serving universal ideals, civilizing, and preaching love and peace in every direction. The Ecumenical Patriarchate belongs to the Church, which was founded by the God of love, whose peace "surpasses all understanding" (Phil. 4:7). We "pursue what makes for peace" (Rom. 14.19). We believe that "God is love" (1 Jn. 4.16), which is why we are not afraid: "perfect love casts out fear" (1 Jn. 4.18).

We close with the admonishment of the Apostle Paul, which we heard in the beginning of today's epistle reading: "Brethren, be watchful, stand firm in your faith, be courageous, be strong. Let all that you do be done in love" (1 Cor. 16.13–14).

Religion and Law

Message to the International Congress of the Chamber of Lawyers in the Federal Republic of Germany, held in Frankfurt am Main, October 29, 2009.

It is with great joy that we greet the distinguished participants of the prestigious and unique International Congress of the Chamber of Lawyers in the Federal Republic of Germany, gathered in Frankfurt am Main from October 29 to 31, 2009, to address the crucial topic "The Influence of World Religions on the Legal Systems of Nations." Although, owing to prearranged commitments, we are, unfortunately, unable to be among you in person, we can assure you of our presence among you in prayer and spirit, inasmuch as the subject of your deliberations touches a deep chord within our heart. For, throughout our humble ministry, we have earnestly labored and grappled with such issues related to interreligious tolerance, human rights, and environmental protection.

The world of faith can undoubtedly prove a powerful ally in efforts to address issues of social justice. It provides a unique perspective—beyond the merely social, political, or economic—on the need to eradicate poverty, to provide balance in a world of globalization, and to combat fundamentalism and racism as well as to develop religious tolerance in a world of conflict. In fact, it is rare instance when a faith institution is not a defining marker of the space and character of a community. Religion is arguably the most pervasive and powerful force on earth. This is why religion and the faith communities are proving to be the subject of renewed interest and attention in international relations and global politics, directly affecting social values and indirectly impacting state policies.

And so, standing at the crossroads of continents, civilizations, and faith communities, the Ecumenical Patriarchate has always had as its vision that it embrace, and accept as its responsibility, the idea of serving as a bridge between Christians, Muslims, and Jews. Since 1977, then, the Ecumenical Patriarchate has either pioneered or been involved in a bilateral interreligious dialogue with the Jewish community (on such topics as law, tradition, renewal in a modern world, and social justice); since 1986, we have initiated bilateral interfaith dialogue with the Islamic community (on such matters as authority, coexistence, peace, justice, pluralism, and the modern world); and, since 1994, we have organized a number of diverse multifaith convocations, in particular hosting several international gatherings, which have made possible deep, multilateral conversations between the Christian, Jewish, and Muslim communities (particularly on such issues as tolerance and peace).

Freedom of Conscience in a Secular World

Moreover, freedom of conscience and the free practice of religious conviction are fundamental principles, which from an Orthodox Christian perspective derive immediately from the words of Jesus Christ: "Whosoever wants to follow me . . ." (Mt. 16.24). The sacred freedom originally conferred by God at the moment of creation, and the freedom subsequently confirmed by the Son of God at the moment of the divine incarnation, cannot be ignored or withheld without at the same time denying and rejecting the very presence of God. Emphasizing the element of freedom in God's relationship with the world, the second-century *Epistle to Diognetus* affirms:

> God persuades; God does not compel. . . . For, violence is foreign to God.

This attitude should also determine our relationship with every human being.

Finally, while secular culture sometimes maintains that the relationship between God and humanity is individual or private, the Orthodox Christian faith offers an alternative worldview, perceiving the entire cosmos—including everyone and everything within it—as a seamless garment of God's vast creation. And so individuals exist not separated or isolated from the rest of creation and their fellow human beings but in constant relationship with the entire natural world. Within this context, human beings are valued as part of the cosmos. It is, therefore, within such a context that a just society is also founded and sustained. For the Orthodox concept of *theosis* (deification) is more than merely individual or personal; it is also deeply communal and, indeed, cosmic inasmuch as it extends to and embraces all of God's natural creation.

Nevertheless, since we live in a fallen world, where the presence of evil is real and people are easily swayed to avoid their divine and human obligations, there can be no doubt that the formulation of appropriate legislation as well as the enforcement of relevant policies and laws is a critical aspect of civilized life within a global world. The involvement of law inevitably enables the proper balance in these spheres, encouraging greater interfaith tolerance and understanding and respect for human rights and religious freedom as well as for the sustainable use of the world's natural resources for the sake of the survival of our fragile planet and the future of our children.

In this regard, then, the assembly of prominent leaders within the legal community at your historical congress is both timely and important in a world where the boundaries of right and wrong are often blurred. Permit us to remind you that no single sector can resolve such critical issues alone. All of us—faith communities and churches, political and legal authorities, together with representatives of every discipline—must be willing humbly to cooperate in order to ensure the peaceful and fair coexistence of all people in God's world.

Twenty Years after Chernobyl

Message to an international conference, Twenty Years of Chernobyl Catastrophe: A Look to the Future, Minsk, Belarus, April 17, 2006.

The ancient spiritual bonds between Ukraine and the Ecumenical Patriarchate permit and indeed demand a constant mutual interest. Furthermore, we would reemphasize all that we have declared at other times and in other forums concerning the necessity that the Orthodox Christians of Ukraine should proceed in harmony and look forward with confidence to their ecclesiastical future and their worthy past—and that, moreover, in line with current demands, they should work creatively, with other Christians and believers of other religious persuasions, toward common actions which signify that healing of old wounds and toward the crystallization and establishment of definite, positive objectives for the noble and glorious Ukrainian people and the wider region.

As we write these things, we also hasten to pay our respects and, with fatherly solace, offer our sympathies on the twentieth anniversary of the Chernobyl disaster. We offer fervent prayers for the blessed repose of the victims of the awful catastrophe as well as for the comfort and healing of those who suffer still. And we pray for divine enlightenment for all those who, whether in science, technology, politics, or in other fields, are involved with nuclear power.

As is well known, the Ecumenical Patriarchate interprets the biblical commandments and the patristic legacy through the prism of current events and needs. The Ecumenical Patriarchate calls all people—both in and out of season—to be mindful of their responsibility to manage all things relating to the natural environment with greater respect.

The Ecumenical Patriarchate encourages scientific research and blesses all those who work responsibly, and within the full realization of their lofty mission, to uncover and sustain the potential that God has placed in the material creation for the service of humankind.

The Ecumenical Patriarchate applauds every effort that contributes to the general advancing of humanity in a spiritual fraternity, one characterized by mutual respect, justice, and common concern for the peace and security of the whole world.

World Energy Crisis

Message to the Twentieth World Energy Congress, Rome, November 2007.

It is with particular pleasure that we congratulate the organizers and greet the participants of this prestigious international gathering and exhibition, which are hosted by the World Energy Council in the historical city of Rome and aim at an exploration of the future of energy development in an interdependent world.

The proper development and distribution of the energy resources of our planet is clearly one of the most critical and urgent problems facing our world. We are in the throes of an energy crisis, and we can no longer afford to risk moving along our present path of indiscriminate waste and devastation. We are obliged to review our ways radically, something that in our theological tradition is called "repentance." This is precisely why it is a source of great joy and personal satisfaction to observe the stated goals of your world congress: namely, "debating and solving economic issues of both industrialized and developing countries" as well as "seeking ways for a sustainable use of energy resources to the benefit of the entire world."

These two fundamental goals also articulate—in an eloquent and at the same time powerful manner—the spiritual conviction and sacred worldview that our Ecumenical Patriarchate has propounded in recent decades. For there is no doubt that, first of all, in raising ecological awareness among people throughout the world, we have endeavored to draw the essential and intimate connection between sustainable development and social justice. Indeed, the energy problem is invariably connected to the social problem of poverty. This is because all ecological activity is ultimately measured by its impact on other people, especially the poor. And, in this regard, industrialized nations are called to bear the burden both of greater responsibility and greater sacrifice. Interdependence implies greater initiative on the part of the privileged.

Second, the phrase "to the benefit of the entire world" is reminiscent of the biblical phrase in the New Testament, which is also the root and source of liturgical practice in the Orthodox Church. The phrase "for the life of the world"—found in the Gospel of St. John (chapter 6, verse 51)—at once determines and defines our understanding of a spiritual worldview, which calls for communion and sharing in a world of division and inequality, challenging us to work for a just society where everyone has sufficient means for survival, where the natural resources of our planet are plentiful for all.[31]

The energy crisis of our age is not primarily an ecological or economic matter. Rather, it is a spiritual crisis relating to the way we perceive our planet's resources. We are treating our world in an inhumane, godless manner precisely because we fail to see it as a gift received from above, which it is, in turn, our obligation to respect and return to future generations. It is our fervent prayer, then, that your congress will explore possibilities and discern ways of changing the way we perceive the world. Otherwise, we will continue to deal with symptoms and not their causes.

The Role of Religion in a Changing Europe

Address at the London School of Economics at the invitation of the London Hellenic Society, November 3, 2005.

You have chosen a topic that is of vital importance to all of us without exception: "The Role of Religion in a Changing Europe." This is, needless to say, a subject that is of burning concern to me personally in my ministry as Ecumenical Patriarch. In all the countries of Western Europe, the Orthodox flock that is under the spiritual care of the Ecumenical Throne is rapidly growing in numbers. It is, therefore, natural and necessary for us to ask ourselves: What is our vocation as Orthodox Christians in Europe as a whole?

The title of my lecture tonight refers to "a changing Europe." In what particular ways is Europe undergoing change? Two features come at once

31. See Alexander Schmemann, *For the Life of the World: Sacraments and Orthodoxy* (Crestwood, N.Y.: St. Vladimir's Seminary Press, 1973).

to mind: multiculturalism and secularization. First, the national boundaries separating one European country from another are becoming less sharp and clearly defined, and this is happening on many different levels—political, economic, and social. None of us are living any more in a monolithic, pan-ethnic cultural milieu; all of us belong to or find ourselves cast into broader cultural currents. This is true not only of the countries of Western Europe such as Britain, France, and Germany but of the traditional Orthodox lands such as Greece and Romania as well. One aspect of this multicultural trend is the ever increasing scale of immigration. In Europe today, for example, there are between fifteen and twenty million Muslims: in Britain they constitute 2.7 percent of the population, but in most other countries the proportion is higher—in Germany, 4.9 percent, and in France as much as 8.3 percent (no less than five million). Surely we should see this not as a threat but as an opportunity.

Does Religion Have a Role in Europe?

Alike as a result of immigration and of other factors, we Europeans are coming to recognize—in a way that we have never done before—that we belong to one another and need each other. Nations in the contemporary world are not self-sufficient but interdependent. To Cain's question in the Old Testament story of Cain and Abel—"Am I my brother's keeper?" (Gen. 4.9)—there can today be only one answer, equally on the personal and the international level; and the answer has to be "Yes, I am."

This does not mean that national loyalty, patriotism, and love of one's native land have ceased to have any meaning. On the contrary, what Alexander Solzhenitsyn said in his Nobel Prize speech thirty-five years ago still remains fully valid today: "The disappearance of nations would impoverish us no less than if all humans were to become alike, with one personality and one face. Nations are the wealth of humankind, its collective personalities; the very least of them wears its own special colors and bears within itself a special facet of divine intention."[32] But our experience of our own national identity has today to be lived out within a pluralistic and multicultural context.

---

32. See Leopold Labedz, ed., *Solzhenitsyn: A Documentary Record* (Harmondsworth, U.K.; Baltimore, 1974), 314.

The most striking contemporary expression of this multiculturalism is of course the emergence of the European Union. From its beginnings on May 9, 1950—when Robert Schuman, as French minister of foreign affairs, proposed the establishment of the European Coal and Steel Community—it has now come to embrace no less than twenty-five member states, and it continues to expand. As a Turkish citizen, we would like at this point to express my hope that in due course Turkey will become a full member of the E.U., when the necessary preconditions of such membership have been met, including in particular the recognition of the religious and other rights of minority communities. The admission of Turkey to the E.U., so we are convinced, will significantly contribute to rapprochement and reconciliation between the Muslim world and the West.

It is true that, during recent months, the E.U. has been passing through a time of crisis. The idealistic vision of the Union's founders has sadly faded. Political leaders in the different states have to ask themselves why so many of their citizens are strongly hostile to the proposed Constitutional Treaty. Yet this should not blind us to the remarkable achievements of the E.U. For more than sixty years there has not been a major war in Europe; probably, since the fall of the Roman Empire, there has never been in Europe such a prolonged period of peace. With a minimum of violence and bloodshed, the Iron Curtain has been torn down. To a degree unthinkable in the 1930s, the peoples of Europe are today committed to the principles of freedom, justice, and democracy. When we Orthodox pray, as we do at every celebration of the Divine Liturgy, "for the peace of the whole world," we have good reason to reflect with gratitude on these developments. Yet we know that there is no room for complacency: peace and freedom are not only a gift from God but an unceasing task.

Along with multiculturalism, a second major feature in today's changing Europe is the growth of secularism. In most countries, especially in the western part of Europe, there has been a dramatic decline in churchgoing. Almost everywhere, with certain notable exceptions, religious groups in Europe are lamenting a dearth of candidates for the priesthood and the monastic life. In education and in the whole life of society, Christianity is becoming marginalized. All of this leads us to ask: Does religion any longer have a role in the future of Europe? It is surely disquieting that, in the proposed Constitutional Treaty, despite protests from many church leaders, there is no explicit reference to the contribution made by Christianity to the formation of the European heritage.

Yet we must take care not to exaggerate. Even if levels of churchgoing have fallen in many places, the majority of Europeans—as recent surveys indicate[33]—still affirm that they believe in the existence of a God. In some countries, the proportion of those who do so is surprisingly high: in Malta, 95 percent; in Cyprus and Romania, 90 percent; in Greece and Portugal, 81 percent; and in Poland, 80 percent. In E.U. countries as a whole, an overall average of 52 percent state that they believe there is a God, and only 18 percent declare that they do not believe in the existence of any sort of God, spirit, or life-force. Of course by no means do all those who accept God's existence actively practice their faith. Interestingly, in Turkey the number of those expressing belief that there is a God is as high as 95 percent, and of these the great majority are indeed practicing their faith. A modern and democratic political and social structure has to respect the religious wishes and sentiments of its citizens. Religious freedoms cannot be curtailed in the name of secularism.

Does Orthodox Christianity Matter in a United Europe?

Even if, in all too many European nations, organized religion is passing through a time of difficulty, religious belief is by no means merely a thing of the past. Christianity in numerous European lands is like a sleeping giant, and according to all indications the giant is going to wake up soon. Indeed, this has already been happening since the fall of communism in the former Soviet Union: in Russian and Ukraine, since 1989 the number of Orthodox parishes has increased nearly threefold and now exceeds 20,000; whereas in 1989 there were only eighteen monasteries, today there are more than six hundred. Let us not underestimate the resilience of Christianity. And let us not forget that the founding fathers of the E.U., such as Konrad Adenauer and Alcide de Gasperi, were profoundly Christian in their vision of a unified Europe.

With approximately 300 million faithful in Eastern Europe, the Balkans, the Middle East, and also the New World, the Orthodox Church is a force for unity, a stabilizing influence and an essential component in

33. See, for example, the special report in *Eurobarometer* 225 (2005): 7–11.

the ongoing process to create a new European reality bridging the eastern and western Christian cultures and traditions of the continent. Under the leadership of the Ecumenical Patriarchate, Orthodox dioceses have also been present for a long time in almost all the countries of Western Europe, providing spiritual guidance to the Orthodox faithful. Because of its decentralized structure, Orthodoxy is in a position to reach, in a much more direct and effective manner, its faithful through its sixteen local churches operating under the coordination of the Ecumenical Patriarchate, first among the equal churches of the Orthodox commonwealth.

Given the global revival of religious faith and attachment to spiritual values in recent decades, the Orthodox ecumenical message and cultural legacy has gained greater credibility and has turned into a bulwark against extreme nationalistic, confessionary, and religious dissension and conflict. In this respect, the patriarchate of Constantinople upholds the work of the conciliation of all mankind, the propagation of peaceful coexistence, and the preservation of the natural environment. Toward those ends, the Ecumenical Patriarchate has been undertaking multifaceted activities, organizing international environmental conferences since 1992, cosponsoring a dialogue between the Orthodox Church and the European People's Party and the European Democrats since 1996, and promoting interfaith dialogue beginning with the Bosphorus Declaration of 1994, an interfaith document that condemns as a crime against religion all crimes committed in the name of religion.[34]

Historical Constantinople and modern-day Istanbul is a city where religions and cultures converge. The Ecumenical Patriarchate, with its seat in this city for seventeen centuries, has coexisted peacefully and constructively with Islam and Judaism. While contact between Orthodox and Muslims has been an everyday business in multicultural Istanbul, an academic dialogue of friendship and mutual understanding between Christians and Islam was begun in 1986 in the Orthodox Center of the Ecumenical Patriarchate in Chambésy-Geneva.[35] Under these circumstances, Orthodoxy, headed by the Ecumenical Patriarchate, whose headquarters are situated in a predominantly Muslim city, has all the

34. For the full text, see Chapter 6, "Major Declarations: Public Proclamations."

35. The Interreligious Dialogue between Islam and Christianity has held several international academic consultations organized by the Royal Academy for Islamic Civilization Research (Al-Albait Foundation in Amman, Jordan) in collaboration with the Orthodox

credentials to assume the role of a bridge between Europe and Islam. In the same manner, the staunch support extended by the Ecumenical Patriarchate to the cause of Turkey's membership in the European Union is linked to the belief that Europe will benefit greatly by integrating a predominantly Muslim country, willing of course to adopt European principles such as respect for religious freedom and minority rights. A similar dialogue between Orthodoxy and Judaism has been proceeding with the blessings of the Ecumenical Patriarchate.[36]

The Spiritual Foundation of Europe

Europe, it has often been said, is not simply a geographical area but an idea. What, then, we ask, is the fundamental "idea" that gives unity to Europe, that constitutes the "soul" of Europe, and that the European Union is seeking, however imperfectly, to embody?

The answer can be found in a Jewish saying recorded by Martin Buber in his *Tales of the Hasidim*. "What is the worst thing that the evil urge can

---

Center of the Ecumenical Patriarchate in Chambésy-Geneva, Switzerland (1986–98) and, since 2001, in collaboration with the Kingdom of Bahrain and the Office for Interreligious and Intercultural Relations of the Ecumenical Patriarchate in Brussels, Belgium. The dialogue has included meetings in Chambésy on "Authority and Religion" (1986), in Amman on "Models of Historical Coexistence and Common Humanitarian Ideals" (1987), in Chambésy on "Peace and Justice" (1988), in Istanbul on "Religious Pluralism" (1989), in Amman on "Youth and Values of Moderation" (1993), in Athens on "Education for Understanding and Cooperation" (1994), in Amman on "Educational Systems" (1996), in Istanbul on "Perspectives of Cooperation and Participation" (1997), in Amman on "Modern Society and the Meaning of Co-Citizenship" (1998), and in Bahrain on "Peaceful Coexistence" (2002). A further meeting was organized in Athens (2008) to launch the Interreligious Training Partnership Initiative.

36. The Interreligious Dialogue between Judaism and Christianity has held several international academic consultations between the International Jewish Committee for Interreligious Consultations (IJCIC) of the World Jewish Congress and the Orthodox Center of the Ecumenical Patriarchate in Chambésy-Geneva, Switzerland (1977–2001) and, since 2001, with the Office for Interreligious and Intercultural Relations of the Ecumenical Patriarchate in Brussels, Belgium. The dialogue has included meetings in Lucerne on "Law" (1977), in Bucharest on "Tradition and Community" (1979), in Athens on "Continuity and Renewal" (1993) [see *Immanuel*, vol. 26–27, 1994], in Kibbutz Maaleh Ha-Chamisha on "The Encounter with Modernity" (1998), in Thessaloniki on "Faithfulness to our Sources: Commitment to Peace and Justice" (2003), and in Jerusalem on "Religious Liberty and the Relationship between Freedom and Religion" (2007).

achieve?" a rabbi is asked; and he replies, "To make us forget that we are each the child of a King."[37] As human persons, we are each of us from royal lineage, in the spiritual sense; that is to say, we are each and every one of us *free*. This notion of personal freedom—of the free dignity and integrity of every single human being—lies at the heart of what we mean by the European idea, and it is the primary guiding principle of the E.U.

It is precisely from this perspective that we can begin to appreciate the role of religion in Europe, for personal freedom is fundamental likewise to the Christian doctrine of human personhood. "The truth will make you free," states Christ (Jn. 8.32); "Am I not free?" asserts St. Paul (1 Cor. 9.1). Emphasizing the element of freedom in God's relationship with the world, the second-century *Epistle to Diognetus* affirms, "God persuades, he does not compel; for violence is foreign to him."[38] This is indeed a golden saying: would that Christians over the centuries had paid more attention to it! The cardinal significance of freedom is vividly underlined in "The Tale of the Grand Inquisitor," in Fyodor Dostoevsky's masterpiece, *The Brothers Karamazov.* For the Christian tradition, freedom—the ability to make decisions consciously and with a full sense of responsibility—is the most tremendous thing granted by God to human persons. Without liberty of choice there is no authentic personhood. As God says to the people of Israel in the Old Testament:

> I call heaven and earth to witness against you this day, that I have set before you life and death, blessing and curse; therefore *choose*. . . . (Deut. 30.19)

If, however, we are to appreciate the true meaning of this personal freedom, we have to ask further what is meant by "a person." Here again the testimony of the Christian tradition is of decisive significance. Is the human animal merely a political animal, *politikon zōon*, as Aristotle says,[39] or a logical and rational animal, *logikon zōon*, to use the Stoic phrase?[40]

---

37. Martin Buber, *Tales of the Hasidim: The Early Masters* (New York: Schocken Books, 1968), 282.

38. *Epistle to Diognetus* 7.4. This letter is by an anonymous Greek author of the late second century, possibly earlier, and represents one of the earliest examples of Christian apologetics.

39. Aristotle, *Politics* 1.1.9 (1253a)

40. *Stoicorum Veterum Fragmenta*, ed. H. von Arnim, III (1903), 95, §390.

Are we no more than an animal that laughs and weeps, as some have thought? Is the human animal to be seen simply in materialistic and economic terms, as a consumer? Such, unfortunately, is exactly the approach of many citizens today within the E.U.: they think almost exclusively of what they can get out of the Union in terms of material advantages, not of what they can contribute on a spiritual level, and that is perhaps the chief reason why the E.U. at present is passing through such a severe crisis.

Against this concept of the person as merely an economic entity, a consumer, Christianity insists that as human beings we are *zōon theoumenon*, to use the words of St. Gregory Nazianzus[41]—"an animal that is called to be deified," that is invited to share in God's glory and to become a "partaker of the divine nature" (2 Pet. 1.4).[42] The most important fact about our humanness is our transcendent dimension: we are formed in the image of God (Gen. 1.26). We are endowed, that is to say, with God-consciousness, and so we are capable of prayer. We have the capacity to offer the world back to God in thanksgiving, and it is only in this act of offering that we become genuinely human and truly free.

We do not expect all this to be stated explicitly in the Constitution of the E.U.; for the Constitution is a legal document, not a theological treatise. But it is our hope that, implicitly if not explicitly, the foundational documents of the E.U. will at least be open to such an interpretation. We trust that full recognition will be given to the fact that man does not live by bread alone.

Hitherto, we have spoken of "personal freedom," but it also needs to be said that our freedom is not only personal but interpersonal. As human beings, we cannot be genuinely free in isolation, repudiating our relationship with our fellow humans. We can be genuinely free only if we form part of a community of other free persons. Freedom is not solitary but social. We are free only if we become a *prosopon*—to use the Greek word

41. *Oration* 38.11. Gregory Nazianzus (330–90), one of three saints given the title "theologian" by the Orthodox Church, was archbishop of Constantinople during the Second Ecumenical Council (381). See Andrew Meredith, *The Cappadocians* (Crestwood, N.Y.: St. Vladimir's Seminary Press, 1998).

42. *Zōon Theoumenon* is the Greek title of Panayiotis Nellas. Panayiotis Nellas, *Deification in Christ: Orthodox Perspective on the Nature of the Human Person* (Crestwood, N.Y: St. Vladimir's Seminary Press, 1987).

for "person," which means literally "face" or "countenance"—only if we turn toward others, looking into their eyes and allowing them to look into ours. To turn away, to refuse to share, is to forfeit liberty.

This indeed is specifically what is implied by the Christian doctrine of God. According to the teaching of the Greek Fathers, "in the image of God" means primarily "in the image of Christ"; to be human is to be Christlike, for Christ is the supreme model of what it is to be a person. But the phrase "in the image of God" means also "in the image of God the Trinity." As Christians, we believe in a God who is not only one but one-in-three. The Christian God is not merely personal but also interpersonal; God is not just a unit but a union. As Trinity, God is not simply the Monad, unique, self-sufficient. God is the Triad of Father, Son, and Holy Spirit, the three divine persons united to one another in the unceasing movement of mutual love that the Greek patristic tradition terms "coinherence" or "co-indwelling" (*perichoresis*). God is communion (*koinonia*). In the words of Saint Basil of Caesarea: "The unity of God lies in the communion (*koinonia*) of the Godhead,"[43] in the interrelationship of the three persons. As Metropolitan John (Zizioulas) of Pergamon expresses it:

> The being of God is a relational being: without the concept of communion it would not be possible to speak of the being of God.[44]

Now, if as humans we are formed in the image of the Trinity, then it follows that everything that has just been said about God should be applied also to humankind. We are called to reproduce on earth, so far as this is possible for us. The *perichoresis*, or movement of mutual love that in heaven unites the three persons of the Trinitarian God—this we seek to do not only on the level of our interior life of prayer, not only within the immediate circle of our family and friends, but also more broadly on an economic and political level. Our social program is the doctrine of the Trinity. Every form of community—the workplace, the school, the city,

---

43. *On the Holy Spirit* 18 [45]. Basil (330–79), one of the Cappadocian Fathers, is also known as Basil the Great for his ecclesiastical and monastic reforms. See Meredith, *The Cappadocians.*

44. John D. Zizioulas, *Being as Communion: Studies in Personhood and the Church* (Crestwood, N.Y.: St. Vladimir's Seminary Press, 1985), 17.

the nation, even the European Union—has as its vocation to become, each in its own way, a living icon of the Trinity. Nations are called to be transparent to one another, just as the three persons of the Trinity are transparent to one another. Such is the role of religion in a changing Europe.

To some of you, we fear, what we have just been saying about the imitation of God the Trinity may appear remote, unreal, overidealistic. Of course we do not expect such language to be used in the legal formulations and the official documents of the E.U. Yet such are the decisive inner convictions that inspire our commitment as Christians to a united Europe.

State and Church: Separation or Cooperation?

Accepting, as we do and must, the pluralistic and multicultural character of Europe today, what should be our understanding of the relationship between the state and organized religion? There are in principle three main systems for regulating this relationship. There is first the *confessional* system, whereby the state gives official recognition to one particular religion or church. Second, there is the *non-confessional* system, whereby the state is separated from religion and assumes an attitude of neutrality toward all expressions of religious belief and practice. In the third place, the state is officially *atheist.*

Within the European Union, only the first two systems exist; there is within it no example of a state that is officially atheist. As examples of the first system, the confessional, we may take Great Britain, Denmark, and Greece. Within these three countries there is of course full freedom of religious worship and observance—indeed, this is presupposed by the basic principles of the E.U.—but a special position is assigned to one particular religious body: to the Church of England in Great Britain, to the Lutheran Church in Denmark, and to the Orthodox Church in Greece.

Most countries in the E.U., however, follow the second system, the non-confessional. This is the case, for instance, with France, Germany, Portugal, Belgium, Holland, and Luxembourg. In the 1970s, Ireland,

Spain, and Italy abandoned the confessional pattern whereby special recognition had been given to the Roman Catholic Church. More recently, in 2000, Sweden ceased to be a confessional state. Even in confessional states such as Great Britain and Greece, the link between church and state is being gradually weakened: now in Great Britain the state plays a far smaller role in the appointment of bishops; in Greece the president of the state is no longer required to be a member of the Orthodox Church. Increasingly, the norm within the E.U., and within Europe generally, is coming to be the non-confessional pattern.

Both in the confessional and the non-confessional systems, there are of course many variations in detail. Even where the non-confessional system prevails, it is usually accepted that religion cannot be simply a private matter for each citizen but that it has implications for the public life of the state, implications that may be recognized on the legal level. In some non-confessional states, for example, religious bodies continue to play an official role in the educational system. Thus, even in non-confessional countries, usually there is no attempt to establish a *total* separation between religion and the state.

Indeed, as we may legitimately ask, is *separation* the most appropriate word for us to employ in this context? Instead of using what is essentially a negative word, would it not be better to speak in terms of mutual respect and cooperation? It is significant that, in what is for Eastern Orthodoxy the most important statement of political philosophy—the Sixth Novel issued by the Emperor Justinian around the year 534—the key word is the term *symphonia*, "concord" or "harmony." Justinian begins by distinguishing the roles of the emperor (the civil authority) and the clergy (the religious authority): "The greatest gifts that God in his *philanthropia*[45] has given from above to human beings," he says, "are the priesthood [*sacerdotium*] and the imperial authority [*imperium*]." He goes on to specify the respective spheres in which each authority is competent to act, and he emphasizes their reciprocal interdependence: the emperor watches over the good order of the Church, and in their turn the clergy pray for the work of the emperor. He continues:

45. Greek for "loving-kindness."

> For if the priesthood is in all respects without blame and full of faith before God, and if the imperial authority rightly and duly adorns the commonwealth committed to its charge, there will ensue a *happy concord* that will bring forth all good things for humankind.[46]

We would like to underline in particular the phrase used here by Justinian, "a happy concord." Between sixth-century Byzantium and Europe in the twenty-first century, there are obvious and profound differences. But in speaking of "a happy concord," Justinian in his Sixth Novel offers us a paradigm for the relationship between the state and religion, a paradigm that is still valid today. Whether we are living in a confessional or a nonconfessional system—and as Christians we can accept either situation—it is our hope that there will exist between religion and the state a *symphonia* of active collaboration. We should not think only of separation, neutrality, or mutual tolerance but of a relationship that is far more dynamic and creative. Our Christian attitude toward the total society in which we live is expressed exactly in the statement of St. Paul (he was speaking, it is true, of membership within the Church, but we are justified in giving his words a wider application):

> If one member of the body suffers, all suffer together with it; if one member is honored, all rejoice together with it. (1 Cor. 12.26)

All that we have been trying to say this evening can be briefly summed up. Freedom, respect, and the dignity and integrity of each human person are fundamental to our vision of a united Europe. It is equally fundamental to our religious understanding of the relationship between the divine and the human: "God persuades, he does not compel." But freedom is not only personal, it is also interpersonal. The Self has its being and its fulfillment in the Other. We cannot be truly free, truly personal, unless we are in communion with other persons. We need you in order to be ourselves. If we make that the guideline in our personal religious life—and if we make that our guideline as citizens of our own nation, of Europe, and of the world—then without doubt religion will have a vital role to play in a changing Europe.

---

46. See Ernest Barker, *Social and Political Thought in Byzantium, from Justinian I to the Last Palaeologus: Passages from Byzantine Writers and Documents* (London: Clarendon Press, 1957), 75–76.

European Identity: The Welfare State and Religious Communities

Message to the Euroconference, University of Florence, Italy, February 25, 2001.

We are pleased to take this opportunity to address all the distinguished participants of this Euroconference. We witness that, at the outset of the new millennium, political, economic, and social forces are reshaping the European identity. We pay tribute to the efforts of visionaries like Jean Monnet, who, following the destruction wrought by World War II, sought to establish an integrated Europe in which interlocking political interests and economic interdependence would render another European war impossible. This vision was realized with the creation of the European Economic Community, now known by all as the European Union.

Yet this integrated Europe is not just an economic entity; rather it is also both a "political Europe" and a "social Europe." After fifty years of integration, Western Europe has experienced unsurpassed economic affluence and social stability. The European Union is today a shining example and a beacon of hope to the eastern half of Europe liberated from four decades of communist bondage. We also realize that all is not positive in Europe. We observe the troubles relating to nationalism in southeastern Europe; family and social breakdown; the diminishing role of religion and traditional values; soaring crime rates; alcohol and drug abuse; and the spread of AIDS. We need to ask ourselves: What path should Europe strive for in this millennium? How could religion, and in particular the Orthodox Church, accentuate the positives while reducing the negatives in Europe? Can secular civil society, government, and religion work together in a common endeavor to redefine the European identity?

The Orthodox Church follows the immutable and timeless principles espoused by our Lord Jesus Christ two thousand years ago—namely, those of love, compassion, tolerance, selflessness, and moral rectitude. Let us remember that our Savior sacrificed his life on the cross in order to lift the burdens of sin from the shoulders of his children. We recognize that such principles should remain at the core of the developing European identity. To put it another way: We need to apply established values in a modern setting. The great traditions of the Orthodox Church are a clear example of how religion could act as a positive influence on society.

The Values of Christianity

Take, for instance, Orthodoxy's direct and authentic link with Greek and Roman cultures—the foundation of European civilization. This religious and intellectual movement fostered the respect and support of cultural diversity within a single religious identity. It contributed to the evolution of Slavic culture, represented an important chapter of Arab civilization, and nurtured distinct local cultures in African countries. In short, for more than fifteen hundred years the Orthodox faith has preached love, reconciliation, and mutual understanding, irrespective of personal background, race, or gender.

Our vision is that the new Europe must be based on these Christian values, according to which government, civil society, and religion are partners and not rivals. We should harness the power of technology, especially the Internet, to spread Christ's message to all Europe's peoples. We should dispel the notion that Christ's teachings have no relevance in the new Europe or that a conflict between science and religion is inevitable. These teachings are relevant today as much as yesterday, in all spheres of human conduct. Let us not fall into the trap of thinking that religion cannot contribute to the ethical and moral debates of the day, debates ranging from genetic engineering to economic globalization.

We believe that the challenges of the twenty-first century are soluble through Christian ideals. Of particular satisfaction to us, and a source of pride, joy, and hope, is the spirit of reconciliation permeating the Balkans. We will leave no stone unturned to advance the cause of peace in this region. With an open heart, the Orthodox Church always extends a hand of trust and friendship to all religions, civil societies, and governments who share our vision of love and compassion for Europe. We are all children of the Almighty God. In the words of Aesop, "Together we stand, divided we fall."

4

Church and World: Global Perspectives

Another Way of Living

Invited op-ed, Washington Post, *Easter 2008.*

While many Christians have long celebrated Easter, this year Orthodox Easter takes place on April 27—much later than normally, as a result of ancient calendar calculations and regulations requiring the prior celebration of the Jewish Passover, in accordance with their traditional interpretation of scriptural record. Thus, at midnight on Saturday, April 26, the night that is said to be brighter than any sunlit day, some 300 million Orthodox Christians will crowd churches to hear the words: "Come, receive the light!" Throughout the world, entire congregations, previously waiting in darkness and anticipation, will light up in splendor and people's faces will shine with joy and hope. All of them will chant the familiar hymn of triumph:

> Christ is risen from the dead, trampling death by death, and granting life to those in the tombs.

For Orthodox faithful, Easter is the feast of feasts. As one Orthodox Easter hymn says, the feast of the Resurrection proposes "another way of seeing" and "another way of living." Yet, the secret of that new life is already foreshadowed in the previous day, when the Orthodox Church recalls the harsh reality of the Cross.

Faced with the seeming inevitability and impasse of global suffering, it is so easy to be cynical; it is tempting to dismiss issues like climate change or global conflict or world hunger, to criticize those who sentimentalize such issues.Yet, while people have become insensitive to sermons about the gloom and doom of our world, the reality of evil transcends any act of war or terrorism and every expression of violence or suffering. These are but symptoms of a deeper reality, which is overcome on the Cross on Good Friday (or Holy and Great Friday, as Orthodox Christians prefer to call it) through the radical power of forgiveness, tolerance, and compassion.

The Reality of Resurrection and the Global Reality

The truth is that the gospel message is as simple as it is radical. We are called to stand for love where there is hatred, to preach compassion where there is injustice, and to insist on dialogue where there is division. This at least, as we have been assured, is how people should recognize those who call themselves Christians (Jn. 13.35). In fact, however, as uncomplicated as this may sound, it is a much harder gospel to live by. It is far easier to proclaim a gospel of power and might. It seems far less challenging to be dismissive of efforts to sustain conversation among unlikely partners from radically different religious or cultural backgrounds (even among the great monotheistic traditions, particularly Christianity, Islam, and Judaism) and conservation of natural resources (whether such conservation is undertaken because it is fundamental to our survival as human beings, or in response to developing nations that experience poverty or hunger, or because it is supportive of our lifestyles). It is certainly far less intrusive in our personal lives to resist changes to our habits. People have far too much at stake.

Hoping for change invites challenge in our worldview and lifestyle. But how willing are we to pay a price for our selfish consumption, our wasteful pollution, and our prideful discrimination, both racial and religious? When will we stop and be silent long enough to notice the direct impact of our way of life on the poor among us and on the poor of the world? Do we even recognize the wounds we have wrought on the flesh of our brother and sister as well as upon the body of the world? Is it that difficult to discern the arrogance of our behavior, conveniently and complacently overlooking the damage that results from our silence or ignorance?

When Orthodox Christians recall the Resurrection, they are not primarily concerned intellectually with how that miracle actually took place. In fact, they think less of an empty grave and more of an open tomb, which remains an open invitation to those who believe. The miracle of resurrection calls for an openness to confess the reality of the darkness within us and around us, to admit our role in and responsibility for refusing to eradicate the suffering in our world. Then, when we stand honestly before the reality of our evil—in earnest recognition and prayerful confession both of the hurt we inflict on our neighbor in society and in the global community and of the abuse with which we treat the earth's resources—at that very moment of realization we are also able to perceive the hope and light of the Resurrection. Only then are we able to apprehend the relationship between the Resurrection and the presence of war, racism, global warming, and terrorism in our world. For then we shall also be able to discern the light of the Resurrection in our hearts and in our world.

This is why, for forty days after the bright night of that Easter vigil, Orthodox Christians will continue to greet one another with the words "Christ is Risen! Truly, He is Risen!"

Moral Dilemmas of Globalization

Address to the meeting of the World Economic Forum, held in Davos, February 2, 1999.

We should first like to express our joy that this meeting of distinguished and dynamic economists, political figures, and other eminent dignitaries has included on the agenda of its discussions the human dimension of globalization of the economy as well as noneconomic values. There is no doubt that, when values are ranked, the human person occupies a place higher than economic activity; neither is there any doubt that economic progress, which is present when there is growth in economic activity, becomes useful when—and only when—it serves to enhance the noneconomic values that make up human culture. This is the reason that justifies our Modesty's presence among this luminous gathering of eminent economic activists, even though we bear no relation to economic matters.

The advance of humanity toward globalization is a fact arising primarily out of the private sector, particularly from the desires of multinational economic giants. This fact finds support in the incredible development of communications. Already the role of states is being constantly downgraded, with few exceptions; the role of the economically powerful is growing in magnitude, even among the larger states.

As the primate of the Ecumenical Patriarchate and the first bishop of the Orthodox Church throughout the world, we assure you that the Orthodox Church has experienced and cultivated the idea of spiritual ecumenicity, a form of globalization that proclaims that all human beings of every race and language and of all cultures should be united by bonds of love, brotherhood, and cooperation.[1] It is true that the Church invites all to one faith, but it does not make brotherhood and love and its concern for people contingent on their joining this faith. Because the Church loves everyone, it also experiences the unity of humankind to its fullest. From this point of view, Christian ecumenicity differs substantially from globalization. The former is based on love for one's brother and sister and respects the human person whom it also seeks to serve. The latter is motivated primarily by the desire to enlarge the market and merge different cultures into a new one, in accordance with the convictions of those who are in a position to influence the worldwide community.

Unfortunately, globalization tends to evolve from a means of bringing the peoples of the world together as brothers and sisters to a means of expanding the economic dominance of the financial giants even over peoples to whom access to economic opportunity was denied because of national borders and cultural barriers. It is not our intention or responsibility to suggest ways and means by which this danger can be contained or eliminated. We do, however, have a duty to point out and proclaim that the highest pursuit of humanity is not economic enrichment or economic expansion.

The Gospel saying "Man does not live by bread alone" (Mt.4.4) should be more broadly understood. We cannot live by economic development

1. See Archbishop Anastasios Yannoulatos, *Facing the World: Orthodox Christian Essays on Global Concerns* (Crestwood, N.Y.: St. Vladimir's Seminary Press, 2003).

alone, but we must seek the "word that proceeds from the mouth of God" (Mt.4.4)—that is, we must seek the values and principles that transcend economic concerns. Once we accept these, the economy becomes a servant of humanity, not its master.

We believe that it can be understood by all, regardless of religious conviction, that economic development in itself and the globalization that serves it lose their value when they lead to deprivation for the many and an excessive concentration of wealth in the hands of the few. Moreover, evolution in this direction is not without limitation, because beyond a certain limit the person dealing with financial matters receives a response well known since ancient times: "You can not take from one who has not."

Solon the legislator, declaring that Athenian society was not functioning properly because of the excessive indebtedness of the majority of its citizens to the few, instituted what was known as *seisachtheia*,[2] the writing off of all debts. Although this seemed at first to be to the disadvantage of the rich, in the end it benefited the entire Athenian community because it allowed its members to act as free, creative, and self-motivated citizens and not as each other's slaves. Also well known is the decision of that pioneering American industrialist, the inventor of the assembly line, who raised the wages of his workers to make them capable of purchasing his products. (We are, of course, referring to the automobile manufacturer Henry Ford, who based his ideas on Taylor's views on the rationalization of labor.) These examples and many others show that economic progress is morally justifiable and successful only when all the members of the global community participate in it.

Moral Dimensions of Economy

This situation sets before us new dimensions of economic morality of a global magnitude. But although we are speaking of new challenges, we are dealing essentially with an aggravated form of ancient problems. The ancient Athenians excelled "not by bestowing any advantage on the rich, but by the poor sharing equally with the rich."[3] When Athens fell into an

2. Laws instituted by the Athenian lawmaker and statesman Solon to correct by means of debt relief the problem of serfdom and slavery.

3. Euripides, *Suppliants*, 407.

anarchic democracy controlled by demagogues, its former glory was eclipsed, just as it was and still is in those societies that Aristotle called "oligarchies," the presupposition of which is the possession of wealth.[4]

It is a fact that, as soon as respect for the human person is abandoned as an inviolable presupposition of our ethos and the principle of economy, power and the ability to influence the masses are made into idols and worshipped as such. There arises an insatiable cupidity, which inevitably leads the "haves" to increase what they possess, whether it be wealth, political or military power, the power to shape ideas, or, generally, the power to influence the whole world. We ought, however, to preserve all the remaining cultural values that pertain to humanity without, of course, putting up unnecessary barriers to useful economic development. But we also ought to be aware that the globalization of abilities is morally justified only when accompanied by the global distribution of the benefits that flow from it.

Globalization thus proves to be a new vision for some and a new threat for others—a vision that promises much to a few and very little to many, a vision impressive to some extent in its conception and in its realization. At the same time, however, it is also frightening to the degree that the dynamic of globalization exceeds the limits acceptable to the moral conscience and the limits of regulatory rules and mechanisms. What is impressive, for example, is the almost automatic globalization of information. Yet, at the same time, the potential for intentional misinformation is alarming. What is impressive is the globalization of knowledge and the participation of many in the farthest reaches of the macrocosm and the innermost depths of the microcosm. But what is also fearful is the threat posed by the possible misuse of this accumulated knowledge.

The visions, the dangers, the threats, the dilemmas rise up before us. The achievements—of international cooperation in the sectors of economy, commerce, telecommunications, and trade in general—that are attributed primarily to the phenomenon of globalization are wonderful. What, however, is the true gain for humanity as a whole if the economy, in succumbing to the sickness of elephantiasis, devours the other sectors of culture—namely, thought, the artistic will, and the contemplative side of human life? What is the true gain for humanity if it causes its creative

4. Aristotle, *Politics* IV, 8, 1294a.

powers to wither and enfeebles the fundamental principles of coexistence and survival such as justice, reciprocity, solidarity between individuals and peoples, and respect for the human person, that truly unshakeable bedrock of our existence and coexistence?

As a representative of the Orthodox Church, we are not opposed to the economic progress that serves humanity, nor are we bigoted or timorous in the presence of other faiths and ideologies. Our desire, however, is to safeguard the possibility for the members of every religious or cultural minority to maintain their distinctiveness and the particularity of their culture. We are in absolute agreement and are prepared to move ahead when globalization opens doors for the cooperation of peoples. The Ecumenical Patriarchate and we personally have already frequently invited adherents of divergent faiths and ideologies and interests to put aside their differences and reconcile and work together on a practical level. Globalization, however, as a means of making humanity homogeneous, of influencing the masses and causing a single, unified and unique mode of thought to prevail, will find us opposed. We also regard the use of globalization exclusively for the enrichment of the few to the detriment of the many as something impermissible and to be avoided. And we invite all, rich and poor, to cooperate for the improvement of the standard of living of all people, for this is also in the interest of the "haves," more so than is the one-sided increase in their economic worth. May God enlighten us all to be able to understand this truth.

Cultures in Conflict and Dialogue

Address at the International Conference on Islam in a Pluralistic World, held in Vienna, November 16, 2005.

We would like to thank the honorable government of Austria and especially Her Excellency Ursula Plassnik, the federal foreign minister of Austria, as well as the Austrian Organization for the Middle East for inviting us to participate in this international conference on Islam in a Pluralistic World. We thank you even more for offering us the floor to express our thoughts on this topic, especially with respect to "cultures in conflict and dialogue."

Such gatherings prepare the way for the peaceful cooperation of peoples. They bring cultures into proximity with one another and the faithful of the various religions to a definitive understanding that all human beings as individuals face the same problems in life and that they ought to help one another, instead of provoking and persecuting. We need to emphasize the important role of dialogue among religions and civilizations as the only means of arriving at a peaceful coexistence. In our contribution at this final session on "cultures in conflict and dialogue," we will endeavor to emphasize this need for a sincere and open dialogue between the two religions.

Interreligious dialogue takes people who have religious beliefs different from those of the majority and removes them from their isolation. It prepares them for mutual respect, understanding, and acceptance. We have expressed ourselves many times on this subject of dialogue and of the possibility for the coexistence of peoples who come from different cultural traditions. We are glad that once again an opportunity is given us to repeat in the presence of so many distinguished individuals our unswerving conviction that, if we so desire, if our hearts accept it, we can coexist in peace and profitable cooperation, despite the difference of our faiths.

We wholeheartedly greet the prominent Muslim brothers who participate in this meeting, some of whom we have met in other similar conferences, during which all together, they and we, try to infuse the world with the spirit of reconciliation and peaceful coexistence among all. And we believe that the two cultures, the Christian and the Islamic, the primary topic of our discussion these three days, have within them the elements of peaceful coexistence.

It is well known that the Qur'an, the sacred book of Islam, defines explicitly that the Christians and the believers of Judaism, the so-called monotheists, must not be forced to become Muslims. In general it says that religion is not coerced. Furthermore, it describes the New Testament as an "illuminating book" (chapter 3, verse 184), and it recognizes that Christians are those who are mostly disposed to love the faithful (chapter 5, verse 82). Therefore, there is no religious reason, according to the faith of Islam, for disputes and conflicts between Christians and Muslims. There are of course differences in faith and conviction, but Islam does not exalt them to the level of reasons for conflict. The conflicts between

Christians and Muslims that are mentioned in history have their roots in politics and not in religion. Every time religion has been used for inciting enmity and misfortune, it has been a matter of taking advantage of the ignorance of the masses and of misleading them into actions of intolerance and fanaticism. If we examine these cases with a clear and healthy mind we see that they are unjustifiable.

There are no religious reasons that would justify a violent conflict of the Christian and Muslim cultures. Regarding the the theory of the clash of civilizations, an opinion that has been expressed, publicized, and become known to the entire world, we say that it is not valid, inasmuch as it refers to religion as reason for such a supposedly expected and supposedly unavoidable conflict. If the aspirations of the nations and the geopolitical correlates of those aspirations lead to isolated or generalized conflicts between the Muslim and Christian peoples, or between some of them, and if politicians mobilize religions for the reinforcement of "otherness" and of hostility between nations—that is a totally different issue and irrelevant to the true nature of religion.

Christians and Muslims lived together in the same areas in the context of the Byzantine and the Ottoman Empire, with the consent or the assistance of the political and the religious authorities of the two monotheistic religions.[5] And the example, as was already mentioned, of the coexistence of the three monotheistic religions in Andalusia in Spain in the Middle Ages shows the possibilities offered even today. Despite the occasional explosions of phenomena of religious intolerance and fanaticism, the contemporary interreligious dialogue between Christianity and Islam rightly seeks in the previously mentioned historical models the criteria for the necessity of dialogue as well as for the identification of suggestions for peaceful coexistence of peoples and nations in the contemporary world, globalized and pluralistic as it is.

We see, then, that there are no religious reasons for the realization of the previously mentioned foreseen conflict. But even if there were reasons for such a conflict, then we, as religious leaders of both religions, have a duty to try and prevent such an outcome. A fundamental way of settling

5. See Steven Runciman, *The Great Church in Captivity: A Study of the Patriarchate of Constantinople from the Eve of the Turkish Conquest to the Greek War of Independence* (Cambridge, U.K.: Cambridge University Press, 1968).

any national, economic, or ideological difference, or a difference of any nature, is to develop a serious and fair dialogue between the parties involved. Dialogue resolves superstitions and biases, contributes to mutual understanding, and paves the way for finding a peaceful solution to all problems. Fear and suspiciousness are ill advisors and can be cast out only by getting to know people better on a deeper level and by cultivating good and truly friendly relations. Deep and meaningful relations will affirm either the honesty or possibly the dishonesty of one's interlocutor.

Religious Freedom and the Freedom of Religion

Many people have such strong convictions that they would rather sacrifice their own life than change them. Now, the following question is raised: Do we, by mentioning this, introduce a sense of instability and variability into one's faith? No, we do not introduce any such concept. We introduce only a closer examination, a continuously deeper understanding of the truth. Those who examine truth closer come to the conclusion that many times, ideas that up to a point seemed contradictory and mutually exclusive are in fact harmonized.

Let us give an example. It is written in the gospel that "whoever desires to save his life will lose it" (Mt 16.25). It is as if the person who wants to save his or her own life must accept to sacrifice it, for life is won only when it is sacrificed and not when it is preserved from danger with petty feelings and fear of loss.

Hesiodus in ancient Greece said that night and day are one and the same.[6] If that is so, then why are not Jew and Greek, slave and freeman, male and female, human being and human being of any race, language, and religion—why are they not one and the same thing? Ancient Greeks distinguished themselves by their ability to take knowledge and ideas from neighboring peoples and develop them without the fear that by doing so they would undermine or undervalue their own convictions. The rapid and inspired development of the ancient Greek spirit during the classical age is due also to their character. It was their character that allowed them to intercross their ideas with the ideas of other peoples and civilizations

6. Classical Greek didactic poet who lived in the eighth century B.C.

and, with great discernment, to take on and reshape into a new composition all that was good outside of Hellenism.

This freedom of spirit is found at the foundation of all spiritual progress. We believe that wherever there is the Spirit of God there is also freedom. The danger that lies in spiritual freedom is not worth taking into account if compared with all the good that this freedom has to offer. Unfortunately, though, as we have already mentioned, many people construct a spiritual and ideological stronghold and shut themselves inside its walls to safeguard their spiritual wholeness and integrity.

We have to clarify that a closer and deeper examination of the truth does not necessarily imply a change of religious affiliation. In ecclesiastical language we use the word *metanoia*, which means, literally, a shift of the mind, of our mentality. According to the Church Fathers, this is necessary even for those without sin. It is this shift of mentality that the dialogue helps realize, and that is why we hope that, by continuing with these dialogues, we will achieve a better, closer, and deeper examination of those truths that facilitates the peaceful coexistence of peoples.

Over the last three days, we have had the beautiful opportunity to talk with one another peacefully and to listen to distinguished speakers developing their positions on important issues that are raised by the coexistence and cooperation of Christians and Muslims. What should be highlighted is the development of the issues relating to the position of Christians in Muslim countries and to the position of Muslims in Christian countries. It seems that the position of Christians in certain Muslim countries is vulnerable and needs important improvement, so that Christians as well as the other minorities there will be able to enjoy the rights and possibilities that Muslims in Christian countries do.

It was only a week ago that we had in Istanbul the second conference on the topic of "Peace and Tolerance," which, while also condemning terrorism and violence, affirmed, among other things, the respect for life by the proverbial expression "Live and let live"; the respect for human rights, especially the rights of minorities; and religious tolerance.[7] Furthermore, it also pointed out the Christian saying "Blessed are the peacemakers, for they will be called Children of God" as well as the Muslim saying "Allah summoneth to the abode of Peace." Finally, we expressed our

7. For the full text, see Chapter 6, "Major Declarations: Public Proclamations."

gratitude to God, for he gave us the opportunity to verify our decision to cooperate for the increase of peace, justice, and human dignity.

It is therefore necessary that we move in that direction, beyond the difficulties and hindrances of the past. Objective, impartial history has of course registered behaviors of Christian nations and governments that are incompatible with the gospel as well as behaviors of Islamic nations and governments that are incompatible with the Qur'an. The time has come to act for God. We will both converge to what the will of God commands for all.

Those who have opened their hearts to God feel that the merciful and loving God is pleased not by bloodshed but by peace, which is the ultimate good and divine present. Christians and Muslims greet one another using the word *peace*. And it is with this greeting and with this wish that we will end our speech. Peace be unto you. Peace be unto the whole world.

Religious Communities and Building Peace: I

Address at the United Nations Luncheon, New York, October 27, 1997.

As leaders of the international community, you have an awesome responsibility to ensure peace throughout the world. As the successor to the Apostle Andrew, the First-called disciple of Jesus Christ, we also have a similar responsibility. Our Modesty is charged by Christ to preach the message of peace, hope, and love. We do this recognizing that our message must be set within the realistic setting of people's lives. We are committed to the universal cause of freedom, religious and political self-determination, and justice.

We have this day spoken with the secretary-general of the U.N., Mr. Kofi Anan. We thank him for his warm welcome. We look forward to working with him on any and all issues that touch on the fundamental message of our Lord's commandment to love one another. We represent the 300 million communicants of the world's Orthodox Christians who span the planet's many continents.

Certainly, the United Nations has recognized the increasing importance of religious communities as partners in the conflicts marking the post–Cold War world. It is a tragic fact that religion has contributed to cycles of violence and fragmentation between and within nation-states, before and since the end of the bipolar international order. However, it is also true that the end of bipolarity has produced new social and political circumstances. Recently, religious entities have directly cooperated with temporal powers in developing principles, language, and concrete policies premised on the rejection of categories of power that lead to separation, exclusion, disintegration, and conflict.

During the mounting chaos that was part of the implosion of Albania during much of 1997, the Orthodox Church of Albania was the first voice in civil society to call on all citizens to refrain from acts of violence. Since 1991, the country's Orthodox leadership has worked steadily with its Muslim counterparts.

In Turkey, the Ecumenical Patriarchate has led the way in its efforts to promote interfaith tolerance by convening the Conference on Peace and Tolerance—peace and tolerance among Christians, Jews, and Muslims. This forum produced the Bosphorus Declaration, whose signatories proclaimed that crimes in the name of religion are crimes against all religion. The Bosphorus Declaration condemns all religious violence.[8]

Similarly, only a short week ago, the Greek Orthodox Church in America inaugurated an official dialogue with Muslim leaders in America.

On a global scale, the International Orthodox Christian Charities (IOCC)[9] is a transnational NGO. This organization, very dear to our hearts, is vigorously opposed to proselytism. It is committed to interfaith cooperation, via philanthropic and welfare projects for improving literacy and life expectancy and for combating infant mortality and disease.

The Ecumenical Patriarchate and Peacemaking

The Ecumenical Patriarchate has worked to promote an awareness of the global ramifications of environmental issues. We see this God-inspired work as integral to the goal of world peace. We mention these positive examples of the Orthodox Church's involvement in worldly affairs to

8. For the full text, see Chapter 6, "Major Declarations: Public Proclamations."

9. An agency of the Standing Conference of Canonical Orthodox Bishops in the Americas (SCOBA), IOCC is an international humanitarian organization established in 1992.

underscore the fact that our faith offers a rich set of resources useful in promoting the U.N.'s noble agenda of conflict transformation and peacebuilding.

Unfortunately, the unique resources of the Orthodox Church remain relatively unknown to the U.N. and therefore underutilized by it. This has led to some situations where Orthodoxy has not had the support it might have had, support that would have helped the Church's message of love prevail in the face of historical animosities.

As the Mother Church of Orthodoxy, the Ecumenical Patriarchate of Constantinople is ready to expand any and all efforts to rebuild the moral and ethical well-being of long-suffering peoples everywhere. We say this without any intention of transgressing the fundamental rights of spiritual self-determination. However, we would hope that the West would make an effort to understand the unique hardships that the Orthodox Christian East has suffered during its long decades of persecution. We ask that noncoercive aid programs be extended to Orthodox Christians in areas where they are recovering from decades of repression and persecution.

We believe that Orthodoxy's rich theology of creation rests on the assumption that the entire cosmos is an integrated whole. The Orthodox Church's theological and existential goal of the integrity of all creation is constant with the U.N.'s goal of peacebuilding.

Orthodoxy's understanding of the human being as person, as a microcosm of the cosmos, assumes that our humanity is existentially meaningful only through the free and conscious engagement with others. The Ecumenical Patriarchate is committed to transforming the human condition. Our vision of freedom and relationality is consistent with U.N. efforts at transforming post-conflict situations, as it includes within its scope the restoration of the torn fabric of individual and community life.

The Orthodox Church transcends linguistic, ethnic, and national divisions. Our Orthodox Church is modeled on the Trinitarian principle of unity in diversity, whereby heterogeneity and uniqueness are fundamental aspects of our humanity. The Church's experience is comparable to that of the U.N. itself, an entity whose unity is the result of the diversity of its membership. Dear coworkers in the vineyard of peace, our presence here today is meant to reaffirm the commitment of the Holy Orthodox Church to the U.N. agenda. We humbly serve notice that our Church is capable of offering much to better the health of the U.N. family.

We exhort you to take up the responsibility that has been given to us by God, our Creator, to collectively renew our commitment to restoring the peace, justice, and integrity of all creation. We ask you to consider the creative gifts of the Orthodox Christian community as a resource for change. We respectfully offer you the spiritual resources of the Ecumenical Patriarchate.

Religious Communities and Building Peace: II

Message to the Eighth World Assembly of the World Conference of Religions for Peace in Kyoto, Japan, August 21, 2006.

It is with honor and a sense of responsibility that we address the Eighth World Assembly of the *Religions for Peace,* in an effort to appeal to the conscience of our world to confront violence and advance shared security at a time that this is much needed. It is with deep sorrow and frustration that we have recently witnessed the tragedy in the Middle East, where war has once again broken out and uncontrollable and indiscriminating violence has taken a great toll in lives, those of hundreds of people. Let us all pray to God and ask for his mercy in the hope that he will shine in the hearts of the parties involved in this bloodshed and give them the strength to commence peace talks once again and spare the lives of innocents. It is such violence that we have to strive to overcome, and we must join our efforts to find ways to bring peace to all.

The wealth of the variety of religious traditions that are being represented in this World Assembly can become a beacon to many and can prove that, despite our differences, our common goal and aspiration—namely, that of establishing a peace that will enable us all to share in the gifts that God offered to all of humankind without any exception—is much stronger. We all realize that we live in a world where change is constant and inevitable, and this change must be achieved without violence, for this is essential to our survival. We might seem very different in many ways, yet we share the same frustrations and hopes for the future. Our common vision of peace and prosperity for our world, which is experiencing turmoil, division, and conflicts, is in the heart of everyone.

We are called to raise our voices and object to the use of violence, any form of violence, whether it is armed conflict, poverty, or diseases such as

HIV/AIDS. There have been claims that violence can be used for a good purpose. Nevertheless, even if it appears to do good, this good can only be temporary, whereas the evil that it does remains with us permanently. As Albert Einstein once said, "Peace cannot be achieved through violence, but it can only be attained through understanding." It is this understanding we are trying to promote.

We have always welcomed all forms of dialogue and cooperation among religions, and it is our unshakable conviction that religion can be a key factor and a solid foundation for peace and dialogue among civilizations; we are to be a people who pursue righteousness and justice and who therefore pursue peace. The Ecumenical Patriarchate, in its dedication to support a constant pursuit for peace and reconciliation among peoples, has an ongoing interreligious dialogue, particularly with Judaism and Islam, that began almost thirty years ago and has always been collaborating with the World Conference of Religions for Peace.

It is written in the scriptures that "terror and violence make havoc of riches; similarly, desolation overtakes the houses of the proud" (Sir. 21.4). We have gathered once more to find ways to prevent this from happening, for we witness on a daily basis the sweeping reality for millions of our brothers and sisters all over the world. One of the major roles of religion is to bring the peace of God into the world on a local, regional, and global level. Our purpose is to continue our constructive dialogues which benefit the world. We must teach our people tolerance, which is ultimately based on respect for the sanctity and rights of individual human beings.

Indeed, if there is one place where the spiritual and secular universes converge, it is in the individual, in the human person. This reality cannot be overlooked. At least it cannot be overlooked without detriment to the planning of the relations among religions, because then the context of peaceful coexistence of peoples is not really constructed but, on the contrary, there is an aggravation of the conflicting relations, with unpredictable and definitely painful consequences for the common vision of peace. To be sure, religious leaders do take the initiative in establishing dialogue, but their cooperation with political authorities would give a more immediate social context to the political declarations for the protection of peace, social justice, and human rights without any ethnic, racial, religious, social, or other unacceptable discrimination.

We assure you, fellow travelers on the road to peace, that we will always work with you—not only in the spirit of peace and tolerance but, more so, in the spirit of divine love itself. The Ecumenical Patriarchate belongs to the living Church that was founded by the God of love, whose peace "surpasses all understanding" (Phil. 4.7). We "pursue what makes for peace" (Rom. 14.19). We believe that "God is love" (1 Jn. 4.16), which is why we are not afraid to extend our hand in friendship and our heart in love, as we proclaim that "perfect love casts our fear" (1 Jn. 4.18).

There is more that unites us than divides us. We have within our grasp the vision of the Psalmist: "Behold, how good and how pleasant it is for brethren to dwell together in unity" (Ps. 133.1). We pledge to you today that the Orthodox Church will do everything in her power to fulfill that vision. Certainly, there are peacemakers among us. Certainly, there are those who cry out in a seemingly lonely voice to heaven for God to establish peace. Certainly, there are men and women in this world who, in the spirit of the prophets, seek justice in order to lay the foundation for peace. If we are true to our respective faiths, to seek peace must be our task.

Let us seek peace. Let us work for peace. And let us pray for the peace of God, which is the basis for all peace on earth.

Religious Communities and Building Peace: III

Address to the Religions and Peace Conference in Mardin, May 13, 2004.

With profound appreciation for this opportunity to share with you a reflection on our father, Abraham, I greet you in peace! For it is indeed peace, together with justice and righteousness, that is central to Abraham's legacy, which we share as his sons and daughters in faith. As we all know from the ageless story handed down to us, the Lord came to visit Abraham and his wife Sarah in the form of three men.[10] Of course, tradition has identified these men as angels of the Lord, and in Christian theology these angels form the symbol of the Trinity, as artistically represented in the Trinitarian icons so familiar in Orthodox churches worldwide.

---

10. See Genesis, chapter 18.

During this visit, according to the Hebrew scriptures, the Lord made an interesting comment as he contemplated telling Abraham of his intentions for the city of Sodom:

> Shall I hide from Abraham what I am about to do, seeing that Abraham shall become a great and mighty nation, and all the nations of the earth shall bless themselves by him? No, for I have chosen him, that he may charge his children and his household after him to keep the way of the Lord by doing righteousness and justice; so that the Lord may bring to Abraham what he has promised him. (Gen. 18.18–19)

"That he may charge his children and his household after him to keep the way of the Lord by doing righteousness and justice." This is a legacy left to us by our father, Abraham. If we are to be recognized as his descendents—either by blood, by promise, or by adoption—we are to be a people who pursue righteousness and justice and who therefore pursue peace. Jews, Christians, and Muslims all claim to be descended from Abraham. Our faiths are very clear that we are all somehow his children. But it is interesting to note in this passage that what is characteristic of his children is that they are pursuers of peace. In other words, what should characterize us, his children, is our dedication to the pursuit of peace.

In today's world, it seems that pursuers of peace are few. Terrorists wantonly kill innocent people to make a political statement. Countries go to war against other countries without justification. Ethnic groups commit genocide against other ethnic groups. Racism still causes enmity between people. Children are killed daily, either in war by conventional weapons or in urban street violence by small arms. Even religious rhetoric is often filled with hate speech directed against other religions. And the list of horrors goes on and on.

Religions and Peace in the Light of Abraham

In the midst of all these troubles, where are those who pursue peace? Certainly, there must be peacemakers among us. Certainly, there are those who cry out in a seemingly lonely voice to heaven for God to establish peace. Certainly, there are men and women in this world who, in the spirit of the prophets, seek justice in order to lay the foundation for peace.

If we are true to our respective faiths, Jews, Christians, and Muslims have no option. If we are true to our father Abraham, to seek peace must be our task.

I once heard an interpretation of the Lord's visit to Abraham that might be useful in the context of our reflection. What if, the story goes, the three angels returned to visit Abraham and one of them was a Jew, one a Christian, and one a Muslim? What would Abraham say to them? The question I would pose to you, my friends, is this: what would Abraham say to the three visitors today? What would he say to us if we were standing in his presence? What would be our response? What, moreover, would be our responsibility?

Theologically, our answer would be based on the principles that all of us hold in common. Indeed, we may differ theologically—we each profess ultimate truth claims that cannot be entirely reconciled, either through the covenant with Moses, the revelation in Jesus Christ, or the words of the Prophet Mohammad. But we also share theological principles that must be affirmed, especially in light of our common ancestor Abraham.

We all uphold belief in God as that which leads to the fulfillment of the human person. We all uphold the dignity of the human person as the basis for relationship among all people. We all uphold justice for all people as the goal of our efforts as faithful children of God. Certainly based on at least these three, shared principles, we can stand together before our father, Abraham. These three theological principles lead to the search within our respective traditions for imperatives that motivate us to pursue peace. And these imperatives lead us to concrete action.

Belief in God, and in his sovereignty and love, compels us to love one another and to desire for the well-being of all. This leads us to work on behalf of the others whose fulfillment is thwarted by evils in the world. For example, it leads us to do all we can to minister to those suffering from HIV/AIDS, to teach and preach against the stigmatization that this disease often brings, to care for the families of those affected by the disease, and ultimately to support the scientific research that would eliminate the scourge of this disease from the earth. Some might ask why I include responding to HIV/AIDS as an example of peacemaking. To me, the answer is clear: HIV/AIDS is destroying the infrastructure of countries throughout the African continent. If we do not find a solution, the hopelessness and violence that result there will affect all people of the world.

Belief in the dignity of the human person demands that we treat all people with respect. This leads us to speak out against those who would humiliate, oppress, and commit violence against others. For example, it leads us to condemn terrorism and war, comfort prisoners, and seek to heal the divisions among people. I am sure that no one in this room, given current events, would question the importance of this example.

Belief in justice requires that we bring an end to injustice. This leads us to seek sustainable development for the economic well-being of all. It leads us to address the root causes of terrorism. It leads us to foster reconciliation among enemies. For example, it leads us to try to eliminate the crushing poverty that is the cause of alienation, desperation, and all other manner of hopelessness, and, therefore, of the spontaneous eruptions of violence that result from such hopelessness. It is up to religious communities to call on societies to solve these problems, so that all people experience the wholeness that is offered by God to his creation. To raise this example, which is often lost in secular circles, is certainly the responsibility of religious voices.

Even as we pursue peace through these types of action, religious communities have other resources that they have traditionally shared, and must continue to share, with those in need. Religious communities offer refuge to those affected by the storms of life. Religious communities offer charity to those who hunger and thirst. Religious communities offer healing to those who are sick, those who mourn, and those who are at enmity with one another. Certainly there is much that we have done; certainly, however, there is much more that we can yet do.

These resources have over the years demonstrated the faithfulness that is at the heart of every religion. Not surprisingly, they are at the heart of what it means to be the inheritors of Abraham's legacy. For as Jews, Christians, and Muslims recall, Abraham offered to his heavenly visitors shelter, a meal, and even a challenge to overlook the sins of others. If Abraham could be so faithful in the presence of the Lord, it is incumbent on us to be so faithful in the presence of all people created in the Lord's image.

This is what it means for religions to seek peace in the light of Abraham. As war rages on the biblical home of our father Abraham, the importance of this legacy is even more pronounced. Let us seek peace. Let us work for peace. And let us pray for the peace of God, which is the basis for all peace on earth. In this way, it can be as it is written in the Hebrew Scriptures: "and by your descendants shall the nations of the earth bless themselves" (Gen. 22.18).

Religious Communities and Building Peace: IV

Message to interreligious meeting, Cyprus, November 11, 2008.

It is with honor and a sense of responsibility that we address this interreligious meeting, gathered today on the island of Cyprus to participate in this Day of Prayer for Peace, in an effort to appeal to the conscience of our world to confront violence and promote peace at a time when it is much needed. We would like to welcome those who initiated and organized this event and to further underline the yearlong dedication and sincere interest of the Community of Sant' Egidio in such important matters that concern our society.

From the prophet Isaiah we know that the "prince of peace" (Is. 9.6), our Lord Jesus Christ, declared blessed the peacemakers, promising that they "shall be called sons of God" (Mt. 5.9). The peace of God is the most perfect of blessings and manifests itself as steadfastness of the free will of the human person.[11] As such, it surpasses all understanding (see Phil. 4.7) and does not have any limit (Is. 9.7). "It is extended from age to age, being limitless and endless."[12] There is no such peace "if virtue has not been previously achieved,"[13] because this peace is the fruit of grace, the grace that operates in those who have been delivered from evil desires and internal war. Wrongful desires beget internal turmoil even in the absence of any intruder from the outside, and they cause external war when they mislead the will to act toward actualizing them (see Jm. 4.1).

As you are well aware, establishing peace is our common goal and aspiration, peace that will enable us all to share in the gifts that God offered to all of humankind without any exception. We all realize that we live in a world where change is constant and inevitable, and this change must be achieved without violence, for this is essential to our survival. We

11. Basil the Great PG30.305.
12. Basil the Great PG30.513.
13. John Chrysostom PG62.73.

might have our differences, yet we share the same frustrations and hopes for the future. Our common vision of peace and prosperity for our world, which is experiencing turmoil, division and conflicts, and grave financial crisis as of late, is in everyone's heart, and we greet wholeheartedly this initiative of promoting a civilization of peace, which can be brought into being through an honest and constant dialogue between faiths and cultures. Especially in view of the contemporary financial crisis, which is shaking the very foundations of our society and is the result of manic profiteering and corrupt financial activity—lacking an anthropological dimension and sensitivity, it does not ultimately serve the real needs of mankind—we have to remember that working together may well be the only solution available and possible.

The Orthodox Church has from the very beginning inscribed "its contribution to the realization of the Christian ideals of peace, justice, freedom, fraternity and love between the nations as well as to the elimination of racial discrimination" in the agenda of the Holy and Great Council. Needless to say, this concern is not limited to the Orthodox Church. Peace is a matter of concern for all Christians and for all religions, and it reflects, in diverse shapes and forms, the preoccupations of humanity as a whole.

More than the Absence of War

However, when we speak of peace, let us not limit it to the neutral and negative concept that defines it as the mere absence of war. It must be emphasized that we refer to the biblical notion, which does not coincide with that simplified definition. The biblical notion of peace implies the restoration of all things to the original wholeness they enjoyed before the Fall, when man still lived and inhaled the life-giving breath of creation in the image and likeness of God.[14] In other words, peace is understood as the restoration of the relationship and peace between God and mankind.

We have always welcomed all forms of dialogue and cooperation, and it is our unshakable conviction that religion can be a key factor and a solid foundation for peace and dialogue among civilizations; we are to be

14. On the consequences of the Fall in Orthodox theology, see John Romanides, *The Ancestral Sin* (Ridgewood, N.J.: Zephyr, 2002).

a people who pursue righteousness and justice and who therefore pursue peace. The role of religions in the contemporary world requires the transcendence of all morbid manifestations of religious fanaticism and intolerance of the past, which are alien to the spiritual mission of religions and have heaped many woes on humanity. The role of religions requires as well their full-hearted support of peace, social justice, and human rights, which are called for in the teachings of all religions to a greater or lesser extent and constitute a common basis for their constructive dialogue with contemporary political ideology vis-à-vis the relations between human beings and between peoples.

We, at the Ecumenical Patriarchate, will continue our efforts to be peacemakers and to light the lamp of the human spirit. We, like all of you who have gathered here on the historic island of Cyprus on this Day of Prayer for Peace, wish to be a religious and spiritual institution, teaching, edifying, serving universal ideals, civilizing, and preaching love in every direction. We assure you, fellow travelers on the road to peace, that we will always work with you—not only in the spirit of peace but, more so, in the spirit of divine love itself.

After all, there is more that unites than divides us. We pray that this meeting will become yet another beacon of hope, especially since it is taking place during this Year of Intercultural Dialogue, and we welcome all the sincere efforts of the political world to contribute to the promotion of such a dialogue. Intercultural dialogue is at the very root of what it means to be a human being, for no one culture of the human family encompasses every human person. Without such dialogue, the differences in the human family are reduced to objectifications of the "other" and lead to abuse, conflict, persecution—a grand-scale human suicide, for we are all ultimately one humanity. But where the differences between us move us to encounter one another and where that encounter is based in dialogue, there is reciprocal understanding and appreciation—even love.

Certainly, there are peacemakers among us. Certainly, there are those who in a seemingly lonely voice cry out to heaven for God to establish peace. Certainly, there are men and women in this world who, in the spirit of the prophets, seek justice in order to lay the foundation for peace. If we are true to our respective faiths, to seek peace must be our task, for we are faced with times that entail every kind of hardship, and such a task is a noble one.

Therefore, we call on all of you to pray "again and again" that peace, justice, and God's love may finally prevail in people's lives. "Glory to God in the highest, and on earth, peace and goodwill toward men."

Religious Communities and Building Peace: V

Address to the Sixth World Conference on Religion and Peace, Riva del Garda, Italy, November 4, 1994.

In the days ahead, as you discuss various problems, keep in mind that no member of the human family has a monopoly on malice. We are all sinners and stand in desperate need of God's grace in our quest for a better world. The representatives of many civilizations have gathered here today in a spirit of brotherhood and harmony to reaffirm that humankind is the culmination and recapitulation of divine creation and, as we were created in the image and likeness of our Creator, the restoration of humankind to our primordial magnitude and beauty is our common mission. May our heavenly Father grant us the faith and strength to maintain this fraternal spirit and common mission as we work together in the years to come.

Dear brothers and sisters, we live in an age of wonder and glory. Justice has rolled down like waters, and righteousness like an ever-flowing stream (see Am. 5.24). A tide of tears has washed over our world, and as it recedes it sweeps away much sorrow and pain. The curse of communism has practically disappeared. Palestinians and Israelis have taken steps to make peace, and now Jordan has joined them. In Haiti, the sword of the generals has yielded to the ploughshare of democracy. In South Africa, hatred, intolerance, and violence are giving way to brotherhood, democracy, and understanding. For the first time in memory, the people of Northern Ireland are finally working to solve their problems with words rather than with weapons. We could grow accustomed to such a steady diet of miracles!

What for Christianity is the "recapitulation," or unity, of all things in Christ (Eph. 1.10) is for all humankind as well the earnest beginning of restoring the sacredness and exceptional magnitude of the human person. At the same time, the world that knows disruption, alienation, racial discrimination, and hatred clearly knows that there is no place for those things and that they must be abolished. The human race and the world once again can constitute an organic unity in one body, for, as the Apostle Paul says:

> There is neither Jew nor Greek, there is neither slave nor free, there is neither male nor female; for you are all one in Christ Jesus. (Gal. 3.28)

We do not ignore, however, the tragedies that continue in Bosnia, East Timor, Sri Lanka, and so many other places—indeed, too many other places. But amid the rubble of our tragic century, the heart of humanity still beats: we must not fail to hear it. Amid the gravestones the human spirit is emerging: we must not fail to see it.

Crisis as Challenge

We have been given a rare opportunity. "Thou hast made thy people suffer hard things; thou hast given us wine to drink that made us reel" (Ps. 60). Somehow the world is growing weary of bloodshed; it is tiring of fanaticism; it is reeling from the wine it has drunk. We must build on this. There is a great hunger for spirituality, for transcendent meaning. We must satisfy it. There has never been a greater need for spiritual leaders to leave their cloisters, come together, and take action. Too many crimes are committed in the name of faith. "Beware of false prophets, who come to you in sheep's clothing but inwardly are ravenous wolves" (Mt. 7.15). Those words come from the Christian tradition, but their truth is transcendent.

There is no lack of false prophets today:

Drugs and their handmaiden, *crime*—an international problem that grows with each passing year.

Cults and their charismatic leaders—in the last two years, in Waco, Texas, in Switzerland and in Canada, we have seen the spark of faith transformed into the flames of fanaticism, claiming scores of lives, young and old.

Nationalism—which began as a positive force for the construction of democratic states but turned out to be the most destructive force in human history, killing 75 million human beings between 1914 and 1945 alone.

Religious *extremism* and *terrorism*—the chosen instruments of perhaps the most wicked false prophets of all, for, not only do they commit horrible crimes against humanity, they do so in the name of a lie. When a bus in Tel Aviv is deliberately blown up or a mosque on Mt. Hebron fired on, more than precious lives have been stolen; faith, which is the only way to break the cycle of hatred and retribution, has been undermined. We must dispel fanaticism and intolerance while defending the human and civil rights of people everywhere.

War—arms buildup and, particularly, atomic warfare are followed by the devastation of creation and the annihilation of life from the face of the earth. In the aftermath of an atomic war, not only would there be loss of countless lives, but, for the survivors—if there are any—life would be unbearable. War—or anything that destroys—is a crime against humanity and a mortal sin against God.

Hunger—if feeding ourselves is a material matter, then caring for the feeding of our fellow human beings is a purely spiritual matter. The economically developed world unjustly and often criminally distributes and mismanages material goods, and so those responsible are guilty of offending not only the image of God in themselves but also God Himself.

Some of you were with us earlier this year in Istanbul when we signed the Bosphorus Declaration.[15] We proclaimed that a crime committed in the name of religion is a crime committed against religion. We were pleased to hear these words echoed just last week by President Clinton in his address to the Jordanian parliament and agree with him wholeheartedly that

> Terrorists and extremists are the past. Peacemakers are the future.

Peacemaking and the Responsibility of Freedom

We are not immune to the forces of history, but neither are we helpless before them. We must answer the fratricide and fragmentation of the current age with the brotherly love and reconciliation taught by our timeless traditions. We must renounce and condemn violence and we must teach our people the blessing of peace, which is ultimately based on respect for the sanctity and rights of individual human beings. Indeed, if

15. For the full text, see Chapter 6, "Major Declarations: Public Proclamations."

there is one place where the spiritual and the secular universes converge, it is in the human person.

The completeness of the human person, both as a singular bearer of the image of God as well as a community of persons, is for Christianity a reflection of the Holy Trinity. For every man, woman, and child, this completeness constitutes the divine gift of freedom—the freedom that allows humankind, conscious of his or her own self, the possibility to choose between what is good and what is evil; the freedom that gives one the ability to strive toward spiritual perfection.

Simultaneously, however, this freedom demands responsibility and contains the danger of disobedience, autonomy from God, a falling away. Evidence of this may be seen in the traumatic role that evil plays in humankind, especially with regard to issues of peace and freedom. Consequences of this evil are the imperfections and deficiencies in today's life: secularization, violence, demoralization, the problems of today's youth, phyletism, arms buildup, wars, and the social evil that is a result of them—namely, the oppression of the masses, social inequality, economic disaster, the unfair distribution or lack of consumer goods everywhere, hunger among millions of undernourished people, forced relocation, chaos involving refugees and the migration of peoples, the destruction of the environment, the problems of developing societies within an unequally industrialized and technological world, and the expectations of futurists—all these weave the unending anxiety of contemporary anguished humanity.[16]

Among those of us who place our faith in spiritual institutions, this means that, of all the precepts of our diverse religions, the first principle must be the divinity of each and every one of God's children. Among those who place their faith in temporal institutions, this means that, of all political principles, primary emphasis must be put not on collective but rather on individual human rights.

The Role of Religion in a Secular World

This is one of many areas in which we as a community of faith have something to teach secular leaders. In recent years we have heard some

---

16. See the report of the Inter-Orthodox Preparatory Commission, Chambésy-Geneva, 1986.

say that human rights are relative—an unfortunate and potentially catastrophic idea. Humanity was created in the image of God, and there cannot be one standard of treatment for those human beings who happen to be Asian, another for Africans, and yet another for Europeans. Culture may be relative, but humanity certainly is not. Christians believe that God "made from one blood all nations of men to live on all the faces of the earth" (Acts 17.26) and that God does not accept the notion of racial discrimination in any form whatsoever, since this would suggest a marked difference among the human races and would encourage a graduated classification of rights.

Eastern Orthodoxy has never encouraged racist ideas and theories, nor has it practiced racial discrimination, social marginalization and isolation, prosyletism, persecution, or genocide of people who belonged to a different culture or worshipped God in a different manner. Humankind must make every attempt to substitute incredulity and enmity—which poison the international atmosphere—with friendship and mutual understanding. Today, we are still working energetically to promote ecumenism and love over extremism, nationalism, hatred, and war. This is why we convened an unprecedented Pan-Orthodox *synaxis* (an assembly) of the heads of the world's Orthodox patriarchates and autocephalous churches in March of 1992—an unusual display of Christian solidarity and a return to the ecumenism of centuries past. We will repeat this act of unity by convening another *synaxis*, this time on the sacred island of Patmos, in September 1995, to celebrate the 1,900th anniversary of the writing of the Book of Revelation, the concluding book of the Holy Bible.

The Ecumenical Patriarchate and the Way of Unity

Brothers and sisters, the watchword of the Holy Orthodox Church today is unity. For this reason, the Ecumenical Patriarchate has established an academic dialogue with both Muslims and Jews. We hope to put behind what is unpleasant while putting forward the best values of humankind. As leaders, we must stand prophetically and, for the benefit of all, work for brotherly and sisterly coexistence among those of different faiths. We must set aside our differences and learn to "speak the truth in love" as children of the one true God.

In June of 1995, we will continue the "dialogue of love" with our brother, the bishop of Rome, Pope John Paul II—a tradition established by Patriarch Athenagoras and Pope Paul VI, both of blessed memory. Six months later, we will meet with His Grace the archbishop of Canterbury, Dr. George Carey, to continue our ecumenical dialogue; and, immediately after, we will visit the World Council of Churches in Geneva, Switzerland, thereby further promoting understanding and unity through bilateral and multilateral dialogues.

We are committed to unity, and on our pilgrimage we have taken as our motto the words of Ephesians 4.3, that we are "eager to maintain the unity of the Spirit in the bond of peace." We will continue to seek unity and peace, to denounce violence and discredit false prophets, and to act as a bridge of understanding among people belonging to various faiths. We have always lived on the fault line between East and West. We have witnessed great suffering on both sides, as we see again today in Bosnia, but we have witnessed also the most extraordinary acts of tolerance, such as the historic peace between Muslim and Jew in the Middle East even as we speak.

We must help bring the spiritual principles of ecumenism, brotherhood, and peace to the fore. Indeed, this is why we are gathered here! This is one way that we of the cloth can help those in government. Our deep and abiding spirituality stands in stark contrast to the secularism of modern politics. The failure of anthropocentric ideologies has left a void in many lives. The frantic pursuit of the future has sacrificed the stability of the past. Religious bodies have at their disposal a variety of spiritual possibilities that stand in contrast to what international organizations and governments can offer. These possibilities arise from the very nature of our being men and women called by God. As a community of faith, we can counter secular humanism and nationalism and temper the mindless pursuit of modernity with love, ecumenism, and our own healthy respect for tradition.

However, we can do this only if we are united in the spirit of the one God, "Creator of all things visible and invisible," to adopt the opening words of the Symbol of Faith, the Nicaean-Constantinopolitan Creed. Roman Catholic and Orthodox, Protestant and Jew, Muslim and Hindu, Buddhist and Confucian—it is time not only for rapprochement but even for alliance and teamwork to help lead our world away from the false prophets of extremism and intolerance.

We at the Ecumenical Patriarchate have a strong sense of social mission for peace, freedom, justice, and brotherhood among peoples. Over and above this, however, there must be a witness of love. This witness must be borne regardless of the conditions under which any of us live today. A witness of love means that we must respect the human person and the image of God engraved in each of us; that we must serve our fellow human being who is weak, hungry, and oppressed; that we must relieve malady, misfortune, and suffering. We cannot be indifferent just because this virtue seems to be lacking in contemporary society.

On the contrary, because we have benefited from divine justice, we must struggle for a fuller justice in the world and for the neutralization of every kind of oppression. Any attempt on our part to behold the divine presence of God without a relationship with one who is in need would prove nothing but simply theoretical. Love is what will galvanize the desire of the Orthodox Church to work in close cooperation with the other churches and confessions as well as with all people everywhere. This is at once our mandate and mission as members of the family of God.

Beloved brothers and sisters, the spiritual gift of peace depends on our willingness to be coworkers. We believe that this unity is not static or monolithic but powerfully dynamic. Today, fear is giving way to hope and our worst pockets of despair have become our greatest sources of inspiration. Let this conference mark yet another turning point in this age of miracles. We have within our grasp the vision of the Psalmist: "Behold, how good and pleasant it is when brothers dwell together in unity" (Ps. 133.1). Let us, therefore, become what Clement of Alexandria calls "the peaceful race" and "peaceful soldiers"—for peace, he said, is synonymous with justice.[17] Nothing is more characteristic of the Christian—as it is of every God-fearing person on earth—than to make peace. Today the Orthodox Christian Church will do everything in her power to fulfill this vision.

We greet you, dear brothers and sisters, with the words of Jesus Christ, "Peace I leave with you; my peace I give to you; not as the world gives do I give to you" (Jn. 14.27).

---

17. Clement of Alexandria (150–215) was the head of the catechetical school of Alexandria and teacher of Origen of Alexandria (185–254).

Religious Communities and Building Peace: VI

Address to the Ministry of Foreign Affairs in Iran, January 12, 2002.

It is indeed with great emotion that we take up the discourse at this time, responding to an invitation of the Islamic Republic of the glorious and historic Iran to dialogue with you, to express our convictions on the subject of "the role of religion in the establishment of peace in the contemporary world," and thereby to contribute in a heartfelt manner to the mutually desirable dialogue, between Islam and Christianity, on this practical and social topic, without entering into theological and dogmatic questions of faith.

This invitation and this meeting are truly of historic significance, because they confirm the constant persistence of the honorable government and of the beloved people of Iran to pursue dialogue as a means of promoting common understanding among peoples and the advancement of culture. This initiative of the honorable government of Iran will be recorded in the annals of history as most important, as the proposal of His Excellency the president of the Islamic Republic of Iran Mr. Mohammad Kathami to the United Nations has already been recorded, as, by virtue of it, the past year was declared a year of dialogue. This meeting, too, is aligned with other similar meetings and discussions organized by the same honorable government of Iran and the International Center of Dialogue and held among cultures based in Iran. This center constitutes a very honorable achievement for the Islamic Republic of Iran, which we wish many would emulate.

Between outstanding representatives of Christianity and Islam there have certainly been other such meetings and dialogues, which have been recorded in remote as well as in recent history. Nevertheless, the need for a systematic implementation of dialogues, which are on the increase today, is the fruit of the contemporary efforts of enlightened persons, including the aforementioned president of the Islamic Republic of Iran. All these efforts bear witness, on the one hand, to the free spirit exhibited by outstanding Islamic leaders in all peacemaking discussions, and, on the other hand, to the truly praiseworthy enhancement of the ability for dialogue that God has implanted in man.

We express, therefore, our deepest joy and satisfaction in this truly historic and most laudable initiative of the honorable government of the

Islamic Republic of Iran, and we extend again our warm thanks to its most honorable members for the precious invitation of our Modesty to participate in this dialogue, to expound to you from this position our views and convictions on the said topic—not, of course, to add anything new and unknown but to confirm, both in a heartfelt manner and officially, that, according to our Christian faith as well, dialogue and mutual understanding are God-loving works and the obligation of every human person who loves God. Consequently, we all are obligated to listen in good faith to our fellow human beings, with attention and sympathy and a disposition to understand them, and to speak to them the truth sincerely and in a human-loving manner, without arrogance or fanaticism, so that through dialogue we may demolish prejudices and whatever else inhibits peaceful cooperation and coexistence or leads to spiritual and material conflicts and lamentable bloodshed and destruction.

Logos *and* Dialogos*: Human Reason and Human Dialogue*

And now let us turn to our topic. Humanity, as we all know and acknowledge, is endowed by God with the capability for reasonable discourse (*logos*). Reasonable discourse is the means whereby we communicate with our fellow human beings, and our consultation with each other on this basis is called dialogue. Dialogue is characteristic of human beings, and we can say that it constitutes one of the greatest gifts of God to humanity. If we were to imagine ourselves deprived of the ability to dialogue with our fellow human beings, we would feel suffocated and our life to be unbearable.

Nonetheless, there are found, from time to time, people who attempt to deprive others of the inalienable and divine privilege of dialogue. This tactic is damaging not only to those who are forced to keep silent but also to those who oppress them, because they deprive themselves of all those good things they could learn if they would dialogue with their fellow human beings.

It is known that the entirety of human knowledge—the secrets of the arts, religious faith, and human emotions—are expressed and passed on through rational discourse and dialogue. And so the free and self-sufficient person, who is fearless about himself, is usually open to dialogue and, from whatever he hears, selects what he deems to be right and useful, while he rejects what he determines to be erroneous and harmful. He never rejects dialogue as such, since it is the source of his spiritual cultivation. Even when we read a book or pray to God, we are in dialogue with the author and with God. Again, when we observe with an investigating eye the starry sky, or the immensity of the oceans, the flora of the mountains, the infinite multitude of living creatures, we are in dialogue with their creator, on the one hand glorifying him, and on the other hand being taught by him.[18] "The heavens declare the glory of God and the firmament proclaims the creation of his hands" (Ps. 19.1), as David exclaims, while our predecessor St. John Chrysostom, archbishop of Constantinople, adds that God "is always in dialogue with us."

Let the above serve as an introductory encomium to dialogue. And let us now turn to the topic of how dialogue is used in practice. It is a fact that within the soul of every human being there are formed various perceptions, viewpoints, desires, and aims that often conflict with the corresponding perceptions and aims of others. Confronted with this multiplicity of opinion and opposing aims, we find ourselves at a fork in the road. One way leads to the violent imposition of our viewpoints and aims, and the other to dialogue with those who disagree with us about finding a means of peaceful coexistence.

On matters of scientific or philosophical truth, dialogue has been ongoing and encouraged since ancient times. It is conducted sometimes on a high level and sometimes on an inferior one but almost always with a mutual effort to understand the ideas of the other and, if need be, to oppose them with proper arguments. Nevertheless, among co-religionists, the recurring different interpretations of the content of their initial common faith, each interpretation claiming to be exclusively faithful to the truth, are not always met with sobriety and proper argumentation but with disputations and jealousy, which often inhibit sober judgment.

Although no one can deny to the faithful the right to be jealous of his faith, no one would also contest one's obligation to discuss or search with his co-religionists, at least, concerning the truth, so that they can all arrive at a common understanding of their faith. Indeed, it is not reasonable to

18. See Philip Sherrard, *Human Image, World Image: The Death and Resurrection of Sacred Cosmology* (Ipswich, U.K.: Golgonooza Press, 1990).

accept that all opposing views are equally correct. And yet, despite the obvious reasonableness of this outlook, it often happens, unfortunately, that fanaticism seizes those holding opposing views concerning their religion, so that they turn against each other, sometimes shedding blood, as happened, for example, in Western Europe at the time of the so-called Holy Inquisition or the wars of the Reformation.

The Threat of Fanaticism

On the other hand, the phenomenon of fanaticism appears with greater intensity among the followers of different religions who oppose each other. In this case, dialogue is again preferable to fanaticism, because it is only by means of it that the heterodox can understand the points where their faiths fall in line and the points where they really differ. Many times, however, ignorance or (still worse) erroneous and distorted information that the followers of one religion have about the content of another religion predominates, especially among the uninformed masses, and as a consequence the one party is drawn into thoughtless condemnation of the other and not infrequently into fanaticism and intolerance. Through dialogue, mutual understanding is achieved, as is the knowledge necessary for accepting not the faith of another but rather the person himself.

We all believe that religion is God's gift to humankind. That we have many religions and many dogmatic divisions within any one religion automatically raises the question whether all of them are equal revelations of God or whether we need to exclude all the rest of them except one, or some, and to accept only one or some? Christianity's answer to this question, like that of Islam, is that, to begin with, it contains the full revelation of God and that many truths are included in the other religions, especially the monotheistic ones, and also exist in all human conscience as a seed of God. This is why Christianity calls these very truths the "seminal word" (*logos spermatikos*)[19]—a word of truth sown by God into the souls of human beings.

Knowledge of the divine truth is a process that is indeed endless. Each of us journeys along this path ceaselessly and at any given moment is

19. The fundamental teaching of Justin (100–165), the early apologist, philosopher, and martyr.

found at a certain point, which, however is not firm. This is why one never accuses any companion on the journey who is found at another point along this path, either moving ahead or following behind. That one should not judge one's fellow traveler for the condition in which he is found is a basic teaching of the gospel. In addition, offering help to a fellow traveler so that he may journey successfully toward God is generally a recognized duty of all responsible religions.

The Primacy of Religious Freedom

Each individual, of course, is personally responsible for choosing his faith and relation to God and for his choice of which of God's commandments he is to keep. We, however, as religious leaders, ought to help each man understand that the truth of the one God is perceived and appropriated in life differently by each particular person according to one's spiritual condition. Jesus Christ said to his disciples that he had many things yet to reveal to them, that they were not able to uphold them, and that therefore he would send the Holy Spirit to lead them to the whole truth. The truth exists and has been revealed, but penetration into the depth of this revealed truth is possible only to those who have a pure heart, to the saints. All the rest of us take from it only a part, a part corresponding to our spiritual age and to our spiritual condition in general.

In this connection also the Apostle Paul writes to Christians that he fed them with spiritual milk, because they were not able to absorb solid food. And St. Gregory of Nyssa explains in his *Life of Moses* that the teaching of truth is transformed along with the dispositions of those who receive it.[20] Just as pupils at school advance from one grade to another and progress according to their comprehension of the lessons, so also all of us human beings advance toward understanding the truth and appropriating it in our lives. It is exactly for this reason that the Qur'an says that religion is not imposed. Religion is embraced and appropriated voluntarily, while its truths are absorbed gradually during a long evolutionary process, which is as much individual as it is corporate. It is, in other

20. The younger brother of St. Basil the Great, Gregory (330–95) was a philosopher and mystic. See Andrew Meredith, *Gregory of Nyssa* (London; New York: Routledge, 1999).

words, possible for religious viewpoints that were dominant during a certain era to be developed subsequently, not because God's revealed truth has changed but because the appropriation and absorption of it by human beings becomes less affected by their particular wills. Indeed, we are obligated to observe that God often tolerates conditions that are contrary to his first and perfect will, because he sees that man is not willing or is not able to observe it. And so God grants him an alternative, second will, in order to prevent man from falling into total evil. This second will of God—or possibly third or fourth or so on—is in each case preferable to the evil that follows, but in no case can this replace his primary, proper, and holy will. Consequently, if we see God in history allowing certain actions that to our present sensibilities are puzzling, we ought to ask ourselves whether such actions were permitted as a concession because of the hardness of heart of the men of the given time, who were not able to realize the usefulness and the magnitude of his initial high will. In such cases, which are far too many, we as contemporary religious leaders ought to seek first the highest will of God, which is in full harmony with his goodness, and not be carried away by historical precedents that express a concession to human weakness in other eras.

God's Authority and Human Authority

This way of looking at things removes from man the arrogance of his authority and preserves only God's authority, which is difficult to approach in the fullness of its revelation. It also leads to the rejection of arrogance, because it enables us to see other human beings as fellow pilgrims, who, evolving and progressing, are called to the truth of God and have the possibility to come to it in time, even if they may be at a distance from it at the present moment. As a result, this way of seeing things entails magnanimity, tolerance, and hope and opposes any violent means of imposing religious convictions, which, under such conditions, would not lead to a sincere faith that is acceptable to God, as experience bears witness.

Our realization that we appropriate and experience the truth of God gradually and progressively, and to the measure of the purity of our inner disposition toward it, humbles our mindset and restrains our self-confidence as perfect spokesmen for the will of God. Furthermore, it prevents us from committing the terrible error of attributing to God decisions and objectives that are purely our own—an error that verges on idolatry. It was such an error that made an ancient poet, satirizing the low manner that his fellow citizens had of perceiving God, the Most High, say that if the oxen were able to describe God they would turn him into an ox. Unfortunately, however, there is no era that is deprived of men who have such misguided self-confidence that they attribute even their criminal actions to God. It is this fact that made Jesus Christ predict the coming of the hour when anyone that kills his disciples (and, by extension, any fellow human being) will think, mistakenly of course, that he offers service to God.

These erroneous views concerning God, which overlook that God is long-suffering and merciful, led certain Western philosophers to speak about the death of God and many Western citizens to abandon religious faith. If we wanted to speak accurately, however, we would say that this case is not really about the death of God but about the destruction of a false image of God, by which, owing to an error committed by many religious leaders, he is presented as rigid, inhumane, and even bloodthirsty.

If, on the other hand, we turn to the experience and teaching of the saints—those, that is, who came closer to God and came to know Him better—we would see that they all converge on the point that he is good and human-loving, longsuffering, merciful, and eager to apply his righteousness but that he waits for the repentance and conversion of human beings. The religions, then, whose destiny is to announce to humanity the existence of the one God and his true character as longsuffering, as not rejoicing at the loss of any human beings but rather as well pleased with their salvation and well-being, are obligated to watch constantly that their spokesmen not describe malicious, merely human ideas and objectives as being the will of God. It is only when religions reveal the person of God as full of goodness that they make people's relation with him and faith in him attractive and contribute to the peaceful coexistence and cooperation of peoples and cultures.

On the contrary, when religions submit to human choices and especially to human objectives and assent to be used as a means toward their realization, they are forced to change their teaching to make them fit the aims pursued, and so, conforming to merely human interests, they falsify the truth of God. Fortunately, however, there have always been and still are in all religions purer spirits and especially poetic ones, many of whom have emerged from the people of Iran, who grasp the magnificence of God's goodness and loving-kindness toward humanity and can serve as guides to their co-religionists.

We are all obligated to turn to these higher spirits. It is our duty to seek the will of God, the good and perfect one. Whenever we disagree, dialogue is the God-given means to common deliberation. Our target should always be truth and righteousness together with God's mercy and loving-kindness toward humanity. Whatever is merciless is not derived from the long-suffering and merciful God, because the tree produces fruit that is proper to its nature, and the long-suffering and merciful God produces long-suffering and merciful actions. If we continue to disagree, despite our efforts at dialogue, we are obligated to tolerate each other in peace. Peace is the highest good, and the peaceful coexistence of human beings is one of the highest intentions of God's will. If we act on this we will contribute greatly to the peace of the contemporary world, and we will certainly please God, the King of Peace. And then religions will indeed play a positive and essential role in establishing peace in today's world.

We pray from the depths of our heart that the God of all goodness, who is the source of all good things, may present his goodness in the hearts of us all, so that we all, free from our own personal willfulness and objectives, may hear God's voice and conform to his peaceful will. Then we will be peacemakers, we will be called children of God, and peace will reign in our hearts and in our nations as well as in the entire contemporary world. May it be so.

Religious Communities in the European Union: I

Address to the Plenary Assembly of the European Parliament in Brussels, September 24, 2008.

Permit us to express our sincerest appreciation for the extraordinary honor of addressing the Plenary of the European Parliament, especially on this occasion that commemorates the European Year of Intercultural Dialogue. As a purely spiritual institution, our Ecumenical Patriarchate embraces a truly global apostolate that strives to raise and broaden the consciousness of the human family—to bring understanding that we are all dwelling in the same house. At its most basic sense, this is the meaning of the word *ecumenical* (the *oikoumene* is the inhabited world)—the earth understood as a house in which all peoples, kindreds, tribes, and languages dwell.

As is well known, the origins of our religious institutions lie at the core of the Axial Age, deep in the history of the Christian faith—with the earliest followers of Jesus Christ. Inasmuch as our see, our institutional center, shared the center and capital of the Christian Roman Empire, it became known as "ecumenical," with certain privileges and responsibilities that it holds to this day. One of its chief responsibilities was to bring the redemptive message of the gospel to the world outside the Roman Empire. Before the age of exploration, most civilizations had a bicameral view of the world—as being "within" and "without." The world was divided into two sectors: a hemisphere of civilization and a hemisphere of barbarism. In this view of history, we behold the grievous consequences of the alienation of human persons from one another.

Today, when we have the technological means to transcend the horizon of our own cultural self-awareness, we nevertheless continue to witness the terrible effects of human fragmentation. Tribalism, fundamentalism, and phyletism, or extreme nationalism without regard to the rights of the other—all these contribute to the ongoing list of atrocities that give pause to our claims of being civilized in the first place.

And yet, even with the tides of trade and migrations, the expansions of peoples, religious upheavals and revivals, and great geopolitical movements, the deconstruction of rigid and monolithic self-understandings of past centuries has yet to find a permanent harbor. The Ecumenical Patriarchate has sailed across the waves of these centuries, navigating the storms and the vicissitudes of history. For twenty centuries—through the Pax Romana, the Pax Christiana, the Pax Islamica, the Pax Ottomanica (all of them epochs marked by intercultural struggle, conflict, and outright war)—the Ecumenical Patriarchate has continued as a lighthouse for the human family and the Christian Church. It is from the depths of our experience on these deep waters of history that we offer to the contemporary world a timeless message of perennial human value.

Today, the ecumenical scope of our Patriarchate extends far beyond the boundaries of its physical presence at the cusp of Europe and Asia, where Istanbul has been the center and residence of our see for over seventeen centuries. Though it is small in geographical size and worldly power, the historical and spiritual dimension of our experience brings us before this august assembly today, in order to share from that experience and offer insight on the necessity of intercultural dialogue, a lofty and timely ideal for the contemporary world.

As you yourselves have said, in the very words of this most esteemed body:

> At the heart of the European project, it is important to provide the means for intercultural dialogue and dialogue between citizens to strengthen respect for cultural diversity and deal with the complex reality in our societies and the coexistence of different cultural identities and beliefs.[21]

And we would humbly supplement this noble statement, as we did last year in our address to the Plenary of the Parliamentary Assembly of the Council of Europe in Strasbourg, by adding that authentic dialogue is the very language with which human beings communicate not only with one another but also with God.

Dialogue is necessary first and foremost because it is inherent in the nature of the human person. This is the principal message that we propose for your consideration today: that intercultural dialogue is at the very root of what it means to be a human being, for no one culture of the human family encompasses every human person. Without such dialogue, the differences in the human family are reduced to objectifications of the "other" and lead to abuse, conflict, persecution—a grand-scale human suicide, for we are all ultimately one humanity. But where the differences between us move us to encounter one another and where that encounter is based in dialogue, there is reciprocal understanding and appreciation—even love.

In the past fifty years, our human family has experienced leaps of technological achievement undreamed of by our forebears. Many have trusted that this kind of advancement will bridge the divides that fragment the human condition—as if our achievements had given us the power to

---

21. Decision No. 1983/2006 of EP and CEU.

overcome the fundamental realities of our moral and our spiritual condition. Yet, despite every conceivable benefit and technological skill, we still behold the universal banes of hunger, thirst, war, persecution, injustice, planned misery, intolerance, fanaticism, and prejudice.

The European Project: A Significant Way Forward

Amid this cycle that cannot seem to be broken, the significance of the "European Project" cannot be underestimated. It is one of the hallmarks of the European Union that has succeeded in promoting mutual, peaceful, and productive coexistence between nation-states that less than seventy years ago were drenched in a bloody conflict that could have destroyed the legacy of Europe for the ages. Through the Council of Europe, nearly a billion persons in forty-seven nations work to find means of integration and cooperation at every level of human interaction. Yet the concept of the nation-state is by no means coextensive with and inclusive of the human condition. Nations can provide systems of economics and justice, methodologies of security and interdependence, but the sum of every part of a society never reaches the whole of the individual. Just as Plato[22] sought the perfect society by looking at the condition of the human person "writ large," so we must discover in the human person the very qualities that will enable us to transcend division and achieve not mere unions of cooperation but the fundamental unity that links every person to one another.

Here, in this great hall of assembly of the Parliament, you strive to make possible the relationships between states and political realities that make reconciliation between persons possible. And so you have recognized the importance of intercultural dialogue, especially at a time in the history of Europe when transformations are taking place in every country and along every societal boundary. Great tidal forces of conflict, combined with economic security and opportunity, have shifted populations around the globe. Of necessity, then, persons of differing cultural, ethnic, religious, and national origin find themselves in close proximity. In some cases, populations are excluded from the broader societal context. In some cases, the same populations shun the majority populations and close

22. 427–347 B.C.

themselves off from the dominant society. But in either case, as we engage in dialogue, it must not be a mere academic exercise in mutual appreciation.

For dialogue to be effective, to be transformative in bringing about deep change in persons, it cannot be done on the basis of "subject" and "object." The value of the "other" must be absolute—without objectification, so that each party is apprehended in the fullness of his or her being.

For Orthodox Christians, the icon, or image, stands not only as the summit of human aesthetic accomplishment but also as a tangible reminder of this perennial truth. As in every painting—religious or not, and notwithstanding the talent of the artist—the object is displayed as two-dimensional. Yet, for Orthodox Christians, an icon is no mere religious painting—and it is not, by definition, a religious object. Indeed, it is a subject with which the viewer, the worshipper, enters into wordless dialogue through the sense of sight. For an Orthodox Christian, the encounter with the icon is an act of communion with the person represented in the icon. How much more should our encounters with living icons—as persons made in the image and likeness of God—be acts of communion!

In order for our dialogue to become more than mere cultural exchange, there must be a more profound understanding of the absolute interdependence not merely between states and political and economic actors but between every single human person and every other single human person. And such a valuation must be made regardless of any commonality of race, religion, language, ethnicity, national origin, or any of the benchmarks by which we seek self-identification and self-identity. And in a world of billions of persons, how is such interconnectedness possible?

Indeed, there is no possible way to link with every human person—this is a property that we would ascribe to the divine. However, there is a way of understanding the universe in which we live as being shared by all, as a plane of existence that spans the reality of every human person—an ecosphere that contains us all.

The Ecumenical Patriarchate and Ecological Concern

And so it is that the Ecumenical Patriarchate—in keeping with our own sense of responsibility for the house, the *oikos* of the world and all who dwell therein—has for decades championed the cause of the environment, calling attention to ecological crises around the globe. And we engage this ministry without regard to self-interest. As you know so well, our patriarchate is not a "national" church but rather the fundamental canonical expression both of the ecumenical dimensions of the gospel message and of its analogous responsibility within the life of the Church. This is the deeper reason that the Church Fathers and the councils have given this Patriarchate the name *Ecumenical.* The loving care of the Church of Constantinople exceeds any linguistic, cultural, ethnic, or even religious definition, as it seeks to serve all peoples. Although firmly rooted in particular history, as any institution is, the Ecumenical Patriarchate transcends historical categories in its perennial mission of service.

In our service to the environment, we have to date sponsored seven scientific symposia that bring together a host of disciplines. The genesis of our initiative grew on the island that gave humanity the Apocalypse, the Book of Revelation—the sacred island of Patmos in the Aegean Sea. And it was in the Aegean that we commenced, in 1995, an ambitious program of integrating current scientific knowledge about the oceans with the spiritual approach of the world's religions to water, particularly the world's oceans.

In 1997, we pursued our ecological odyssey on the Black Sea, where after a journey of more than one thousand nautical miles, through the lands and seas of twenty-five hundred years of Greek colonies and the Roman, Byzantine, and Ottoman Empires, we ended in Thessaloniki, the cultural capital of Europe for that year. Currently in the City (Istanbul) we are experiencing great joy and enthusiasm as we are all preparing for its celebration as the European capital of culture in the year 2010. The City, which has a long history, was a crossroads for gatherings of people and served as a place where diverse religions and cultures dwelt together. This past week, we attended a luncheon that the prime minister of Turkey hosted in honor of the prime minister of Spain. As is public knowledge, both are cosponsors of the Alliance of Civilizations under the auspices of the United Nations. We heard their wonderful presentations, which were consonant with the timeless and tolerant spirit our City. Since Thessaloniki was the culture capital of Europe, we have traversed the Danube, the

Adriatic Sea,[23] the Baltic Sea, the Amazon, and the Arctic Sea, and we are making preparations even now to sail the Nile in Egypt and the Mississippi River in the United States.

Through all of these remarkable symposia, we have brought together into dialogue disciplines that hitherto had understood themselves as being unrelated to one another. Through their communing together in dialogue, scientists and theologians, politicians and philosophers, businessmen and educators have found common ground for understanding and practical programs that lead to solutions. Just as intercultural dialogue strives to reconcile forces and groups that may believe they are in opposition, so does our Ecumenical Patriarchate seek to unite seeming opposites.

In the final analysis, however, what we seek is not only an ongoing dialogue that is serviceable for the purpose of meeting practical necessities but also one that raises human consciousness. While we strive to find answers to ecological concerns and crises, we also bring the participants into a more comprehensive sense of themselves as belonging to and relating to a greater whole. We seek to embrace the ecosphere of human existence not as an object to be controlled. We do so as a fellow struggler on the path of increase and improvement. As the Apostle Paul, whose two-thousand-year legacy both the Orthodox and the Roman Catholic Churches are celebrating this year, says in one of his most famous epistles:

> For we know that until now, the whole of creation groans with us and shares our birth pangs. (Rom. 8.22)

Every ecosystem on this planet is like a nation—by definition limited to a place. The estuary is not the tundra, nor is the savanna the desert. But like every culture, every ecosystem will have an effect that goes beyond, far beyond its natural—or in the case of cultures, national—boundaries. And when we understand that every ecosystem is part of the singular ecosphere that is inhabited by every living breath that fills the world, then do we grasp the interconnectedness, the powerful communion of all life, and our true interdependency on one another. Without such an understanding, we are led to ecocide, the self-destruction of the one ecosphere that sustains all human existence.

---

23. See Neal Ascherson and Andrew Marshall, eds., *The Adriatic Sea: A Sea at Risk, A Unity of Purpose* (Athens: Religion, Science and the Environment, 2003).

Wider Ramifications and Sociopolitical Dimensions

And so it is that we come before you today, highlighting this Year of Intercultural Dialogue, bringing parables from the natural world to affirm your transcendent human values. As an institution, the Ecumenical Patriarchate has lived as a relatively small ecosystem within a much larger culture for centuries. Out of this long experience, allow us to suggest the most important practical characteristic that enables the work of intercultural dialogue to succeed.

Chiefly and above all, there must be respect for the rights of the minority within every majority. When and where the rights of the minority are observed, the society will for the most part be just and tolerant. In any culture, one segment will always be dominant—whether that dominance is based on race, religion, or any other category. Segmentation is inevitable in our diverse world. What we seek to end is fragmentation! Societies that are built on exclusion and repression cannot last. Or, as the divine Prince of Peace said, "Every kingdom divided against itself is brought to desolation; and every city or house divided against itself shall not stand" (Mt. 12.25).

And this holds true for the European Union as well. As the E.U. has expanded, there have been severe challenges to the sense of what the E.U. really is. From the countries of the former Soviet bloc, we see from some a headlong rush to embrace the E.U.—in many ways hoping for economic benefits. But from others we see reticence and even resentment. From our own country, Turkey, we perceive both a welcome to a new economic and trading partner, but we also feel the hesitation that comes from embracing, as an equal, a country that is predominantly Muslim. And yet Europe is filled with millions of Muslims who have come here from all sorts of backgrounds and circumstances, just as Europe would still be filled with Jews, had it not been for the horrors of the Second World War.

Our counsel to all is to recognize that only when we embrace the fullness of shared presence within the ecosphere of human existence are we then able to face the "otherness" of those around us—majority or minority—with a true sense of the consanguinity of the human family. Then do we behold the stranger among us not as an alien but as a brother or sister in the human family, the family of God. St. Paul, addressing the Athenians, expounds on pan-human relation and brotherhood quite eloquently and concisely:

> And He made from one man every nation of mankind to live on all the face of the earth, having determined their appointed times and the boundaries of their habitation, that they would seek God, if perhaps they might grope for Him and find Him, though He is not far from each one of us; for in Him we live and move and exist, as even some of your own poets have said, "For we also are His children." (Acts 17.26–28)

This is why Europe needs to bring Turkey into its project and why Turkey needs to foster intercultural dialogue and tolerance in order to be accepted into the European Project. Europe should not see as alien to itself any religion that is tolerant of others. The great religions, like the European Project, can be a force that transcends nationalism and can even transcend nihilism and fundamentalism by focusing their faithful on what unites us as human beings and by fostering a dialogue about what divides us.

Indeed, it is not only non-Christians whom Europe must encounter but also Christians who do not fit into the categories of "Catholic" or "Protestant." The resurgence of the Orthodox Church in Eastern Europe since the fall of the Iron Curtain has truly been a marvel for the world to behold. The segmentation of Eastern Europe has led to fragmentation in many places. Not only does the center not hold; it is hardly discernible. Through this process, as nation-states strive to reestablish themselves in the Balkans and beyond, it is the Orthodox Christian faith that has risen to a new status that could not have been predicted even twenty years ago.

One of the vital roles of our Ecumenical Patriarchate is to assist in the process of growth and expansion that is taking place in traditional Orthodox countries, by holding fast as the canonical norm for the worldwide Orthodox Church, comprising more than a quarter of a billion people across the globe. At this moment, we wish to inform you that in October, at my invitation, all the heads of the Orthodox patriarchates and autocephalous churches will meet to discuss our common problems and to strengthen pan-Orthodox unity and cooperation. Simultaneously, we will also concelebrate the two thousand years since the birth of the Apostle Paul. Whether it is by reestablishing the Church of Estonia to its state before the Second World War, or by helping the Ukrainian nation and people on their course for self-determination in matters of national faith, our Ecumenical Patriarchate seeks not to advance nationalist, or ethnophyletistic, causes at the expense of any portion of a society. We uphold the canonical tradition of the Orthodox Church, which seeks order without tyranny, liberty without license, and justice yoked to mercy and compassion.

This is why in July we journeyed to Kiev, Ukraine, at the invitation of President Yushchenko, to preside over the celebrations surrounding the one thousand and twentieth anniversary of the Christianization of Kievan Rus. Like all human societies, Ukraine's presents remarkably complex political, cultural, and social phenomena. The antiquity of Kievan civilization requires cultural sensitivities that are often lacking in a modern world that presses for immediate results. The Ecumenical Patriarchate possesses the institutional memory and fortitude to assist in the resolution of deep-seated issues. Our active and vital participation is designed to enhance the process of self-determination within the broader context we have spoken of before: an ecosphere of communion.

Your Excellencies, honorable members of the European Parliament: the Ecumenical Patriarchate stands ready to make vital contributions to the peace and prosperity of the European Union. We are prepared to partner with you in constructive dialogues such as this and to lend willing ears to the concerns of the day. In this spirit, our patriarchate for the past twenty-five years has been cultivating and developing academic dialogues with Islam and Judaism. We have realized many bilateral and trilateral meetings. In early November in Athens, we will have the twelfth stage of our dialogue with Islam. Some of the issues we have examined together so far are common humanitarian ideals for Muslims and Christians, peace and justice, youth and the values of moderation, educational systems in Islam and Christianity, principles of peaceful coexistence, and so forth.

In our dialogues with Judaism, some of the subjects that were discussed so far have been continuity and renewal, religious freedom and the relationship between liberty and religion, the encounter of Orthodoxy and Judaism as well as of Judaism with modernity, and so on. Parallel to the aforementioned dialogues, we continue theological dialogues with the Roman Catholic, Anglican, Lutheran, and Reformed Churches. In October, at the invitation of the pope, we will have the opportunity to address the Twelfth General Ordinary Assembly of the Synod of Bishops at the Vatican.

In summary, then, the Ecumenical Patriarchate is very active in the sphere of ecumenical dialogue with the purpose of contributing to reconciliation, peace, solidarity, better understanding among people, and their separation from fanaticism, hatred, and all forms of evil.

We thank you for this singular opportunity to address you today, and we pray for the abundant mercy of God and his blessing on all your righteous endeavors. Please allow us from this honorable podium to offer our best wishes to the Muslim faithful around the globe for the upcoming great feast of Ramadan and also our best wishes to the Jewish faithful throughout the world for the upcoming feast of Rosh Hashanah.

We are all brothers and sisters with one heavenly Father, and on this beautiful planet, which we are all responsible for, there is room for everyone, but there is no room for wars and killing of one another.

Religious Communities in the European Union: II

Opening Address to the Seventh Dialogue between the Orthodox Church, the European People's Party, and the European Democrats, Istanbul, October 16, 2003.

It is with particular pleasure and satisfaction that we greet you on the occasion of the Seventh Dialogue between the Orthodox Church and the Members of the European People's Party and Christian Democrats of Europe, in this great and hospitable city on the Bosphorus, as we address the particularly timely issue of the position of religious values in the new Constitution for Europe. A very wise decision was made to have this meeting in this place and at this time. It was wise in terms of place because for approximately sixteen centuries this historic city was the capital of two empires, the Byzantine and the Ottoman, and made a major contribution to the establishment of Roman law, not only among the Christian peoples of Europe but also among the peoples of the other religious traditions in the East. It was also wise in terms of timing, because it coincides with the brave and historic initiative of realizing the dream of a united Europe after the painful experience of the tragic consequences of two world wars in the twentieth century. It is our hope that there will be a place for Turkey in this united Europe, when our country meets the necessary criteria.

This great vision for all the peoples of Europe was not generated out of a void by political planning technocrats but had a centuries-long gestation in the consciousness of the peoples of Europe, who at all times and everywhere sense the various political and spiritual processes of their common cultural heritage in a positive or negative way. And so any new theory in the uninterrupted dialectic between the traditional and the new in politics, culture, or society constitutes a specific proposal that always embraced aspects of people's public and private lives, even when it was in the form of theoretical opposition to existing traditions.

It is very significant that this dialectic between the traditional and the new, notwithstanding that in modern political theory it has taken on the nature of acute ideological confrontations, or clashes, has remained in the popular imagination a permanent dialectic between the old and the new in the spiritual heritage of European peoples. Although their spiritual awareness is attuned to the new, they do not sacrifice the old to the attractions of the new, because they have preserved their historical memory intact and do not in their lives espouse uncritically the extreme and morbid deviations of ideological antagonism.

In this sense, the secularized political theory of modern times, although it came into being as an adversarial questioning or rejection of the traditional patterns of the Greco-Roman world—as a means for serving the "new ideas" of the European intelligentsia or ideology—was nevertheless not strong enough to strike at the historic depth of the European peoples' memory or cut them off from their timeless cultural and spiritual heritage.

It is now obvious that religion, the undisputed wellspring of the European peoples' timeless spiritual heritage, is at the center of the dialectical confrontation between the old and the new views, by virtue of its neutralizing objections to "new ideas" or of its weakening their social influence, or both. Nevertheless, under the pressure of the "new ideas," religion has become dissociated from the obsessions of the historical past and has strengthened its relations with society. It has become more or less attuned to the new conditions of the democratic political system and the legal culture of the modern theory of the secularized, or people's, state. Consequently, despite ideological pressure, religion has been able to preserve intact the innermost core of its spiritual relation with the community of citizens, as has been confirmed in a striking way particularly after the collapse of the atheist socialist regimes.

Indeed, the rich modern experience of the dialectical confrontations between ideology and religion leads readily to the conclusion that persistence in disputing the institutional role of religion in modern society could be described as a groundless ideological superstition, an extension of old-fashioned ideological patterns that no longer correspond to the real modern demands of the citizens' society. The theoretical circumvention of the issue by means of constitutional provisions to protect the principle of religious freedom for citizens or religious communities without any corresponding expressed guarantee of the institutional role of religion—granted, the lack of any such guarantee may have been necessary in difficult times—nevertheless constitutes a shortcoming of the democratic political system today. This is because neither religious communities nor religious values exist in themselves alone but always in reference to the religion to which they belong.

The Legitimate Place of Religion

The legitimate claim of religion and the consistent stance of the political authority come together in the urgent need for an express constitutional acknowledgment of the institutional role of religion in the modern citizens' society—on the one hand, because it is dictated by the confirmed, striking historical durability of the spiritual relations between religion and the society, and, on the other, because it is necessitated by the political realism of a visionary democracy that seeks the fuller utilization of religion in modern intercultural dialogue. Moreover, the undeniable and profound relationship between religion and civilization, a relationship embodied in the religious values in people's lives, makes fiction of any tendency to confuse them in the cultural heritage of the European peoples in particular, because religion has always had, and persists in, its independent spiritual relationship with society.

In this spirit, our patriarchate, as the First Throne of the Orthodox Church, as part of its due care to promote the Orthodox proposal for the draft Constitution of the European Union, conducted specific and official initiatives—to the president of the Constitutional Convention, His Excellency M. Giscard d'Estaing; to the president of the European Commission, His Excellency Mr. Romano Prodi; to the esteemed members of the European Parliament; and to the European Convention (in October 2002)—regarding official recognition, in the Constitution, of the institutional role of religion and its decisive contribution to the entire cultural heritage of the European peoples.

Moreover, in this spirit, an inter-Orthodox Conference was convened in Herakleion, Crete (in March, 2003), by our patriarchate, and its unanimous constructive proposals were submitted to His Excellency, the chairman of the European Convention, to be taken into consideration in drafting the relevant provisions.

These initiatives were undertaken as a duty, despite known opposition, expressed and unexpressed, to any suggestion of constitutional recognition of the great contribution of religion not only to historical progress but also to the spiritual and cultural identity of the European peoples. Indeed, the prospect of the enlargement of the European Union, through the accession of other Orthodox peoples of Eastern Europe, makes it necessary to ensure the official submission of the Orthodox proposal for the European Constitution, because the Orthodox tradition has always promoted in particular the necessity not only for constructive cooperation between church and state but also the equal guarantee of the freedom of all religions in any well-governed and democratic state, and especially with the prospect of the forthcoming accession of Turkey to the European Union. The new constitutional framework being drafted for the European Union, by putting an end to the dilemmas that arise from the divisions between the Western tradition and modern ideology, could open up new horizons to the institutional role of religion in modern multicultural society.

It is obvious that religious values, unless they serve some expediency foreign to the mission of religion, were inspired and have constantly emphasized the necessity to protect peace, social justice, and human rights in relations between individuals and peoples. Consequently, the insistence of the European Convention on the more effective protection of these ideals, through the relevant provisions of the Constitution of the European Union, makes more egregious the systematic effort to justify avoidance of any reference to the wellspring of these ideas. Therefore, we are of the hope that the present assembly will point out not only any oversights in the past but also the obligation at this time to respect the expressed desire of the European peoples, because only thus will the Constitution for Europe acquire the necessary historical depth as well as modern social dynamism.

The proposed Constitution should contain an express reference to the Christian heritage of Europe, through which the principles and values of the biblical and the Greco-Roman tradition have been perpetuated and which, together with later cultural features, constitute the foundation on which the modern European structure has been built.

The guarantee of the human rights that have been recognized in European and international conventions and declarations and were codified in the Charter of Fundamental Human Rights must continue to constitute the internal law of the European Union. Human rights must, however, be guaranteed in terms of their individual as well as of their collective and institutional expression—as the rights and obligations of the citizens of Europe. In particular, reference is made to the sacredness and inviolability of the human being and to the mystery of life and, by extension, to the responsible management of biotechnological knowledge and applications, to protection of the institution of marriage and the family, and to the compliance of education with the above principles and values.

We wish you every success in this most important and sacred task of contributing to the new Constitution for the future of Europe and invoke for you the wisdom, truth, and enlightenment of Almighty God.

Religious Communities in the European Union: III

Message for the Opening Ceremony of the Tenth Dialogue between the Orthodox Church and the EPP-ED Group in the European Parliament, held in Bratislava, Slovakia, November 9, 2006.

To all the participants of the Tenth Meeting between the Orthodox Church and the Group of the European People's Party and European Democrats, beloved children of our Lord, may the grace and peace of God be with all of you.

We would like to express our joy in welcoming today in Bratislava all the distinguished participants to this Tenth Dialogue, which in itself constitutes a jubilee, for it is an unwavering example of how religion and politics not only can coexist but—what is more important—can, if there is genuine and sincere will, join hands and work together for the benefit of all people.

Please, allow us to take you back on a short journey to our common past of dialogue and cooperation.[24] It was April of 1996 when the presidency of the European People's Party–Christian Democrat Group and

24. For further information (including agenda, reports, and conclusions) of these dialogues, initiated at the invitation of Ecumenical Patriarch Bartholomew, see *Dialogues between the Orthodox Church and the EPP-ED Group in the European Parliament* (Brussels, 2007). See also http://stream.epp-ed.eu/Activities/docs/year2008/dialogues-en.pdf.

the Orthodox Church commenced the First Dialogue of "The Moral Values of Concern to Humanity: The Spiritual Dimension of Europe." These discussions became the basis of an ongoing dialogue that continues today. It was indeed a well-chosen topic to begin our collaboration, for the Orthodox Church has never ceased to wish to contribute to the growing unity of the peoples of Europe. Its moral values are and always will be of concern of the Church and will always be at the foundation of that sought-after unity for which our Lord Jesus Christ prayed:

> That they all may be one, as you, Father, are in me, and I in you; that they also may be one in us. (Jn. 17.21)

The Church, together with the political world, sees the urgent need to form a leadership that understands both modern pluralist democracy, especially in such a multicultural mosaic as the European Union, and the spiritual dimension of society at large, about which the Church cares deeply.

Throughout these past years, we have addressed burning issues such as the collapse of Marxist-socialist values; it was one of the main themes of the Second Dialogue in December 1997. We have shown how Christian values were a way out of the vacuum and we showed the relevance of Christian values, which are diachronic, for our modern societies. We have witnessed the development of church–state relations, particularly in the last century, and we have advocated the application of Christian values to governments today.

The Third Dialogue, which took place in November 1998, dealt with mankind and his environment in Europe of the third millennium. It provided the appropriate platform for giving the Christian Democrat leaders of Western Europe the opportunity to deepen their knowledge of the faith of Eastern Christianity and of its understanding of current issues facing the body politic with respect to uniting the peoples of Europe. The dialogue introduced the leadership of these parties to constructive dialogue with Church leaders and provided the Orthodox Church with an opportunity to familiarize itself with the problems of implementing Christian teaching in public life. It also focused on Christian teaching as the cornerstone of Europe, and it was made clear that the light of the Church should not be kept in the dark, for this would only lead to a negative outcome and would not help the process of integrating the East into the European family.

The Fourth Dialogue, which took place in June 2000, in our beloved city of Istanbul, focused on the protection of human rights, quality of life, and a strong civil society—themes of grave importance to all people but particularly to those who assume leadership responsibilities with respect to the physical, political, and spiritual lives of others.

The integrity of the human person was the focal point of all discussions, and our affirmation that it constitutes the bedrock of all human social and political relationships was of particular importance. Furthermore, as was stated in the conclusions, both parties acknowledged their shared responsibility in the project for union among the peoples of Europe, and we were one in promoting this project as a work for reconciliation among the peoples of Europe and for the triumph of good, which would constitute the basis for freedom and peace in Europe and in the wider world. Let us not forget the words of our Lord:

> Blessed are the peacemakers: for they shall be called the children of God. (Mt. 5.9)

And it is our firm conviction to continue in this path and to proclaim once again the words of Paul, the Apostle of the Nations, that in Christ all are one (Gal. 3.28), and that the union of the peoples of Europe is not and cannot be viewed as static or monolithic but that it reflects great dynamism and diversity, for it is unity in diversity that we are hoping for.

Fundamental and human rights as well as the role of the church and state in their common endeavor to serve civil society were the subject of the Fifth Dialogue, which took place in June 2001 on the island of Crete, Greece. This dialogue offered the possibility for us to reaffirm our steadfast conviction that

> every human being is a person who is a unique irreplaceable being, totally irreducible, free by nature and open to transcendence, and that each human being within society depends on others, with shared rights and duties. They thus have a responsibility to ensure the rights of one another according to the will of God.

Unfortunately, we have witnessed severe violations of those rights throughout the world, and we have raised our voices to protest against these violations. We have seen children and women treated without respect, and we have seen their blood shed without mercy. And we also affirmed the need of the Church to fulfill its role not only in individual nations but on a European level, with the shared aim to construct civil society. We are committed to cooperation for the benefit of society at large and not for personal gain. Political leaders have underlined that the churches are an integral and essential part of European society, and we are here to support, help, and assist the future of all the peoples and not to promote our own position in society. Our vision is of a world, renewed and unmolested from evil, free and united in diversity, respectful and understanding, reconciled with God.

In September 2001 we all witnessed the tragedy that shocked us and that opened wounds that humanity is still attending to. The Sixth Dialogue examined the religious and societal consequences of these events, and we turned our attention to winning peace and overcoming terrorism. The participants had welcomed the Brussels Declaration of December 20, 2001, as an interreligious response to the events of September 11, 2001; the declaration was promoted by the Ecumenical Patriarchate and by the president of the European Commission, His Excellency Romano Prodi.[25] As it was stated in the conclusions, it was deemed very important to refer to the way in which Islam had been evoked and continues to be evoked by the Al Qaeda terrorist movement in order to justify a mission of hate and revenge against certain peoples of the non-Muslim world, a mission aided and abetted by extremist interpretations of the Qur'an that purport to urge, as a means of personal salvation, suicide in the name of religion. The participants recognized that Islam has, with Judaism and Christianity, a shared basis and responsibility in the divine calling to engender love, peace, and goodwill among people, and they felt the need for objective verification of teaching material about other religions for young people of the Judaic, Christian, and Islamic traditions, in order to inform new generations with mutual tolerance and respect for other faith communities. Overcoming terrorism is still a thorny issue in our everyday life since then, and we pray to God that tolerance and reconciliation will prevail, so that a safe future for our children will be ensured.

---

25. For the full text, see Chapter 6, "Major Declarations: Public Proclamations."

In October 2003 the Seventh Dialogue between the Orthodox Church and the Group of the European People's Party and European Democrats took place, once again in our beloved City, and its focal point was on the New Europe after 2004. The participants reaffirmed once again the importance of human rights, in particular religious rights—including the freedom to believe, not to believe, and to change one's religion. They reaffirmed as well the necessity to facilitate the freedom of religious worship, and they appealed for the safeguarding of human rights, which have been recognized by European and international conventions and declarations, by codifying them in the Charter of Fundamental Rights and incorporating them in legislation by the European Union. The participants also focused their attention on the Treaty of the European Union. We have all welcomed the promising recognition given to churches and religious communities and associations in the draft Constitution, and we have expressed our hopes that the New Europe will become as wholesome as it is diverse. We are still hopeful that this will indeed be the case.

The focal point of the Eighth Dialogue, entitled "Building Europe through Reconciliation and Cooperation," was the reconciliation and cooperation among the peoples of Southeastern Europe in the context of a shared desire to embrace these peoples in the process of the growing union of the peoples of Europe. The southeastern area of Europe, in particular the Balkans, has suffered for many years from vicious warfare. The deaths of thousands of innocent people, as well as thousands of refugees, have been creating tragic problems in this sensitive area, and it was considered necessary to further develop the Ecumenical Patriarchate's Vlatadon Initiative, which commenced in 2000 and discussed the theme "Reconciliation and Peace in South East Europe—the Contribution of the Religious Communities towards Multi-Ethnic and Democratic Societies." The participants have worked hard toward bringing reconciliation to the peoples of the Balkans. We witnessed how reconciliation and cooperation, which has to be based on mutual respect, trust, and shared commitment to each other and to the institutions of society, is the only way to reconcile those in strife. But there is still a long way to go, so we must not rest on this matter.

The Ninth Dialogue focused its attention on solidarity and cooperation, which are two components that will enable and make the enlargement of the European family possible. The European family has grown. The number of states that belong to the Union is now twenty-five. The participants, as it is stated in the conclusions of the dialogue, recognized the influence of Christianity, which marked European spiritual, cultural, and social identity. Christianity has truly inspired the fathers of Europe and the founders of European Christian Democracy. The participants saluted the historical role of the founders of European Christian Democracy, among whose heirs are the present membership of the parliamentary Group in the European Parliament, in ensuring the ethical parameter of reconciliation, which had to be nurtured in the human conscience in Europe. Christianity is indeed the main source of inspiration for democratic movements in Central and Eastern Europe, which finally made the reunification of Europe possible. One cannot simply overlook this fact, although there are tendencies to do so.

However, in order to place the foundations for European solidarity and cooperation on a firm footing and to make further enlargement of the European Union possible, it is necessary to reaffirm that the Supreme Good One—namely, God—and morality can meet only in truth and that each woman and each man has to be obedient to that transcendent truth, a truth that alone can guide just relations between people, societies, and nations. There is no doubt that obedience in the search for truth requires religious freedom for its pursuit. It is this search for truth that we are all working for, and it is reconciliation and cooperation that we aspire to. Unfortunately, the Ecumenical Patriarchate is still experiencing obstacles in the struggle for religious freedom, and we pray and hope that we will finally be given the opportunity to fully enjoy our rights as citizens of our country. We hope that those in power will realize the injustice we are being faced with and that tolerance and respect for the other are fundamental rights in a free democratic society.

Through these years we have continued our honest and sincere cooperation, and it is with great joy that we have now arrived at the Tenth Dialogue. The Ecumenical Patriarchate has for ten years now offered its love and support for this ongoing dialogue, and we are hopeful that we will celebrate many more anniversaries to come. Together with the Group of the European People's Party (as Christian Democrats) and the European Democrats, we have recognized and set the example that the religious and political worlds need to understand one another—and that it is only through cooperation that we will be able to improve our world and glorify our Lord in his wisdom.

We would also like to take this opportunity to thank and congratulate the organizers and participants, from both parties, who have honored us with their efforts throughout these Ten Dialogues. Please allow us to thank also the distinguished speakers who have shared with us through the years their thoughts and presented their opinions with love, respect, and tolerance for one another. It is this kind of respectful and fruitful cooperation that allowed us to establish and continue this important relationship between religion (or church) and state. May it serve as a beacon of light for all those who wish to share our vision of a world more just and more peaceful—a world in which human beings should be able to live.

Yet, for this to be realized we must always keep in mind that we aim only for the glory of God, and, for all of us who believe in him to be one, it is yet one more effort to be faithful and follow his will and desire. He himself taught us this: "May they all be one, Father, just as you are in me and I am in you, so that they also may be in us, so that the world may believe it was you who sent me" (Jn. 17.21). It is a sacred goal that we are pursuing, and it is by our determination and unfailing interest that we will see the fruits of the grace of God multiply in our midst. It is our duty to try and see deeper than just the surface and to open our hearts and minds and pray that what had happened on the way to Emmaus will not repeat itself in our dialogues.[26] So we will listen with all our heart, and with our unceasing prayer we will beseech God so that he might grant us a better future, where we will be able to coexist with respect and understanding for one another. For human intellect simply cannot grasp by its own devices the way of existence of the Holy Trinity, and it is with this understanding that we pray that God will grant us the gift of being able to experience and partake of the harmony that the Holy Trinity is showing us. May God bless you all.

Religious Communities in the European Union: IV

Greeting to participants of For the Cooperation of the Churches of Europe, an inter-Orthodox meeting held in Istanbul, April 5, 2000.

With great joy we greet this inter-Orthodox meeting, which has gathered here in our city immediately before the start of the scheduled

26. See Lk. 24: 13–35, where the disciples on the road to Emmaus did not become aware of the presence of Jesus until he disappeared.

meeting of the presidency of the Conference of European Churches. Your participation in this meeting as representatives of our sister autocephalous Orthodox churches on the European continent bears witness also to your regard for their peaceful cooperation, with those European churches of other denominations, on every commonly held matter of concern, particularly on issues of religious freedom and social solidarity but also on the progress of European peoples toward their integration and on the establishment of the fundamental principles of peace, cooperation, justice, and fellowship among them.

Our Church has always supported and continues to support those fundamental principles, unshakably believing that Orthodoxy has a "prophetic witness" and a "witness of love in the service of truth," which unburdens people from all ideological and psychological oppression. As free peoples and citizens of European countries both in the East and in the West, we believe that our participation in building up the common European *oikos* (home) will substantially contribute to the enrichment of the European peoples through the pure evangelical truths as they are experienced in the Orthodox world. And so European civilization will rediscover the nuances of the Christian ethos, which are still being preserved in Orthodoxy, and be grounded in our ancient Christian tradition. The participation of our Orthodox peoples in building up the Europe of tomorrow will not render us spiritually negligible, but it will indeed signify for Europe a new period.

Candidate countries from Central, Eastern, and Southeastern Europe, including Turkey, provide numerous examples of Orthodox civilization, richly witness to the struggles for freedom and justice, and are experienced in respecting cultural diversification as well as the spirit of understanding religious pluralism. We understand the reservations of some, but at the same time we without reservation express the conviction that the participation of the members of the Orthodox Church in European integration is of great benefit to all. This is because the meeting of the Western European understanding of the world, together with that of Orthodox Christianity as expressed in the East, is ground for the fertile reconstitution and reformation of many inherited faulty ideas that asphyxiate certain sectors of Western European thought.

European civil society does not only look to financial development and coherence but also to the social integration of all groups that come under the European banner. In determining social policy, the European Union requires a common sojourning with the churches, which have great sensitivity and experience in this area and indeed are able to constitute its "soul." Our Orthodox Church is certainly able to play an important role in the preparatory induction phase.

The political will of Europe tends to recognize more and more the need to respect the citizen. Our Orthodox Church goes a step further and considers man as the center of all creation. Man, according to the Psalmist, "cannot abide in his pomp; he is like the beasts that perish" (Ps. 48.12). We believe that, for the restoration of man to his primordial glory, the glory of being in the image and likeness of God, it does not suffice for measures to be taken through central authorities and political systems, because these replicate conditions that already exist and do not produce the necessary radical change of mentality—or, in Church terminology, *meta-noia.* The real repentance of the world will occur only through the love of Christ, by our accepting him, by our trusting in him, by his approaching us, and by the identification of the *nous*[27] and the heart of each individual faithful to the *nous* and heart of Christ. And so we are able to respond to our call, which invites us to become "the letter of Christ," which is known and read by all peoples.

The presence of other Christian churches and confessions in Europe guides the Orthodox Church in the need to cooperate and witness together for the benefit of the European citizen. The division of the Christian world is undoubtedly a wound in the common witness of Christian faith to today's world. The division should not be a permanent situation. We as representatives of the Orthodox Church, who contain the fullness of truth, have the responsibility to bear witness to this truth in the world and to seek means of referring all Christian churches to this truth. But, until this happens, we must cooperate with our fellow Christians on a practical level to resolve various relevant issues.

The cooperation of the Christian churches in Europe and in the world will not betray our faith and its fundamental truths. On the contrary, in the spirit of sincerity and without "adding or subtracting or in any way innovating doctrine," it will guide us to mutual understanding and the foundation of social solidarity, reconciliation, and acceptance of the other,

27. Greek for "intellect" or "mind."

regardless of what condition he might be in, even though we might be sorrowful, seeing all the while that it would be possible and desirable for him to improve his condition. Studying together the text of the *Charta Oecumenica*,[28] which is an objective study of this meeting, will give to the Orthodox Church the capability of expressing its positions on this text and of proceeding, if necessary, to essential assessments, additions, and improvements.

We pray from the depths of our heart that your works will be crowned with success and that you will be able in a fraternal spirit to extract, from the wealth stored within you, new and old treasures and to offer them to fellow Christians of the other confessions in Europe—to offer them mutually and definitively in all humility and love for the glory of God and the spiritual tranquility of our brothers and sisters.

Religious Communities in the European Union: V

Homily during the opening service of the Third European Ecumenical Assembly in Sibiu, Romania, September 5, 2007.

We give glory to the All-Good and Triune God, who rendered us worthy—from East and West, from North and South, from all over our historical continent of Europe, to gather for a third time as all of its Christian churches, so that "with one mouth and one heart" we may praise his holy name and offer a common Christian witness.

We give glory to the All-Good God for, through the light of our Lord, God and Savior Jesus Christ, He has guided our steps and thoughts during the last three decades, so that we have developed a worthy ecumenical activity and close cooperation among all Christian churches, with hopeful prospects for the creation of a new Europe. At this moment precisely, we also recall the Christian basis of Europe as well as the light of the gospel message, which was preached from East to West, laying the foundations for European civilization and European identity to this day, even though some people have ignored—and continue to ignore—this reality.

---

28. This Ecumenical Charter, a joint document of the Conference of European Churches and the Council of European Episcopal Conferences, outlines guidelines for cooperation among the churches of Europe. It was issued in April 2001 on the occasion of the European ecumenical meeting in Strasbourg, France.

Today, then, we find ourselves in the beautiful and historical city of Sibiu, as representatives and members of all Christian churches in Europe. Indeed, this city has the privilege of serving, at the same time, as one of the cultural capitals of Europe in 2007.

Hope for Renewal and Unity in Europe

We have reached this point in a spirit of pilgrimage from milestone to milestone. We commenced with the First European Ecumenical Assembly in Basil, Switzerland, in 1989, moving thereafter to Graz, Austria, in 1997, for the Second European Ecumenical Assembly. And today, we are here for the Third European Ecumenical Assembly, via Rome and Wittenberg. Jesus Christ, who enlightens all nations as "the light of all nations" (Is. 49.6 and Acts 13.47) and of the whole world, has this time again led our steps to this blessed gathering. For, truly, the light of Christ shines on all, just as we declare in our liturgical life during Great Lent, as we prepare to celebrate the great feast and wonderful event of our Lord's Resurrection.

We bless and greet this sacred journey of European Christianity, which is guided by the light of Christ, as from one lighthouse to another lighthouse, through which we recognize his own crucified journey through the centuries, especially in the splintering of Christianity into numerous Christian churches and confessions, but also in the increasing desire for, and particularly the obligation to realize, the restoration of Christian communion and unity.

It is a joyous fact, as well as the fruit of the light of Christ and the energies of the Holy Spirit, that ecumenical cooperation among Christian Churches is not something entirely new. The Orthodox Church, at the initiative of the Ecumenical Patriarchate, has for more than one hundred years invited the sister Orthodox churches and also the other churches of Christ all over the world to cooperate in the full restoration of Christian communion and unity as well as in the support of suffering humanity. Moreover, in this movement, the specific problems are not unknown. They have repeatedly been discussed openly in past ecumenical meetings of a pan-European nature, where—with the inspiration of the light of Christ and the illumination of the Holy Spirit—the necessary decisions have been made and the relative conclusions have been drawn. These are summarized in, among other places, the *Charta Oecumenica*, which was published in April 2001, in Strasbourg, France. This has bound the churches of Europe, through particular actions and activities, to serve Christian unity on the basis of the same faith in love and in their journey toward the one, holy, catholic, and apostolic Church, as this is formulated in the timeless Symbol of Faith defined during the Second Ecumenical Council in Nicaea–Constantinople of 381. The goal of the *Charta Oecumenica* is precisely the support and protection of the dignity of the human person as the image of God as well as for the reconciliation among the peoples and cultures of the European continent.

Of course, we are aware that the *Charta Oecumenica* is not a constitution for a super-church; nor do we consider this *Charta* to be an infallible text. Nevertheless, despite its apparent weaknesses, it does not cease to be the outcome of an intense and responsible interchurch cooperation as well as proof of the strong will of all European churches to continue, increase, and strengthen their cooperation for an entirely new European development. The *Charta Oecumenica* constitutes the fruit especially of the Second European Ecumenical Assembly in Graz, Austria—the connecting link between that assembly and our own gathering—and is a fundamental text for the enhancement of cooperation among the churches of Europe.

The Light of Christ Shines Upon All!

For all these reasons, then, it is not by chance that, for this Third European Ecumenical Assembly, the text of the *Charta Oecumenica* was promoted as the basis for determining the study of particular issues: "The Light of Christ and the Church," "The Light of Christ and Europe," and "The Light of Christ and the World."

It is fitting that the deliberations begin with the basic theme of unity among Christian churches—namely, the principal and irreplaceable subject of the ecumenical movement. From this position, therefore, we repeat and emphasize that all of Orthodoxy, and our Modesty personally, remains unwavering and unmoved in our conviction that we are obligated to do everything in our power to promote the sacred work of restoring full ecclesiastical and sacramental communion among churches on the basis of the same faith in love and respect for the particular expressions within which the apostolic faith is experienced.

We expect and hope that this Third European Assembly will also result in specific and positive steps and conclusions toward the same purpose, and that, enlightened by the light of Christ and in recognition of this light, the churches may together agree on the character and form of the Christian unity that we seek, especially since we know that one of the existing and preliminary impediments is precisely the different opinion among Christian churches as to the purpose and goal of the ecumenical movement.

The final prayer of our Lord, as preserved in the seventeenth chapter of the Gospel according the Evangelist John, remains for all of us the criterion and goal as well as the shape of the desired and sought Christian unity:

> I ask not only on behalf of these, but also on behalf of those who will believe in me through their word, that they may all be one. *As* you, Father, are in me and I am in you, may they also be in us, so that the world may believe that you have sent me. (Jn. 17.20–21)

The word *as* here indicates the model for restoring Christian communion and unity, which is the life and manner of existence among the three divine persons of the Triune God. This covenant of our Lord Jesus Christ must be fulfilled in us so that the world might believe in him. Through this prayer, we have received the command; and so through prayer, works, and spiritual contemplation, we too are obligated to proceed with the task at hand, in order together to bear witness to faith and practical service. And so we seek to realize full communion among the churches (and accepting all of the consequences thereof) instead of our individual interest—in the increase of our own power and influence or else in overemphasis on exclusivity and ecclesiastical uniqueness.

It is precisely for these reasons that we unreservedly promote and support every ecumenical theological dialogue, on equal terms, as something absolutely necessary, even in the most critical relations among us, given that without dialogue it is impossible to achieve the desired ultimate goal of Christian reconciliation, communion, and unity.

It is only through sincere and objective dialogue that we will also be able to contribute in a crucial way to the consolidation of reconciliation and communion even among the peoples of Europe, supporting and promoting the creation of a new Europe, where Christian principles and values will rule on the basis of the spiritual heritage of Christianity. Then we will be able to confess and proclaim that, indeed, the light of Christ shines upon all! Jesus Christ himself assures us:

> I am the light of the world. Whoever follows me will never walk in darkness but will have the light of life. (Jn. 8.12)

Consequently, the foundations for a new Europe cannot be confined solely to financial and political or to cultural and national dimensions. This is why—to the best of our ability and in fully Christian conviction—we endorse and contribute toward the creation of a humane and social Europe, enlightened by the eternal and inextinguishable light of Christ, and where human rights and the fundamental values of peace, justice, freedom, tolerance, participation, and mutual support prevail. At the same time, we categorically underscore the importance of respect for life, the supreme value of marriage and family, the support and assistance of the poor, forgiveness, and mercy.[29] If people are not persuaded by our works that those in positions of responsibility take to heart the importance of dignity and specific human problems, there can be neither trust nor essential progress in the new Europe.

The Way of Repentance

We remain firm in these Christian principles and values. For we have in mind the greatly disappointing contemporary reality, wherein there prevails a confusion of values and where the struggle between light and darkness is ongoing. We are profoundly concerned about the human person, created in the image and likeness of God but at the same time daily trampled and ignored. We are also concerned about the family and its indispensable significance. We are concerned about workers, who are used purely as a means toward consumption and production. We are concerned about God's creation, which is constantly and shamelessly rendered the object of abuse; for it is groaning, inasmuch as our planet is being threatened, awaiting protection from us and redemption (see Rom. 8). We are concerned about the climate and other conditions—quite literally, about the air and the oxygen that modern man breathes and that

29. See *Charta Oecumenica*, par. 8.

future generations, we fear, will seek in vain. Finally, we are concerned about humanity's mere survival on this continent and on our planet.

What else must be done, beyond what has already been done, in order for us to become aware and conscious of the drastic conditions that threaten human survival on the planet and on the aging continent of Europe? What else must be done, beyond what has already been done, in order for our eyes to be opened, for us to see the light of Christ and follow it, so as not to walk continually in darkness and deceit? There is no time for waiting or delay. Otherwise, we are willingly and irresponsibly, even dangerously, shutting our eyes. As a result, our responsibility is ever increasing.

What must immediately take place is repentance, together with the change of life that accompanies repentance. The guiding light of Christ always exists. Nevertheless, our eyes have been blinded and are unable to perceive and pursue that light. For they have become accustomed to the prevailing darkness and confusion. Those who have eyes to see, let them see. The judgment of Jesus Christ to his disciples is repeated to us today: "Are your hearts hardened? Do you have eyes, and fail to see? Do you have ears, and fail to hear? . . . And He said to them: Do you not yet understand?" (Mk. 8.18–21). It is nothing new, then, though inconceivable, that those who are considered his own abandoned him who is the light, as St. John the Evangelist narrates:

> He was the true light, which enlightens everyone coming into the world. He was in the world, and the world came into being through Him; yet the world did not know Him. He came to what was His own, and His own people did not accept Him. (Jn. 1.9–11)

In the midst of this condition, therefore, we repeat today, as we did in the past, before all of you, that we will continue without fail to place ourselves personally as well as to place the Ecumenical Patriarchate—and, as we like to believe, together with all the Christian churches of Europe—at the service and ministry of humanity, which is today suffering in manifold ways, and at the service of God's creation, which is groaning together with us. We have no alternative resolution to these problems, but we are absolutely prepared to contribute and cooperate in any constructive and sincere dialogue whatsoever.

In this spirit, we bless and endorse the recommendation proposed by the Orthodox representatives in the Preparatory Inter-Orthodox

Conference, which met last June in Rhodes in light of this assembly, that, as a tangible proof of the concern of the Orthodox Church as well as of all Christian churches of Europe, in return for our destructive and arrogant behavior toward nature and the environment, the following Friday, September 7, be set aside as a day of voluntary fasting for all of us.

At this time, fully conscious of our coordinating service within the entire communion of our Orthodox brothers and sisters, we once again call on all Orthodox churches to assume responsibility for our times and to work together—both within and outside the Orthodox Church, together with all churches bearing the name of Christ, and especially with all churches in Europe—to contribute to the healing of the wounds of suffering humankind. Without this dialogue and the necessary close cooperation with all Orthodox and all Christians, but also without all responsible persons and all proper powers and authorities—religious, political, economic, cultural, and others—our isolated actions are destined from the outset to fail. We confess, proclaim and practice this because we are absolutely convinced that our concern is also the concern of all Christian churches as well as the concern of all rational people—local, national, international, and European leaders in various and manifold administrative positions.

Furthermore, we know and affirm that the basic principles and values of the other monotheistic religions not only permit but demand the mutual respect of human dignity and, by extension, the peaceful coexistence of all people and of all faiths. The results and recommendations of the numerous interreligious dialogues, many of which have been organized with our personal initiative and participation, convincingly assure us of this truth. Every other claim or prejudice—specifically, that religion, or at least some religions, on the basis of their character and principles, contributes to and promotes religious intolerance, fanaticism, nationalist extremism, violence, and wars—does not correspond to reality. Indeed, we repeat the basic principle from the Bosphorus Declaration of the interreligious conference held in 1994, which was signed by, in addition to our Modesty, representatives of Christianity, Judaism, and Islam.[30] This declaration categorically underscores that every crime in the name of religion

30. For the full text, see Chapter 6, "Major Declarations: Public Proclamations." Other meetings of interreligious dialogue between representatives of Christianity, Juda-

is a crime against religion. We are entirely certain that the peaceful coexistence and cooperation among people belonging to different races and different religions is not only possible but also pleasing to the God of peace and justice.

Vigilance, then, and strong resistance are required in order that the religious sense and the popular sense with regard to the same ideals, or political and economic and other interests, may not be abused. Without reconciliation, peace, and justice, it is impossible to construct a new European house or, indeed, any human society.

Based on this conviction, we must also not only proclaim with our words but also witness in our lives that we are all transitional sojourners in this world, "having no lasting city here, but rather looking for the city that is to come" (Heb. 13.14). Accordingly, a new Europe already presents all the dimensions of a society through the transition of peoples from various cultural, social, and religious origins, all of which must be taken seriously for the political and institutional regulations of the new society on the basis of mutual respect and the equality of all people, as our Fathers also emphasized.

We are completely convinced that the light of Christ shines upon all! This confession is part of the preparation for the service of the Resurrection of our Savior Jesus Christ in the Orthodox Church. The light of Christ is more or less the same Christ of the Resurrection, who triumphed over evil and suffering, who "trampled down death by death, granting eternal life to all."[31] This is why we also chant and proclaim on Easter Sunday:

> Everything has now been filled with light—heaven, earth, and all things beneath the earth; let all creation, therefore, celebrate the resurrection of Christ, in which it has been established.

Our faith is also the expectation and hope of us all, the conviction and the future of all.

---

ism, and Islam include the Brussels Conference (2001), the Amaroussion Conference (2004), Peace and Tolerance II (2005), and Religions for Peace (2005).

31. From the well-known Orthodox Resurrection Hymn: "Christ is risen from the dead, trampling down death by death, and granting life to those in the tombs."

Religion and Corruption

Address to the Plenary Assembly of the Thirteenth International Anti-Corruption Conference held in Athens, Greece, October 30, 2008.

We bring you warm greetings from the Ecumenical Patriarchate of Constantinople, from our centuries-old spiritual center in modern-day Istanbul. We thank you for this invitation to be with you today and to address this most respected assembly at the Thirteenth International Anti-Corruption Conference. Since its first meeting in Washington, D.C., in 1983, the IACC has offered the contemporary world a unique forum for confronting the deep-seated condition of corruption on every level of human experience.

As Ecumenical Patriarch, we come to you from an ancient institution of faith that, at many times in our history of seventeen continuous centuries, has struggled with all manner of corruption, from within and without. Not only have we survived all these challenges, but our continuing ministry of service to the world also bears witness to a central theme of our purely spiritual mission. Eloquently stated with unashamed hope by the Apostle Paul, whose footsteps were heard in this very city two thousand years ago when he mounted Mars Hill and addressed the people of Athens, and whose legacy and accomplishment of two millennia the Christian world observes this year, these words from his letter to the Romans bring constant hope and expectancy to the human family. He says:

> The creation itself also shall be delivered from the bondage of corruption into the glorious liberty of the children of God. (Rom. 8.21)

In this brief declaration that affirms a greater destiny for all creation, the Apostle Paul has offered to all of us, and particularly to this assembly gathered here in Athens, a decisive perspective that we are glad to offer to you today.

For corruption truly is a form of human bondage, a slavery that enslaves both those who engage in corrupt and corrupting practices and those whose lives are subject to ruination. The desolation that it wreaks on the human spirit is in fact worse for the one who betrays his or her values and principles than for the ones whose lives are grievously affected by such betrayal. For those who are victims of corruption of any kind—whether this be physical, financial, religious, or political—always have the choice to endure and to vindicate their integrity by the purity of their own motivations, even in the face of abject greed and tyranny. On the other hand, those who perpetrate corruption anywhere across the globe, whether it be through governmental turpitude, ecological depravity, financial and economic vice, or religious hatred, reveal themselves as the most damaged of souls and are often incapable of returning to the sanity—indeed, the health—of their own personhood.

This conference has gathered to examine corruption in institutional, industrial, and governmental systems, but these systems do not exist apart from the individual human persons whom they comprise. As we seek to monitor and check corruption, through transparency, accountability, and enforcement initiatives, let us never forget that there is a fundamental issue of personal responsibility that underlies every system of corruption.

Just as responsible individuals risk position, security, and social status to sound the alarm in cases of corruption—the admirable "whistleblowers"—so it is also true that it is the very lack of such responsibility for the self and for others that gives rise to the machinations of bribery, wastefulness, and criminality. The former risks liberty and ease in the cause of higher principle; the latter mistakes escapism for freedom, as well as ephemeral comfort for the bondage of the soul. But surely the one who recognizes truth, honesty, and justice is the one who has already been, as the Apostle Paul says, "delivered from the bondage of corruption into the glorious liberty of the children of God."

Global Transparency: Fighting Corruption for a Sustainable Future

However, the Apostle speaks in his epistle of a future state when creation itself will be delivered from corruption. You who have gathered for this conference and who work tirelessly through the year in order to eliminate corruption at every level of human conduct are the ones who are sharing in that promise and working to bring about a "glorious liberty" for all of God's children, without respect to their religious persuasion, racial identity, or ethnic origin.

From our City [of Istanbul], the Ecumenical Patriarchate is an active partner with you in the ongoing struggle against corruption, both in a spiritual and a material sense. As St. Paul says in another place:

> For we wrestle not against flesh and blood, but against principalities, against powers, against the rulers of the darkness of this world, against spiritual wickedness in high places. (Eph. 6.12)

The Church takes very seriously our mission to be a positive force for peace, forgiveness, and love in the world. We curse not the darkness, but from the lighthouse that we know as Phanar, the sacred center of our Orthodox faith, we continue to radiate the light of God as we are given grace to do so. Our message is a word, a *logos*, of reconciliation, as the Apostle Paul says in yet another place:

> God was in Christ, reconciling the world unto Himself, not imputing their transgressions unto them; and has committed unto us the word of reconciliation. (2 Cor. 5.19)

And our context of faith does not negate what another human being believes. And in passing no judgment on others, neither do we negate our own faith, the faith of millions and millions of human beings. In fact, our faith is made stronger because we not only act in a spiritual way, but we bring concrete results to our struggle against the corruption of the world.

This is why the Ecumenical Patriarchate continues its program of addressing one of the principal thematic streams of this year's conference, climate change and corruption of the environment. We recognize in our ecumenical mission a responsibility for the *oikos*—the house—of the world and of the *oikoumene*, all who dwell therein. As is well known, our Patriarchate is not a "national" church but rather the fundamental canonical expression of the ecumenical dimensions of the gospel message and the expression of the Patriarchate's analogous responsibility to the world and to the Church. Thus our Patriarchate is called "Ecumenical."

In our mission to the *oikoumene*, the inhabited world, we continue to sponsor the religion, science, and environment movement, joining leaders from all great faith traditions with renowned scientists and political leadership. Our cause is to seek ways in the practical realms of demonstrable science and realpolitik—not mere theory and ideology—in order to cleanse the air, the seas, and the land in the service of the great human good.

Dear friends, we have but one planet to share, one ecosphere of mutual existence. In the Church, we speak of the Body of Christ, where every member is linked to another. And so:

> The eye cannot say unto the hand, I have no need of you: nor again the head to the feet, I have no need of you. (1 Cor. 12.21)

We have traveled from the Aegean to the Arctic Seas, from the Danube[32] to—this coming May—the River Nile,[33] all with the thought to find practical solutions to the corruption of the environment, corruption that threatens every life on the planet, human and animal alike. And yet we know that the transformation of societies and systems begins with each and every person taking responsibility for himself and for the other in his midst.

Therefore, we convey to all of you, the participants in the Thirteenth International Anti-Corruption Conference, our heartfelt blessing on your important work. May the deliberations, workshops, and experiences of all build on the foundation laid in previous conferences and particularly on the declaration that emerged from Guatemala City. It was there that a call was sounded for faith-based entities to become more engaged in the promotion of anticorruption measures in the general institutions of the human family. And we know that, as agents for change in society, institutions of religious faith can have an impact on the governmental, legal, and societal establishments.

In a world of unparalleled technological accomplishment that oftentimes feels more insecure than ever—witness the global credit crisis—the fight for basic human equality is essential to the restoration of balance and harmony among all peoples. Greed, terror, oppression—these are the marks of the *bondage of corruption* that threatens every human soul.

May God grant us the grace, the strength, and the moral courage to breaks these bonds asunder, so that every human person may go forth into the *glorious liberty of the children of God.*

---

32. See Neal Ascherson and Sarah Hobson, eds., *Danube: River of Life* (Athens: Religion, Science and the Environment, 2002).

33. The Nile Symposium was postponed for reasons of regional political instability. The next symposium was organized for October 2009 on the Mississippi River.

Turkey and the E.U.: I

Opening remarks at the Center of Turkish Studies, University of Essen, October 12, 2002.

In addressing you and opening the discussion on a subject of such intimate and far-reaching concern to us, we think back to our student days at the Theological School of Halki, where there is an engraving quoting the father of the country, Kemal Atatürk,[34] which reads: "Peace at home, peace in the world." It harkens back to a tumultuous period in Europe, marked by strife and war, but one in which the founder of the modern Turkish state could join with his bitterest enemy, the Greek leader Eleftherios Venizelos, and pursue the promise of peace.[35]

We have addressed many gatherings related to the European Union and European integration. We have noted before that this great historic mission to organize the unity of the peoples of Europe in peace, justice, and democracy has a sacred aspect in its struggle for the sharing of a common understanding of life, of the sanctity of the human person, and in the reconciliation and solidarity of diverse peoples, religions, and cultures. The Judeo-Christian values embedded in this historical process direct us to the world at large, not simply to the confines of a twelve-nation European Union, or even to a twenty-five-nation European Union.

Our tradition of some seventeen centuries of caring and struggling for the salvation of the world and unity of European civilization, sitting as we do at the crossroads of East and West, North and South, illuminates the understanding that political unity separated from civilization—that is, political unity without a fundamental comprehension of human relationships—cannot lead to the achievement of a true union of peoples. We do not see, as has become fashionable today, the clash of civilizations but rather the challenge of civilization. We are compelled by our very nature to meet that challenge. The Ecumenical Patriarchate belongs to the living Church, which was founded by the God of love, whose "peace surpasses all understanding" (Phil. 4.7).

---

34. Mustafa Kemal Atatürk (1881–1938) was the founder of modern Turkey, the leader and first president of the Republic of Turkey.

35. Eleftherios Venizelos (1864–1936), a prominent Greek revolutionary and charismatic statesman, was elected prime minister of Greece on several occasions.

European Values and the European Union

With respect to Turkey, we stand at a critical juncture. A secular state that is the heir to great civilizations, Christian and Muslim, and that saw the development and defining of the great undivided Church and the flourishing of a tolerant Islam that became a refuge for the Jewish people as well as other Christian and Muslim groups, Turkey shares in those fundamental human, political, and social values on which European societies were so successfully built—values derived from the great Abrahamic faiths and from Athenian democracy.

While Turkey's road has been difficult and the full implementation of these values imperfect, not unlike earlier phases in the history of Europe proper, this vibrant nation is no less a part of the European journey. After September 11, 2001, and with the continued turmoil in the Middle East, it is even more incumbent on us to bring unity and peace to all, given the fundamental belief that the human person is created in the image and likeness of God. We are all God's children. Hence, we must categorically reject all forms of intolerance, racism, and violence.

Our times demand the greatest efforts on the part of all of us to work in collaboration with all religions, with all secularists, with all people, without distinction. More than ever, we must seek to break down the walls that separate us. Germany is a great example. A nation that has seen the extremes of nationalism and imperialism but also the greatest of achievements in human thought and culture embarked on a great experiment in breaking down the wall between what we then called East and West. However significant that was, and it was truly significant, as a united Germany became a good neighbor and a refuge for millions from Eastern Europe and around the world, including many Turkish workers, the breaking down of that wall was symbolic of the end of an internal Western conflict.

Today, we have before us an even greater challenge: truly to break down the wall between East and West, between Muslims, Christians, and Jews, between all religions, all civilizations and all cultures, to bridge the great divide and recognize our common humanity and common values. The peace, stability, and ensuing national prosperity, along with the securing of individual rights, freedom of religion, and freedom of expression—all of these goods that were achieved through cooperation in the

European Union helped remove the poison of hate and suspicion that once characterized the European continent. This solidarity and cooperation must be extended in love and understanding to what may appear to be a different and more complex society. We believe that "God is love," which is why we do not fear to extend our hand in friendship and our heart in love, as we proclaim that "perfect love casts out fear" (1 Jn. 4.18).

We believe that a Europe without Turkey will be in danger of becoming a European fortress without bridges, without that universal aspect and philanthropic ideal that is the very nature of its civilization. We believe that Europe faces a truly spiritual challenge to open its door. Already the union is a union of minorities that have learned to live with common values. With Turkey anchored to Europe, we can anchor the world and extend peace and love and justice East and South. Turkey, for its part, must rejoice in those values, reaffirming the rights and freedoms of all its citizens no matter what their ethnic background or religion. We are confident that Turkey is moving in this direction, perhaps imperfectly, sometimes imperceptibly, but inexorably.

In this great country, one can see the majestic Hagia Sophia, or Church of the Holy Wisdom of God, as well as the Blue Mosque, all of which evoke divine serenity. However, there is another church from deep in our history, Hagia Eirene, the Church of the Holy Peace of God.[36] We must continue the European journey together, East and West, North and South, to that appointed time and place in God's Kingdom of Peace.

Turkey and the E.U.: II

Address to the Abant Platform in Washington, D.C., April 19, 2004. Originally the Opening Remarks at the Palais d'Egmont, Brussels, April 4, 2004.

In addressing you and opening the discussion on a subject of such intimate and far-reaching concern to us, we think back to the two recent tragic terrorist attacks in Turkey and the words of the prime minister of Turkey, Recep Tayyip Erdoğan, who said shortly afterward:

---

36. The names of both churches (*Sophia* and *Eirine*) are also personal names of historical saints. However, in these particular cases, the names refer to the divine attributes of wisdom and peace, both ascribed and ultimately dedicated to the person of Christ.

> I cannot bear it when terrorism and Islam are spoken of in the same breath. . . . The Religions of the Book want to protect life, not destroy it. In Islam, those who take human life are acting as if they are blowing up the House of God.

These words resonate with an attitude that goes to the heart of Turkish Islam, the nature of the secular state, and the principles of democracy. They reflect the profound changes that have taken place recently in Europe and Turkey regarding Islam. Today, the European Union has some fifteen million Muslims, three million of who are Turkish. While its history and culture is interwoven with Europe, contemporary Turkey faces the profound challenge relating to its accession to the European Union. Turkey's is, after all, the only Muslim society that came into close contact with and embraced the ideals of the Enlightenment and the French Revolution. In the Ottoman Empire, the state took precedence over religion, and Turkish Islam remained open to the influence of mystical traditions. While embracing the notion of the modern national state, it resisted incessantly and in so many ways the ideology of political Islam. As a result, Turkey is unique because there is a harmony between traditional Turkish Muslim values and secularism. As a matter of fact, Turkey is "Islamic *and* secular" rather than "Islamic *but* secular."

The Turkish Experience: Secularism and Democracy

The Turkish model shows that the interaction between Islam and the modern world need not be on a collision course. The results of Atatürk's goal for Turkey to join what he called "Universal Civilization" have been impressive, with greater opportunity and better conditions than in many countries where government and Islam remained conjoined. But the roots of secular Turkish Islam go even deeper into the social fabric of the country. Turks themselves are committed to the secular path and a democratic future. Even if there was a period of divergence when the state promoted Islam vis-à-vis the challenges of the Cold War, today the desire is to fulfill the Copenhagen criteria and join the European family of nations. And so Turkey is preparing itself to join the European Union.

Like European identity, American identity cannot be seen in terms of geography or even within the narrow bounds of a specific history and culture. It has a wider context and has to do with espousing the same set of fundamental values and principles—human rights, religious freedom, tolerance, and the rule of law—that are shared by many nations. Turkey readily subscribes to and closely identifies with these values and has repeatedly proclaimed its commitment to apply them equally to all its citizens regardless of race or creed. Christians, Muslims, and Jews in Turkey live together in an atmosphere of tolerance and dialogue. We wish to mention the pioneering work of Fethullah Gülen, who more than ten years ago began to educate his believers about the necessity for the existence of a dialogue between Islam and all religions.[37]

The Turkish model of Islam seeks the legitimization of all religions and the freedom to choose now and forever without coercion from the state, whether in a religious or a secular direction. In other words, the Turkish model envisions Islam as occupying in the Islamic societies the same position that religion does in the Western world today—a world far removed from the concepts of jihad and crusades. Turkey shaped its modern identity out of a struggle with the new political order at the advent of nationalism, and it is being tested again today with the emergence of the post–Cold War era at the advent of a new geopolitical reality, unlike any we have known in the past.

The incorporation of Turkey and the Turkish model into the European Union may well provide a concrete example and a powerful symbol of mutually beneficial cooperation between the Western and Islamic worlds and put an end to the talk of a clash of civilizations. This, in turn, would be a true strengthening of Europe and of the European ideals that are consistent with the values of "the Religions of the Book" spoken of by the prime minister of Turkey.

Today, we have before us an even greater challenge—to truly break down the wall between East and West, between Muslims and Christians, between all religions, all civilizations and all cultures, to bridge the great divide and recognize our common humanity and common values. This is God's model for the world. We must continue this journey together, East and West, North and South, to that appointed time and place in God's Kingdom.

---

37. Fethullah Gülen (b. 1941), a Muslim preacher and educator in Turkey, is leader of the Gülen movement, which is dedicated to peace and unity.

Turkey and the E.U.: III

Video Address for the Young Presidents Organization, Istanbul/Athens, September 29, 2007.

It is indeed a pleasure to address—from a distance through prayer and in spirit, as well as through video communication—the auspicious and international gathering of the Young Presidents Organization in Athens, sponsored by the Young Presidents Organization of Greece. Your conference, as we are well aware, is being attended by successful executives and influential opinion makers from all over the world, while also being honored by the presence of Prime Minister Karamanlis. Therefore, on behalf of the Ecumenical Patriarchate, one of the oldest spiritual institutions in the world, we would like to extend our warmest wishes and most fervent prayers for the success of your deliberations. It is a matter of real regret that these wishes cannot be delivered in person. However, we would like to assure you that the message comes sincerely and from the heart, both because your gathering is deeply important but also because, as talented business leaders, you have a calling that is profoundly influential. In different ways, each of you will make a unique and personal contribution to the history of the twenty-first century.

We would like to take this opportunity to remind you of certain global realities in our modern age, in order to bring to your attention two essential and fundamental concerns of our modern world, which must be considered from a variety of perspectives—not only social or political, and not only economic or global, but also from a religious or spiritual point of view. It is our hope that in this way we will encourage you to appreciate and address these critical issues in an open-minded and open-hearted manner as you move into your respective and responsible positions. For it is our firm conviction that these are concerns that all of us will ultimately encounter and about which all of us should be constantly in dialogue in order to pave the way toward a more peaceful and sustainable world for the sake of the present and future generations as well as for the glory of God. These concerns are also a central priority of the Ecumenical Patriarchate, which has been endowed by history with a special responsibility for the spiritual welfare of the whole inhabited earth, the *oikoumene*.

Protection of the Environment

The first concern relates to the state of our environment and the ever growing risk that human folly or recklessness will do irreparable damage to our beautiful but fragile planet. The Ecumenical Patriarchate has, among other initiatives, already convened seven international symposia on the state of the earth and its waters, most recently in Greenland, where we saw for ourselves the frightening pace at which the Arctic ice is melting. Dear friends, this issue is not about politics; it is about life. Indeed, for business leaders of your generation, it will become increasingly obvious that respect for the environment constitutes a moral duty for all, an expression of both common responsibility and simple common sense.

In recent years, we have learned some important lessons about caring for the natural environment. However, in order to draw your attention to the way in which businesspeople and professionals may respond to this issue, we would add that we have learned especially that environmental action cannot be separated from human relations. What we do for the earth is intimately related to what we do for people—whether in the context of human rights or international politics, whether with regard to poverty and social justice or world peace. It has become clearer to us that the way we respond to the natural environment is intimately and deeply connected to the way we treat human beings. The way we relate to material things and the natural environment directly reflects the way we relate to other people. Therefore, the willingness of some people to exploit the environment, which is the "flesh of the world," goes hand in hand with their willingness to ignore human suffering in the flesh of our neighbor. And, by extension, the willingness to respond to the needs of creation and of our neighbor reflects our willingness to respect the way of the heart and the commandments of God.

In our efforts, then, for the preservation of the natural environment, we must ask ourselves some difficult questions about our concern for other human beings and about our way of life and daily habits. Just how prepared are we to sacrifice our excessive lifestyles—as societies and as individuals—in order that others might enjoy the basic right to survive? Or, at least, just how committed are we to working so that all people may have sufficient resources, so that no person suffers from poverty or hunger or unemployment? What are we truly prepared to surrender in order to learn to share? When will we learn to say "Enough"? How can we direct our focus away from what we want to what the world and our neighbor need? Do we honestly do all that we can to leave as light a footprint as possible on this planet, for the sake of those who share it with us and for the sake of future generations?

Today, there are no excuses for our lack of involvement. We have access to detailed and instantaneous information; alarming statistics are readily available. If we constantly emphasize our freedom, then we must remember that caring is also one of the fundamental choices we are free to make. Do we, therefore, choose to care? If not, then we are denying our prerogative, indeed our very nature as human beings. If we choose not to care, then we are not simply indifferent onlookers; we are in fact active aggressors. If we are not allaying the pain of others and see or care only about our own interests, then we are directly contributing to the suffering and poverty of our world. Where do we stand? Where do you stand?

Dialogue and Encounter

Another concern that you as leaders and as businesspeople will almost certainly face, in one form or another, is the sheer diversity of the human race—the simple fact that humankind is divided into so many different religions, races, ethnic groups, and nationalities. Whatever the nature of your business or profession, your employees and your customers invariably serve as representatives of the human race in all its wondrous variety and mystery. It follows, then, that as business leaders, and quite simply as decent and civilized human beings, you have a strong interest in the avoidance of any so-called "clash of civilizations" between different cultural or religious groups.

We hear it stated often that our world is in crisis. It is sick morally, spiritually, ecologically, economically, and politically. It is said that the crises the world is facing are fundamentally related to the humanity–creation–God relationship and more specifically to human responsibility. Yet, never before in history have human beings had the opportunity to bring so many positive changes to so many people simply through the power of encounter and dialogue. Never before have human beings—and especially influential leaders, such as yourselves—had the opportunity to impact and transform our world so radically, both for better and for worse.

The interaction of human beings and ethnic groups is today alarmingly direct and immediate, particularly as a result of technological advances in the mass media and of the means of travel. People of diverse cultural and religious backgrounds gather in conferences to discuss mutual tolerance, to promote authentic reconciliation, and to negotiate peaceful solutions. So, while it may be true that this is a time of crisis, that the world is sick, it must be equally emphasized that there has also never been greater tolerance for respective traditions, religious preferences, and cultural peculiarities. For this, we must remain deeply grateful to God.

Indeed, the Ecumenical Patriarchate has initiated numerous such dialogues of hope and love with other Christian confessions (such as the Roman Catholic Church and the Anglican Communion) as well as with other religious communities (such as the Jewish and Muslim faiths). Through both unofficial conversations, conducted on a personal level between followers of the world's great religions, and formal dialogues organized internationally by religious leaders and institutions, we have struggled to clarify centuries-old misunderstandings while gradually preparing people's hearts and minds for the possibility of peaceful coexistence and dignified cooperation among all people. Is this effort for encounter not something sacred? Can there be anything more precious in the eyes of God than this struggle to communicate and relate? Is there truly anything more valuable for the future of humankind?

Of course, this is slow and painful work. It does not mean, for example, that differences on the level of doctrine are insignificant or inconsequential. For a difference on the level of doctrine leads to a different worldview and, accordingly, a different way of life. Nevertheless, not to pursue differences does not imply indifference. Rather, this sense of working and living together in peace and solidarity signifies a profound respect for each person and each culture as unique and unrepeatable, as a precious piece in the wonderful tapestry called humanity. Genuine dialogue recognizes the inviolable right of every human being to follow a personal journey of faith, hope, and love.

This is precisely why, in our Common Declaration[38] with His Holiness Pope Benedict XVI, on the occasion of his visit to the Ecumenical Patriarchate last November for the Thronal Feast of St. Andrew, we pronounced our special concern for those parts of the world where people live in poverty, war, and terrorism as well as for the various forms of exploitation of the poor, of migrants, women, and children. We jointly proclaimed that

> we are called to work together to promote respect for the rights of every human being, created in the image and likeness of God, and to foster economic, social and cultural development.

Accordingly, then, we do not approach dialogue in the framework of conflict, to set our arguments against those of our opponents. We approach in a spirit of love, sincerity, and honesty. In this respect, dialogue implies equality, which in turn implies humility. Honesty and humility dispel hostility and arrogance. Just how prepared are we in dialogue to receive others and to respect others in dialogue? How willing are we to learn and to love? If we are neither prepared to receive nor willing to learn, then are we truly engaging in dialogue? Or are we actually conducting a monologue?

Often, unfortunately, Christians (including Orthodox) and other religious groups (especially extremists) who are rather conservative are offended that the Ecumenical Patriarchate has historically given priority to such dialogues with other confessions or faiths. These people believe that there can be no dialogue on equal terms with those who, holding to a different creed, are in their view "heretics." Indeed, the word *heresy* is another term that has been greatly misused, if not widely abused, in the history of religious and theological thought. For we are convinced that in no way are we undermining the importance of theological doctrine and its accuracy when we conduct dialogues and discussions.

Perhaps it may be useful to remember here that the Greek word for "heresy," *airesis*, does not mean primarily erroneous doctrine. Rather, it implies the conscious selection of one aspect of truth, which one absolutizes in a fundamentalist way to the exclusion of all other perceptions of

38. For the full text, see Chapter 6, "Major Declarations: Public Proclamations."

truth. We must humbly admit that all of us—Christians, Jews, and Muslims alike—have, at one time or another, been guilty of the sin of narrow-mindedness, particularly when we feel that our worldview has been threatened. Therefore, we are convinced that the purpose of sincere and open dialogue is precisely to reveal the fallacy and arrogance of this stifling attitude. This is the kind of humility that is expected of all those in dialogue and of all people who live alongside adherents of another faith in our multicultural and multireligious world.

Learning to Share

True dialogue is a gift from God. According to St. John Chrysostom, fourth-century archbishop and predecessor of ours on the historical Throne of Constantinople, God is always in personal dialogue with human beings. In fact, God constantly searches for ways to communicate with his creation. In some ways, the history of salvation is none other than the loving pursuit by God of his creatures. So God always speaks—through prophets and apostles, through saints and mystics as well as through persons such as yourselves, who are in key positions in society, and even through the natural creation itself, for "the heavens declare the glory of God" (Ps. 19.1).

When we are in dialogue with those around us, then we are speaking the language of God! Dialogue is the most fundamental experience of life: from childhood, through education, to maturity. Dialogue is also the most powerful means of communication—not only for the teacher and the preacher but for every leader and member of society. Dialogue promotes knowledge and science, reveals truths and emotions, abolishes fears and prejudice, cultivates bonds, and broadens horizons. Dialogue expands our perception of the world; it introduces new ways of achieving goals. Dialogue enriches; whoever refuses dialogue remains impoverished.

This dilemma concerning the critical need for open dialogue is at the heart of the ministry of the Ecumenical Patriarchate, which is located at a great crossroads of civilizations and therefore continually does everything in its power to promote understanding and mutual respect between all faiths and cultures. As we have already observed, the labor of dialogue between different religions and value systems is never an easy one. It requires patience, humility, and the ability to listen carefully to other people's deepest hopes and fears. But with the specter of ethnic and sectarian conflict looming in many parts of the world, the Patriarchate sees no alternative to patient and persistent dialogue. It is our hope and prayer that you too will contribute in every way possible to the avoidance of any form of racial, religious, or cultural conflict.

Dear friends, the language of God is the language of love, tolerance, and compassion. The only question is: Will we refuse to speak the language of heaven, which includes everyone and excludes no one? Or will we choose to learn new methods of communication and to adopt new ways of cooperation?

As you probably know, in the United States of America, the city of Atlanta likes to celebrate its good race relations and its successful economy by saying it is "a city too busy to hate." It is our paternal wish and Patriarchal prayer that you and the people whose lives you touch—whether your customers, your coworkers, your business partners—will always be too busy to hate but never too busy to love.

We are profoundly encouraged by your thirst to learn new ways and to adopt new expressions of love in the global community. The clear signs of your common commitment to the well-being of humanity truly serve as a beacon of hope in a world of poverty and war. The Young Presidents Organization is an encounter of individuals and institutions that bodes well for our world. Yours is an involvement that highlights the supreme purpose and calling of humanity to transcend political and religious differences in order to transform the entire world for the glory of God.

Turkish–Greek Relations: I

Greeting to the Turkish–Greek Business Council, Istanbul, February 25, 2000.

Though we recall greeting you at your meeting two and a half years ago in Istanbul, it now seems as if we met many decades ago in a different world. And, to tell the truth, it was a different world, and a different time. We can no longer speak of Greek–Turkish relations with the same vocabulary. Everything has changed.

We must acknowledge that the dialogue that was begun between Turkey and Greece during the first half of 1999 was further advanced by the disastrous earthquakes in Turkey and in Greece. So we can say that this warming of relations was, in part, an act of God. But we must further admit that, in part, this is also an act of men—not just the courageous foreign ministers of both nations but also leaders in business and religion, two natural constituencies for peace.

The clergy seeks the peace of the prophets, while businesspeople seek the profits of peace. Beneath the play on words, however, the goal is the same: a better life for all our people, through the exchange of goodwill and the exchange of products, which can be accomplished only through peace. We spoke the last time of a combined history so glorious that we are sometimes hypnotized by it. But while Turks and Greeks gazed backward, other nations moved forward. While Greeks and Turks kept old wounds alive—and continued to argue over who did what to whom, and when, and why—the rest of the world moved forward.

The lesson of history is clear: to face the future we must put the past behind us, which means that, while we cannot denounce the past, we must learn from the lessons of history. And to do so takes great courage. Few people know that better than the business leaders in this room. You know the history of our two peoples. You know the bad feelings that exist and you have been criticized and even vilified for participating in the effort to turn them around.

And yet you are here once again in this room. You are here to say, Enough of the past, enough of strife. Let our children and our children's children grow up without feeling the hatred that has poisoned our relations for so many generations. As we acknowledged two and a half years ago:

> Some people risk everything in war. You are risking everything for peace.

You recognize that nothing was ever gained by hating. But much has been lost. And among the sacrifices one must count the economic prosperity of Greece and Turkey. Both countries have great economic potential, yet both have allowed military rivalry to take a huge toll on their budgets, and both have, until now, forsaken the huge Balkan economic boost that would result if Greece and Turkey were to develop closer ties of friendship and trade.

Once, only conquest united Europe and Asia. Today, commerce can achieve the same result. Instead of ships full of soldiers, let us see ships full of goods crossing the Bosphorus. The modern way to bring about unity and peace is to open our borders to one another, extend the European Union, and allow people, capital, ideas, and products to flow. Much has already been done to foster reconciliation and economic cooperation between Greece and Turkey, from the Helsinki Summit, which opened the door to E.U. membership for Turkey without any precondition and as an equal candidate with all others, to the recent visits and press interviews by foreign ministers Cem and Papandreou.

Although many of these initiatives are led by political leaders, politicians alone cannot heal the rift between Greece and Turkey. We all, and especially you as business leaders, have a role to play if this rapprochement is to be successful. You are uniquely positioned to spell out the real costs to Greece and Turkey of keeping ancient feuds alive. You can help our people focus on real problems like the balance of trade with each other, not the balance of sins against each other. You can channel the two nations' competitive efforts away from the battlefield and into the free market, filling orders instead of graves. We pray that you will succeed in your efforts at peace and reconciliation.

We religious leaders also have a contribution to make to your noble task. We can make it unequivocally clear that our holiest books, the Bible and the Qur'an, support the idea of reconciliation among rivals, undertaken in good faith. We can act as the instigators of peace. And we at the Ecumenical Patriarchate will continue our own efforts to be peacemakers.

As we are about to depart for our visits to the Orthodox faithful in Korea and the Philippines, we have a sense of inner peace and reassurance, seeing mayors, businessmen, athletes, media, and representatives of higher education from these two peoples working together. Businesspeople too must insist on and persist in planting seeds of friendly relations in other areas and domains of society and at the grassroots level. To employ an analogy, our aim must be friendship that indeed is well rooted, but it must also reach every branch, twig, and leaf and not remain only in the trunk of the tree—that is, only at a higher theoretical level. For, although the trunk is the most powerful and massive part of the tree, it is its branches and blossoms that give it its beauty and majesty. It is the duty of each and every one of us to try to win over all those who have not yet espoused this ideal of friendship and cooperation.

Turkish–Greek Relations: II

Opening address at the conference meeting in Istanbul: Present and Future, June 30, 2006.

"Love truth and peace," the Lord says (Zac. 8.19). "The order of the Lord is a source of life" (Prov. 14.27). Based on these two divine truths and orders, we greet the present congress and its participants with the wish that we communicate to each other words of life, in truth and love. . . .

The present time is vital in many ways. It is vital for the City's Greeks. It is vital for minorities in general. At the same time, it is vital for the City itself and for our country, particularly with respect to its European perspective. This perspective is directly linked to commitments and obligations, among which the guarantee of the inviolability of the fundamental rights of minorities is a priority.

It is known that the Patriarchate and we personally have from the very beginning voiced our opinion vigorously and directly, clearly and sincerely, in favor of Turkey's European perspective. We have been criticized for this. We persevere, however. And we wait!

It is also known, or at least it ought to be known and respected, that the Ecumenical Patriarchate, as of its nature and mission, has competencies and obligations far wider than this city's and this country's borders. The universality of our Patriarchate does not result from some conventional latter-day regulations, and it is not a bare title, lacking substance. It is a matter of ecclesiastical substance and order, far and above simple human measures and weights. Precisely for this reason, the refusal of our Patriarchate's universality equals a negation and a violation of a fundamental element of our religious freedom. Each person holding, as we do today, the office of the archbishop of Constantinople, the New Rome, is of course primarily the leader of the local church. Each bishop, however, is at the same time a bishop of the catholic, or universal, Church—namely, of the Church in its totality and not merely of a portion of the

Church.[39] And even for this reason alone, locality and universality are inseparably linked.

Apart from this, though—as is known or ought to be known to all, as we have said—the Ecumenical Patriarchate, precisely because it consists of communities scattered around the globe, in the best interests of which it rightfully discharges its pastoral cares and performs its services, cannot be compared in any way to local religious leaders, respected may they always be. Its nature is of a different order and competency. In addition, the Ecumenical Patriarch, as first in seniority, is bishop of the entire Orthodox Church and has specific, and not random, responsibilities and duties. Our Ecumenical Patriarchate strives day and night in order to respond to continuously proliferating needs and expectations.

Meeting in Istanbul: Past, Present, and Future

This obviously does not mean that we disregard the problems of the City's Greeks—and not only of the Greeks but of all Christians, and not only their problems. Seen from a perspective beyond time and space—that is, from the perspective of eternity—all humans are of course "foreign and alien" in this world. Seen from the perspective of rights and obligations, though, the Greeks in the City are neither foreign nor alien, of course. We are well aware where we come from. We all know the principles and values and the historical heritage we bear. We are aware of where we stand and how we must lead our lives. What is to come might be invisible to man but does not relieve us of our responsibilities for all things present and future. And exactly because of this, we believe in the justification and the particular timeliness and importance of this congress, as we have already indicated.

We are glad to observe that, in expectation of the current congress, scientific research on subjects of vital importance were conducted at the universities of Turkey and Greece, separately or in cooperation. We exalt and praise this last fact, regarding it as especially encouraging as we face the future. The presentation of the results of this research and collaboration, as well as those other notable presentations, will undeniably form a

39. Basic principle in the theology of St. Ignatius of Antioch (c. 50–c.110), author of a series of letters, written on his way to martyrdom in Rome, that deal with ecclesiology, sacraments, and the role of the bishop.

solid foundation for an objective dialogue of truth, responsibilities, and perspectives.

Congresses such as this, which have high scientific standards, have no reason to hide the truth and fail to acknowledge the real nature and extent of the problems they encounter. In any case, even if humans are silent, the rocks cry out and the graves echo in sighs. We beg, however, that we act in accordance now with the comportment and advice—which is necessary but not so easy—of Paul, the Apostle of the Nations, whose holy memory we celebrated just yesterday: I continue, he writes, the fight, "forgetting what lies behind and heading to what is to come" (Phil. 3.13).

We say this addressing in particular the former residents of the City, the beloved children of the Great Mother Church who have come from the lands of their dispersion, from all over the globe. As we have said in another relevant context, the Mother Church receives and welcomes all "from North and South, East and West" who have come here to their spiritual hearth, as to another Zion. You come here just as the myrrh-bearing women hastened to the grave of the rabbi—not, of course, to carry sepulchral incenses to the Mother Church, as they did, but to become once again martyrs of our lives in crucifixion and resurrection. The Mother Church always remembers her dispersed offspring, at each moment and occasion of their and her life; she remembers them in her joy and her sorrow.

The emotions are common: Martyrdom. Witness and sorrow. Nonetheless, let us discourse and fight "with words of truth, the power of God and the weapon of justice" (2 Cor. 6.7). Our aim is the future. And the future can only be common—common for all the inhabitants in this country, common for the whole of humanity. And so the point at issue is, first and foremost, the common construction of this future.

The Greeks remaining here have, as do all other minorities, a right to this future. And we hope that any state, in planning its future with sobriety and sound judgment, far from fundamentalism and preconceptions, far from transient and futile expediencies, will let the light shine on its plans, as the fruit of light are "kindness, justice and peace" (Eph. 5.9).

With this expectation, we thank and congratulate once again everyone. We bless this congress, and we look forward to its beneficial results. Welcome to the city of cities, your city, our land—here, where everything silently testifies in an evocative manner the presence throughout the centuries of innumerable Greeks who lived and excelled, who were glorified and humbled. And who, apart from humans, set their future in the hands of God, while working for this future with hope, faith and optimism.

Youth and Leadership: I

Message to the Sixteenth World Council of the World Alliance of YMCAs in Durban, South Africa, July 10, 2006.

It is with great pleasure that we address and greet the participants of the Sixteenth World Council of YMCAs gathered in Durban for the Youth Council and the World Council. The invaluable outreach and manifold work of your councils have stood for many years as a testimony to human cooperation and fraternal concern for an admirable development of a spirit of fellowship throughout the world. Therefore, it is most appropriate that you celebrate this sense of community through the theme of Ubuntu, which will define the parameters of your deliberations and worship.[40]

There are three simple yet fundamental principles that I would like to like to convey to the delegates and members of your historical gathering in relation to your vital theme of Ubuntu. All three of these principles are derived from the Christian tradition, particularly as it has been experienced and expressed in the Eastern Orthodox Church over the last twenty centuries.

First, *the very concept of God*, and the corresponding concept of humankind, is deeply rooted in a spirit of communion and fellowship. The God of the early Christians was a God understood as Trinity, as a community of divine beings fully sharing the divine nature. It is this "being as communion" that is also reflected in the understanding of human nature. Humankind is created for fellowship and relationship. The Greek word for person, *prosopon*, precisely indicates a human being "looking toward" and "facing another human being."

Second, *the basic teaching of both the Hebrew Covenant and the New Testament* is the command, embraced and conveyed by Jesus Christ himself, that "you shall love your neighbor as yourself" (see Lev. 19.18 and

40. Derived from the Bantu languages of South Africa, Ubuntu is a classical African concept and the basis for a humanist or moral philosophy that focuses on togetherness and cooperation.

Mk. 12.30). In fact, Jesus claims that we should adhere to this command to the very end, even unto death. What few people know, however, is that this teaching does not in any way signify that we ought to love others as much as we love ourselves. The rabbinical interpretation of this commandment implies that we ought to love our neighbor because our neighbor reveals our true self. In others, we learn to be ourselves. By loving others, we become more human. As your theme rightly denotes, "a person is a person only through other persons."

Finally, religious people often wonder what *heaven or hell* might resemble. In fact, the Eastern Orthodox Church understands heaven and hell again in terms of the presence or absence of fellowship and community. There is a beautiful story told by one of the early desert fathers, St. Macarius of Egypt.[41] When asked what heaven and hell were like, Macarius responded by comparing heaven to the ability to look someone in the eyes; to do so, as he believed, was to taste heaven even in this life. By contrast, he said, hell is like being bound back-to-back with another person for all eternity without ever being able to look at that person in the eyes. How many people experience this kind of hell in our world!

In our day and age, when poverty threatens the lives of so many human beings, when violence tears apart families and nations, when war deprives so many of life and peace, and when environmental pollution destroys the natural world for generations to come, fellowship and community are the only way forward. Ubuntu is truly our only hope for the preservation of life and peace in the world, both among people and with the natural environment. The moment we turn our eyes away from each other, the moment we remove our hand from holding the hand of the other, the very fabric of life and peace are torn apart.

I would like to leave you with this final image. Close your eyes and imagine this picture. Remember that, when your hands are clenched tightly, you cannot share your wealth with your brother and sister. When your hands are clenched tightly, you cannot hold the hand of your neighbor. And when your hands are clenched tightly, you cannot stretch them out in prayer to the Almighty, who is the source of all life and peace.

---

41. An Egyptian hermit, Macarius the Great (300–91) is one of the renowned and pioneer desert fathers. See John Chryssavgis, *In the Heart of the Desert: The Spirituality of the Desert Fathers and Mothers*, rev. ed. (Bloomington, Ind.: World Wisdom Books, 2008).

Youth and Leadership: II

Address to the Young Business Leaders of Istanbul, October 15, 2000.

We are pleased to welcome you and acknowledge your great achievements as young business leaders from various countries who value cooperation, progress, and peace. We meet in a historic place at the crossroads of history, of East and West, North and South, where great civilizations have passed and prospered. The countries you represent, and particularly the two neighboring countries of Turkey and Greece, have been swept up in momentous historical changes. We soon come to realize that the course of history can change in a heartbeat, just as you all well know that the circumstances and decisions in the world of commerce, trade, and technology can make or break fortunes.

We still hear the crash of empires old and new in the Balkans and see renewed conflict in the Middle East. The demise of communism has brought new freedom and the promise of peace but also confusion and economic dislocation. All institutions are under scrutiny and found wanting. Human beings still yearn for peace, hope, and direction. God alone, in whose image we are made, shows us the way. In our sacred scriptures, he holds out hope and the promise that we will walk in the light of the city of God and that the kings of the earth will bring the glory and honor of the nations into it (see Rev. 21.24–26).

We believe that true leadership emerges from increased knowledge and through overcoming hardships. If you truly are decision makers, then you are truly leaders. The fact that you are young, idealistic, and dedicated women and men is a great encouragement and comfort to us. Indeed, we believe that you as young leaders have arrived at this moment in history, at this strategic international crossroads of religions and cultures, for a purpose. Whether in times of peace or in times of conflict, our roles may be dissimilar, but certainly our ends are not. All of us here present aim to fulfill the promise of peace to humankind, respect for our environment, and stability to our societies.

New Leadership and the Promise of Peace

We may speak of prophecies; you may bargain for profits, but together we strive for peace and prosperity so that all women and men may realize their vocation and at the same time find hope and belief. Make no mistake; you have a vocation. Leadership emerges from all sectors of society. And real leaders move ahead of public opinion, because they have vision and insight. As a spiritual leader, we must add to this that all true leaders also must seek guidance in their judgments, and we all know from whom this guidance must come.

Again, in our scriptures God tells us:

> Do not forget my law, but let your heart keep my commands. . . . Let not mercy and truth forsake you; bind them around your neck, write them on the tablets of your heart. . . . Trust in the Lord with all your heart, and lean not on your own understanding. In all ways, acknowledge Him, and He shall direct your paths. (Prov. 3.1, 5–6)

In your busy lives, give heed to the deep voice within you; seek wisdom and understanding; be sensitive to your loved ones, and love your coworkers and fellow citizens. Work for peace in your societies, and he will direct your paths.

We are heartened by the recent developments toward amity and cooperation between Turkey and Greece. In the past, both countries have needlessly suffered and sacrificed economic prosperity and environmental improvement because of a lack of cooperation and a misallocation of resources. Together, Turkey and Greece can lead the entire region into a new era of greatness, achieved not by conquest but by commerce. Especially now that rapid globalization wrought by new communications technologies is bringing the world closer together, requiring innovative approaches to commerce and trade, these two countries have a unique opportunity to make trade flourish between here and the Balkans and Eastern Europe.

We have said before on a similar occasion that, instead of seeing ships sailing off to battle, destruction, and loss of life, let us see ships destined for missions of peacekeeping, economic stability, and a higher spiritual life. Let us cross the Bosphorus and Aegean on vessels of goodwill, cooperation, and trust; and let us open our borders and extend the European Union. All have a role to play. Courageous initiatives by political leaders are critical, but they are only the beginning. You, as young, prominent, and promising business leaders, are able to effect true rapprochement, for you are in a position to calculate the real cost of keeping enmities alive, all the while demonstrating how to direct competitive energies into free markets and nation building.

Just think of what could be achieved in this part of the world if the creative energies of Turkey and Greece were to be unleashed. Just think of what could be built here astride the East and the West—a model and a marvel for the world to behold! This can be achieved with your brilliant minds, your able hands, and your open hearts.

In doing so we do not forget our history, for we are heirs to a rich and varied past. Here the ancient Christian Church took shape and spread throughout the *oikoumene*; from here Islam flourished into a world civilization. Whether we are Christians, Muslims, or Jews, we are children of God, and our efforts as peacemakers will be blessed and rewarded by the one God whom we all share as our common Creator. We will continue our own efforts for peace, for the stewardship of our precious environment—God's own creation. We in our own vocation will continue to teach, edify, and serve. We will continue to preach and work in the spirit of divine love.

It is to you, young leaders present among us here today in this holy center of Orthodoxy, that we look. We look to you to do your part in creating structures of peace and cooperation. It is in you, our dear friends, that we place our hope and trust for a brighter economic future, one that would complement the spiritual growth pursued by all men and women of faith. We invite you to join us in this venture, which we see both as a sound business proposition and a critical source for spiritual welfare and wholeness.

Youth and Leadership: III

Address to the members of the Turkish International Model at the United Nations Conference, hosted by the Üsküdar American Academy, Istanbul, December 6, 2001.

It is with great love that we offer words here today as you assemble together for the purpose of understanding the modern world and promoting peace and cooperation among its nations. It is for us a great happiness to be among God's blessed youth, and hence a cause of great grief to be unable, because of prior engagements, to directly enjoy the delightful presence of young people such as yourselves from around the world. We wish you every success and enlightenment from God during the days of this conference.

Indeed, the Model United Nations Conference speaks directly to the contributions and efforts of young people. Your own efforts to promote peace and cooperation among the nations of our world are reflected here, as you gather together to model the United Nations, an organization that itself has been recognized for its efforts to promote peace all over the world. In so doing, you are challenged to understand the global implications of policies that promote peace, reconciliation, and tolerance. You are faced with the responsibility to stress cooperation in the face of conflict. In short, you are presented with the awesome task of heralding the message of God, whose desire it is that all human beings love one another as brothers and sisters, united as his children in his abundant love and mercy.

We live, beloved children, in times of crisis and turbulence. Our world faces new global challenges, where life and peace on our planet are jeopardized by humanity itself. Life is also endangered by the degradation of the environment. Pollution and misuse of scarce natural resources put into doubt the capacity of our planet to sustain and reproduce life. The work of building a sustainable peace is threatened by ongoing conflicts and war. We rediscover day by day with astonishment that, as global as our world may be, our views of others have only become more isolated and confused. Today, it is more apparent than ever that human beings need first to look inward, to explore the abyss of their own existences before conquering the outer world that surrounds them.

This not only brings uneasiness and anxiety but also gives us opportunity for self-awareness, responsible decision-making, and thoughtful action. Adults and especially the youth of our world must realize that any and all acts of wrongdoing will influence and change the lives of many generations to come and literally of the whole of the creation for successive years, decades if not centuries. The converse of this principle is also true. The good that we do today will have lasting effects for the peace of the world tomorrow.

Your gathering shines forth as an example of youth's role in addressing the gigantic problems of our times and in guiding and teaching others.

Each and every one of you is called on to be a force for change, a defender of good, a spiritual leader, regardless of age. Therefore, "let no one despise your youth, but be an example to the believers in word, in conduct, in love, in spirit, in faith, in purity" (1 Tim. 4.12). It is the wordless example—of cooperation, understanding, and goodness—you give that will inspire others to walk the same path.

Your work, owing to its very particular nature, goes beyond the usual limits of everyday life and inscribes in its dimension the future course of relations between peoples, races, languages, nations, and religions and their cooperation and harmonic symbiosis in love, peace, and communication. Contact in love will instill in each individual, despite the confusion and uncertainty of our times, the beauty of human relationship with God, our fellow human being, and the creation. For that is our goal, from youth to maturity to old age—to become increasingly holy, to be pure in mind and body, to live by truth, love, and kindness.

Life and peace are much more than a single process of continuous birth and death, pacification and fight. They are the result of a free will to resist natural and moral corruption, and to resurrect. It is our choice—indeed, it is your choice, beloved children—to create or to destroy, to safeguard or to give away, to die or to live. May your efforts result in good and in the salvation of the creation, so that the name of God may be praised. Because of his great love, he "made every nation of men that they should inhabit the whole face of earth" (Acts 17.26).

Youth and Leadership: IV

Opening address at the Second International Orthodox Youth Conference, Istanbul, July 11, 2007. The First International Orthodox Youth Conference was organized, again in Istanbul, on the occasion of the millennial celebrations in 2000, the first time Orthodox youth were assembled at the invitation of the Ecumenical Patriarchate from every church and from all over the world.

This past summer, almost one thousand young men and women from all over the world attended the Second International Orthodox Youth Conference organized by the Ecumenical Patriarchate and held in Istanbul from July 11 to 16, 2007. The general theme of the conference was

"Members of the Church—Citizens of the World." Delegates to the worldwide gathering represented Orthodox churches, monastic communities, theological schools, ecclesiastical seminaries, youth associations, and cultural foundations as well as local churches, church groups, and ecumenical organizations. Indeed, they arrived from all continents: from north and south, east and west. The conference provided an invaluable forum for mutual acquaintance, self-expression, and open dialogue on fundamental issues—both of regional interest and of universal concern—to Orthodox youth.

It was a particular joy for our Modesty to witness the vibrancy of Orthodox young people throughout the world, who exhibited a sense of profound respect for traditional values and at the same time a sincere desire to contribute in a substantial and critical way to their society as Orthodox Christians. This is why one of our primary goals was to underscore the ecumenical dimension of our Patriarchate, which is not confined to national borders, linguistic barriers, or ethnic problems but rather embraces all peoples within its pastoral responsibility and care.

The Ecumenical Patriarchate is characterized by spiritual prayerfulness and a vigilant attentiveness to the spiritual needs of all of its faithful in a manner that reflects contemporary awareness and responsiveness. It was a matter of urgency that we remind those gathered of their personal place and particular role as young people within the Body of Christ, each according to the unique talent and specific gift with which he or she has been entrusted. As citizens of the heavenly kingdom and yet at the same time as citizens of the present world, young people are called neither to identify with nor to reject the world unconditionally, instead assuming a critical stance in the world, according to the standard imposed by "our citizenship in heaven" (Phil. 3.20).

In this spirit, delegates heard a variety of speakers on a diverse range of topics, such as liturgy and mission, doctrine and spiritual life, personhood and culture, education and holiness, ecology and economy, globalization and secularization, human rights and freedom, poverty and hunger, technology and sociology, sexuality and asceticism, family and health, entertainment and information, interfaith and interchurch relations, communication and ecumenical dialogue. For, if Orthodox Christianity is to be true to its authentic tradition and reflective of its spiritual ethos, it cannot be isolated from contemporary social and moral issues. Moreover, it cannot be disconnected from the modern world, before which it is called to bear witness in a spirit of openness, respectful of the particularity of others and tolerant of the differences among races and creeds.

Members of the Church—Citizens of the World

We observed with particular satisfaction the confidence and dynamism with which young delegates regarded themselves as constructive and contributing members of the Church. As they demonstrated in the conclusions of the conference, they possess an earnest desire to participate and cooperate in the pastoral, communal, and liturgical life of the Church; in no way do they wish to be marginalized or viewed simply as "the future of the Church." Indeed, as their spiritual leader and ecclesiastical head, we are convinced not only that young people constitute the hope of the Church but also that, in a way that mirrors the energy of the Holy Spirit and the life-giving flow of Christ's blood, they constitute the necessary force that sustains the vibrancy and relevance of the institutional Church. For we are all "members of one another" (Rom. 12.5); each of us constitutes a precious stone in the Church, where Christ is the cornerstone (Eph. 2.20). No person is ever alone in the community of the Church and the communion of saints.

We reminded the young delegates that, just as the Ecumenical Patriarchate is neither jurisdictional nor national, so also the Orthodox Church is neither institutional nor confessional but in fact the fundamental canonical expression of the ecumenical dimension of the universal gospel message. While Christians are—in the words of our Lord during his high-priestly prayer at Gethsemane (Jn. 17)—not "of the world." Nevertheless, we are "in the world" and called to serve as "the salt of the earth" (Mt. 5.13) and "the light of the world" (Mt. 5.14) "for the life of the world" (Jn. 6.51). We live in a globalized world that has done away with distance. This, however, is a double-edged sword.

The question remains: What is the role of Christians in a globalized world? The answer is that we must not become secularized or identify with the world. We must use, with discretion and reason, for the glory of God, the instruments that it offers us. Let us not forget that the majority of humankind really does not have even an idea of Christ and his Gospel.

Is it not tragic that the so-called "golden arches" of McDonald's are better known in the modern world than the sign of the Cross?

As the light and salt of the world, we are called—indeed, we are commanded—to touch and transform every element of this life. Christians are not to avoid or reject this world but rather to assume it in its entirety, renouncing only the reality of evil and sin. There is nothing in this world that is either evil in itself or neutral in its essence. Everything has been created good and beautiful by God, who also became incarnate for our sake. In this respect, then, God is at the heart of all things, maintaining and sustaining the whole world. As Christians, we affirm that God is in all people and all things yet also above and beyond all. We repudiate any form of dualism whereby independence is attributed to the prince of darkness or the material creation is regarded as either evil or unreal. We are called, then, not to conform to but to transform the world within which we live.

Our role as Christians is precisely the role of the priest in liturgy—that is, our obligation and responsibility is that of assuming every aspect of this life, transforming it into the body and blood of Jesus Christ, into opportunity for communion with God, with other people, and with the natural environment. There is no person or group in society or on the planet that should be either deplored or despised in this priestly task. Similarly, there is no dimension or detail in this life or in this world that should be either ignored or omitted in this eucharistic task. At conclusion of the Second International Orthodox Youth Conference, we were able to repeat the closing words of the Divine Liturgy of St. John Chrysostom, which we celebrated in the Patriarchal Cathedral of St. George: "Let us depart in peace." It is our fervent prayer that Orthodox youth throughout the world may share and spread that peace—the "peace that surpasses all understanding" (Phil. 4.7), the peace experienced by the saints of the Church, the peace that they tasted during this splendid gathering—everywhere they go and to everyone that they encounter. This will be the source of true joy in their lives and the source of abundant life (Jn. 10.10) for their world.

5

Interfaith Dialogue: Interreligious and Intercultural Dimensions

Interfaith Dialogue

Message to the Interfaith Dialogue Assembly, Ankara, Turkey, November 25, 1998.

We wish to offer our warm and wholehearted greetings to each one of you, the beloved representatives of the major religions, who are distinguished because you have been endowed with minds of the highest caliber but even more so because you have been endowed with superior hearts, you who are gathered here to meet and get to know each other in a more intimate manner and to discuss the problems that emerge because of the coexistence in the world of various religions. Dialogue and conversation—which is necessary for dialogue's being carried out—are a necessary precondition of mutual understanding, and mutual understanding is a precondition of mutual trust as well as of the ability to cooperate and to coexist. With a sense of satisfaction we welcome and applaud this initiative for dialogue, as we do the breadth of the participants and the breadth of perspectives of those who invited us here, hoping and being certain that we will meet their expectations by having a dialogue of the highest caliber.

The primary issue that we must address is absolutism. It is well known that every religion asserts that it holds within its belief system the absolute truth about God and the world, the latter including also humanity. Furthermore, it is also well known that God is the absolute being—in other words, that to which all pure attributes belong and from which all evil attributes are entirely absent. We believe that all here present agree with this.

It is also known that God is one, as we all confess, even though we Christians see and confess the one God in Trinity. All of us, therefore, should have this perception of the one, immutable, and perfect God. Yet it is evident that, for the adherents of one religion, the perception of God and the world differs from the perception that the adherents of another faith community have. This can mean nothing other than that we the "observers" of God and of the world differ from one another. In other words, each of our perceptions is not simply determined by the object observed (if we can even ever say such a thing about God) but by the condition of the observer. The variation of opinions, therefore, does not hinge on the relativity of the true Being and his creation but on the relativity of us, the observers.

The admission of this truth elicits from each one of us personally the Socratic confession of our ignorance—in other words, the humble admission that we speak in absolute terms about truths beyond our intellectual capabilities. Because of this, due to our scientific and personal responsibility to the truth, we are obligated to be open, at the very least, to the views of others, in order that we might not arrive at the same conclusion as did Wittgenstein (in his *Tractatus Logico-Philosophicus*)—which is that we must maintain total silence about God, who is beyond our intellectual capabilities.[1]

We most certainly believe and consider it a given that the truth is singular, as is God, that on every occasion only a single sentence expresses the totality of this truth. We also recognize and believe, however, that this singular sentence has not yet been revealed totally to anyone, even if at any given moment it is repeated by thousands and vociferously. In other words, this sentence has not been apprehended by anyone in its magnificent fullness, even if it is uncontainable and it fills the universe. This, we repeat, is due to our own relativity, to the limitation of the perspicacity

1. Ludwig Wittgenstein (1889–1951), an Austrian-British philosopher of logic and language. His *TLP* was published in 1922.

of us humble human beings, in whose noetic framework the knowledge of the infinite and absolute God cannot be contained. To borrow from the Apostle Paul, who was taken up into the third heaven:

> At present we see only puzzling reflections in a mirror, but one day we shall see face to face. (1 Cor. 13.12)

Truth and Absolutism

God himself has revealed about himself, as it is written in scripture, which is revered by all, that "no one shall see my face and live" (Ex. 33.20). Certainly, scripture here does not speak literally but rather metaphorically, because it is not proper to imagine God as being like us. Consequently, we understand the face of God as being his true nature and his hypostasis. Therefore, we do not know God, or rather we do not know God in his totality. However, we know a few things about God, and from this our differences result; because someone understands one thing while another comprehends something else, and many times—so we must admit—we confuse our imperfect knowledge by conforming it to our desires, and we fashion in ourselves the image of God analogous to our condition, as the ancients also stated. What is worse is that we occasionally desire to impose on our fellow human beings this image of God, who has been refracted through the prism of our personality and deformed, as being the only true and correct one. Moreover, it is not uncommon that we assert without verification that God blesses our activities, even if this simply expresses our own desires and not the reality. Or, as is stated in the Qur'an, "Some falsely refer to the Lord, knowingly" (chapter 3, verse 78).

As religious leaders, responsible before God for expressing divine truth in whatever degree we are cognizant of it—this means consciously rejecting the projection of our personal tastes as being the will of God—we are obligated to humbly accept that we respect our fellow human beings and that we allow them to traverse their own personal path to God. This is necessary and the command of God.

This respect on the part of one person toward the religious life of another is a foundational responsibility of each of us and a fundamental presupposition of peaceful coexistence and good cooperation between people. Moreover, we are able to assert that we do not have evidence from which emerges the idea that God is pleased by the use of coercion or deception to win converts. On the contrary, from the Bible the idea that emerges is of the human being, who is created by God in his image and after his likeness, adorned with the divine characteristic of personal free will; for it would be contradictory for us to accept that, on the one hand, God endowed us with a freedom of conscience while, on the other hand, to accept that he is pleased by the use of force or deception to strangle this same freedom.

Consequently, whatever the modern and for the most part secularized human person projects as his cultural achievement in relation to the inviolability of religious consciousness and faith is in essence a result of the teaching of the three major religions, which are conversing here today. Dialogue between these religions, but initially personal dialogue between those who, as Moses, seek the true face of God, is the only God-pleasing path for transmitting the truth from the adherent of one religion to the adherent of the other. "Truth emanates from God" (Qur'an, chapter III, verse 60), and it is revealed to the saints according to their capacity to receive it.

Each of us offers an encouraging word to someone who asks for a hopeful message about himself, his faith, and his faith experience or about friends whom he trusts. This announcement about dialogue is, we believe, the method most pleasing to God for the transmission of faith. We read in the Qur'an: "Say: Truth emanates from your God, he who so desires, let him believe; he who does not so desire, let him remain in faithlessness" (Qur'an, chapter XVIII, verse 29). We read in the gospel: "Whoever wishes to come, follow me" (Mt. 16.24). And we read in the Old Testament: "When in the beginning God created the human race, He left them free to make their own decisions" (Sir. 15.19). How can we even think to overturn all these things by imposing our faith on others?

Dialogue is the only path pleasing to God. This is because God always and in many ways dialogues with us, seeking the free offering of our heart and not our forced presentation before him. Let us offer our own hearts to Him and not the hearts of others.

Relations between Christians and Muslims: I

In the emirate of Bahrain, September 25, 2000.

We wholeheartedly thank Your Highness, the emir of Bahrain, for the invitation to visit the historic and progressive emirate of Bahrain. Indeed, this visit gives us great joy, since we now have the opportunity to communicate with you in a personal way. Furthermore, we express our joy because we find ourselves in the midst of many good and faithful friends here in the blessed emirate of Bahrain. Indeed, the progress and prosperity seen in this hospitable land creates a most pleasant surprise for the visitor. The same feelings were also our experience. It would seem that these signs of prosperity are the result of a creative and proactive government with policies that benefit the people of Bahrain, who are blessed by God, without whom nothing can succeed.

Of course, this is not the first time that the Ecumenical Patriarchate is conducting a dialogue with our beloved Muslim brothers. As is known, the Ecumenical Patriarchate is located in Turkey, a country predominantly Muslim but with policies strongly rooted in neutrality toward and tolerance of other religions. Furthermore, with the cooperation of notable Muslim organizations, we have organized many academic encounters between Christians and Muslims. For example, the well-known symposium called the Academic Exchange between Christians and Muslims, cosponsored by the Royal Academy of Jordan (Al-Abbait Foundation) and the Orthodox Center of the Ecumenical Patriarchate in Chambésy, Switzerland, has become an institution of great success. In fact, this symposium has been successfully conducted nine times so far, with the participation of important individuals from both sides and with discussions of a high caliber on subjects of common interest.

Moreover, we have supported in the past and support in the present every effort for a peaceful dialogue between the followers of both faiths. In order to contribute as much as possible to reconciliation and peace among peoples internationally, we have traveled to various parts of the world. We have also given witness to our conviction that peaceful coexistence and cooperation between Christians and Muslims is both desirable and pleasing to God.

We say that this is pleasing to God because, according to both the gospel, referred to by the Qur'an as a luminous book (chapter 3, verse

181), and the Qur'an itself, "peace is a great good" (chapter 4, verse 127). According to the Gospel account, when Jesus Christ was born, the angels proclaimed, "Glory to God in the highest and on earth peace among men" (Lk. 2.14). Jesus Christ also blessed the peacemakers (Mt. 5.9) and often addressed a greeting of peace to his disciples. This same greeting is customary to this very day among the peoples of that region.

It is true that during the long history of coexistence of Christians and Muslims, especially in the land of the eastern Mediterranean and the Near East, there have been periods of tension and clashes, the gospel and Qur'an verses about peace notwithstanding. This, however, was due mainly to human weakness and not to God's approval of war as an acceptable condition; for, even when God tolerates war, he does so to enforce justice and peace, not because the condition of war is pleasing to him.

The Primacy of Religious Freedom and Peace

In any event, we believe and have proclaimed, during the Interreligious Conference of the Bosphorus, that war carried on in the name of religion is war against religion, because God is benevolent and merciful and does not delight in bloodshed.[2] Although there are situations when war may in fact be unavoidable, the truth is clearly taught in both the gospel and the Qur'an that God enjoins peace. For example, it is written in the Qur'an that "he who murders one who has not murdered or destroyed, is a murderer of the human race" (chapter 5, verse 35). Elsewhere it is written: "Blessed are the peacemakers, because they shall be called the sons of God" (Mt. 5.9).

All good deeds of humanity succeed during periods of peace, while many disasters occur during periods of war. In view of all the above, it becomes clear that God is pleased by reconciliation, mutual understanding, and peaceful cooperation. However, this presupposes a mutual goodwill, which is dictated by both the gospel, through the commandment of love, and by the Qur'an through the commandment of doing good deeds. Indeed, as the Qur'an itself proclaims: "Christians are those most disposed to love the faithful; and this is because there are among them priests

2. For the full text, see Chapter 6, "Major Declarations: Public Proclamations."

and monks, and because they are not proud" (chapter 5, verse 85). Certainly, this does not pertain to all those bearing the name Christian but only to those pious Christians who follow the commandments of God. Elsewhere we read in the Qur'an: "All the followers of the scriptures do not share the same qualities; some have pure hearts" (chapter 3, verse 109). And further: "There are among the People of the Book, some who can be entrusted with a talent [*kintar*] which they will return to you intact; there are others who, however, if they are not forced to do so, they will not return to you even the deposit of one dinar" (chapter 3, verse 68).

Those who are Christians only in name the Qur'an repeatedly castigates for callousness, injustice, and irresponsibility. Because of their inability to follow the commandments of God, they have proven to be much more cruel and unjust against their own fellow Christians, forcing the latter to seek the protection of the Muslims. This indicates that the content of the faith is not judged by the behavior of those who are faithful in name only, whether Christians or Muslims, but by the teachings of the faith and by its authentic application by those who fear and love God.

As the first among equal hierarchs of the Orthodox Church, we believe, as it is also found in the Qur'an, that "religion is not imposed" (chapter 2, verse 257) but depends on the free will of the human being. We respect an individual's choice with regard to his or her faith, and we do not proselytize anyone, nor do we participate in dialogues between Christians and our brother Muslims in order to convince them to accept our own faith. After all, there is no such intention directed toward us by the Muslim participants in these dialogues.

We conduct these dialogues in order for it to become more widely understood that it is not religious differences that create conflicts among humanity. If indeed the cause of human conflict was the differences between religions, then there should not be any conflict among the faithful of the same religion. However, there are plenty of conflicts and wars even among faithful of the same religion. At times, misinterpretations of the holy scriptures of a religion have been created in order to justify human pursuits and in order to attract the faithful to the support of a particular leader. However, the individual who respects God should be careful not to be fooled but to remain steadfast in virtue, mercy, forgiveness, and compassion.

We express our joy and satisfaction that among Muslim people nonfanatical views and especially the principle of consent prevail, the latter being the means through which freedom of religious conscience becomes respected. Of course, we recognize that, among Christian denominations as well as among Muslims of all persuasions, there are minorities who espouse different views. But we do not give up hope that the evangelical gospel of consent, reconciliation, and peaceful cooperation will prevail. For this is what the Apostle Paul refers to when he writes: "If possible, so far as it depends upon you, live peaceably with all" (Rom. 12.18). The equivalent invitation is found in the Qur'an: "O you people of the Book! Let us unite our efforts in the principle which is common to all of us: that we will not worship anyone except God." This gospel of consent, reconciliation, and peaceful cooperation, if accepted by all, will lead to the consolidation of peace and the prosperity of all people, so that each one can worship the one God as he wishes and, together, be able to cooperate for the common good.

As for us Orthodox Christians who have lived for centuries in the same land with our brother Muslims, we are possessed by this disposition. Especially and personally, we, as the first bishop of the Orthodox Church, continue to work for the prevailing of this spirit, which is shared also by pious Christians of other churches. Related to this was the signing of the Ecumenical Charter by the various Christian denominations of Europe, which includes the following in its ninth clause: "We support interreligious dialogue in order to encourage a closer cooperation among all the people of Europe"—indeed, we would add "and all the world." Especially, we feel the existence of a special relationship between us and the people of the Old Testament. For this reason, we support the dialogue with Judaism, as well as with Islam and other religions, in a spirit of respect and esteem, and we work toward mutual understanding.

For our part, then, we promise and pledge that we will

- recognize and protect freedom of conscience and religion for all of humanity;
- recognize the right of every person to seek the truth and project that truth according to his or her conscience;
- propose, encourage, and support meetings, discussions, and communications among communities that have different views about religion and the world.

In so doing, we separate religion from politics, and we seek to inspire in those politicians found in every religion a divine, merciful, and charitable disposition toward all humanity. If such a genuine spirit of openness and willingness exists within us, then the unavoidably emerging differences among people will be easily resolved.

Relations between Christians and Muslims: II

Address delivered at the University of Qatar, October 16, 2002.

It is with deep joy and satisfaction that our Modesty appears before you. We are grateful to His Highness, the emir of Qatar, because he has nobly invited us to this historic and honored country so that we can participate in a dialogue about the interreligious discussions that the Ecumenical Patriarchate has sponsored for some years now, mainly between the three monotheistic religions, and especially between Islam and the Orthodox Christian Church, in which we are the first hierarch among equals, according to the order of seniority.

We therefore express our warm thanks for this kind invitation and for your asking to hear our views on this subject. This university space reminds us of the importance of objective, dispassionate, and attested knowledge, which is taught in the universities and is the presupposition for right judgment on any subject; and, even more so, it reminds us of the most serious subjects—cooperation among believers of the various religions and the peace among them.

It is well known to everyone that we live in a world that acknowledges that there is one God. Each human being proceeds in his life bearing in mind the teachings of his ancestors concerning God and of the environment in which he was raised. Through the contemporary possibilities of communication, even the remotest inhabitants of earth have come to understand that people in different lands entertain a variety of perceptions about God. Nevertheless, God is one, and people ought not to have different perceptions of him, just as there ought not to exist different perceptions about each of us, given that each of us is a singular, unique person.

It is indisputable, however, that human beings entertain different perceptions about each other and about the person of God. This surely does not mean that each of us exists in as many different iterations as the perceptions that others have of him or, by the same token, that there are as many Gods as there are perceptions of him, or that God reveals himself differently to every human being. It means that the eyes and above all the hearts of human beings are different and that, as a result, they see one and the same object differently. Let us give an example: If one and the same person happens to be loved by one person and hated by another, this person will be beautiful, sweet, and pleasant for the one who loves him but repulsive and ugly for the one who hates him.

What should happen? Should we ignore those whose perceptions of persons, God, and existing things are different from our own? Whose opinion matters more? What is the objective criterion of the truth, so that we can determine that it must be imposed over another, since each of us believes that he possesses the fullness of truth. If we allow anyone to impose his perception on others, then surely, by the same logic, the others will desire to impose their own perceptions on him, and we will arrive at the degenerate state of the European Hundred Years War—from the eleventh to the nineteenth centuries—between Catholics and Protestants, a war whose victims numbered in the hundreds of thousands.

Clashing Creeds—Common Cause

It should be noted here that differences of perception exist not only between the religions—for instance, between Islam, Christianity, and Judaism—but also within each of them. For example, Christianity has three great groups, Orthodoxy, Roman Catholicism, and Protestantism, but even within these groupings there are various subdivisions. Islam has been divided differently, as you well know, and Judaism has its own divisions.

All the adherents of these various creeds, and we ourselves who entertain our own convictions each one individually, have been placed by God on the planet earth—each of us in his place, of course—where there is usually one dominant faith, but we often find the coexistence of adherents of different faiths in the same place. What should we do in light of the fact that we do not agree? Should we let the stronger impose his views on the weaker by force, thus making power the criterion of truth? However, the Qur'an says that religion is not something imposed (chapter 2, verse 257) and the gospel says that he who freely wants to should follow Jesus, which means that violence against one's will is unacceptable.

In addition, history and common experience teach that the man who finds himself closer to God and his truth is often deprived of human material power. As a well-known poet of the Islamic tradition puts it:

> The man of God is a king that wears a humble garment. The man of God is a treasure inside a ruin. (Jalal-ad-Din Muhammad Rumi)[3]

Since, then, material power is neither a criterion of the truth nor a means for establishing it, we need to find a way of avoiding power confrontations. The desired way is, in our view, that of rational discourse, which is exchanged in discussions and dialogue. Rational discourse and discussion is an important gift of God to man. God constantly discourses with man. He addresses him through the silent rationality of his creatures, through the rational discourse of the prophets and the saints, through the words of the wise, and through each man's conscience. Human beings constantly converse with each other on various subjects.

Observing this constant dialogue of personal beings, we thought that the hour has come for us, the faithful of different religions, to engage in dialogue of goodwill with each other in order to remove longstanding misunderstandings and tensions and to improve the conditions of our peaceful coexistence. The hour has not yet come to discuss theological subjects or subjects that are purely matters of faith. We are, though, in a position to discuss whatever contributes to mutual understanding, to improvement of the image that each of us has of the other, and to the correction of situations and problems that hinder the cooperation among peoples.

Dialogue and Discussion

It was with this spirit and disposition that we ourselves together with prominent Muslims convened a good number of academic conferences with leading representatives of the two religions and cultural traditions.

---

3. Rumi (1207–73) was an influential Persian poet, jurist, theologian, and mystic. His name derives from the term *Rum*, meaning *Roman*, because he lived in the region once ruled by the Byzantine Empire. See William Chittick, *The Sufi Path of Love: Spiritual Teachings of Rumi* (Albany: SUNY Press, 1983).

The topics that we have discussed so far in these conferences, two of them held in Istanbul, include

- authority and religion
- historic models of the coexistence of Christians and Muslims and the future prospects for such coexistence
- peace and justice in the tradition of the two monotheistic religions
- religious pluralism
- youth and the values of moderation
- education for mutual understanding and cooperation
- the educational systems of Islam and of Christianity
- perspectives on cooperation between Christians and Muslims on the eve of the new millennium
- Christians and Muslims in modern society—images of the other and the meaning of citizenship[4]

There were also other meetings whose scope was broadened by the participation of representatives of the three monotheistic religions. These include the meeting, in Istanbul in 1994, that produced the Bosphorus Declaration, the meeting in Brussels last December, and others.[5] We are able to say that the idea of an interreligious dialogue is becoming more widely acceptable and that the dialogues, without displaying yet visible results in terms of the peace of the world, prepare hearts to accept the peaceful coexistence of human beings of different faiths and constitute an invitation to reject as false the ominous predictions of certain thinkers who claim that a clash of civilizations with a religious basis is inevitable in the future.

In the context of the widening acceptance of the dialogue, we may also mention the invitation extended to our Modesty to visit the Islamic Republic of Iran and the then emirate and now kingdom of Bahrain. We joyfully accepted these invitations, and during our visits we had interesting and useful discussions with political and religious authorities of each

4. In December 2008, at a meeting of the Dialogue between Islam and Christianity, held in Athens, the Ecumenical Patriarchate and the World Islamic Call Society launched the Interreligious Training Partnership Initiative, which began with a seminar in Athens (December 11–13, 2008) for more than sixty-five participants from each of the autocephalous Orthodox churches as well as from Islamic communities of North Africa, Europe, and the Middle East.

5. For the full text, see Chapter 6, "Major Declarations: Public Proclamations."

of these countries. If the interreligious dialogue is going to lead to certain commonly accepted and applicable conclusions, it ought to remain interreligious. This means that the problems of the present time, which are usually political, ought to remain at the margins of the discussions—not because there is lack of interest in their resolution but because when they are charged with religious coloring they become more difficult or impossible to solve, because those trying to solve them are diverted by the irreconcilability of religious differences.

The average man is simultaneously a member of his country and of his religion. It is difficult for him to determine in each case whether a problem is religious or political and whether the solution he should seek is religious or political. Nevertheless, without a proper analysis, no problem is sufficiently and clearly comprehended, and neither are the elements that constitute it, and without clear comprehension and planning no problem is satisfactorily solved. It is obvious that the religious leader is also a member of a particular society and bears on his shoulders a fair amount of common responsibility for its well-being. The religious leader, however, ought to see things much more analytically and to discern when he acts as a citizen in accordance with the ethnic or cultural interest of his country and when he acts as a religious leader, expressing the will of God according to his perception.

This is not always easy to do. Indeed, it becomes extremely difficult when the same person bears the double identity of political and religious leader. And such cases, when one and the same person has to carry both identities, are quite numerous in the history of both of our religions. In Christianity, however, this phenomenon has occurred mainly in the Catholic and the Protestant churches, whereas in the Orthodox Church it was kept to a minimum. The historical memories of political and interstate clashes that occurred under the leadership of persons who were vested with political and religious authority simultaneously make it quite difficult for us today to discern whether they were directed by God in all their activities, as they claimed, or by their own objectives and desires that they regarded, rightly or wrongly, as commandments of God.

All the same, our purpose at this time is not to judge the actions of persons, actions that God and history will judge and about which each of us has his personal opinion, which is to be respected by all. We only wish to stress the great responsibility that we have as religious leaders when we address the faithful as communicators of the will of God. We have this responsibility both before God and before our fellow human beings, and it is one of the greatest responsibilities a man may assume.

Therefore, in our opinion, it is clear that a religious leader ought to form his judgment concerning the will of God without being led astray by criteria that lie outside his religious faith. But even within his religious faith he can find solutions in various classifications on the ladder of perfection that leads to the highest will of God. There are, however, only a few who are willing to observe fully the perfect will of God. For this reason, the merciful and compassionate God has a second will, which can be more easily accepted and observed, and even a third and a fourth, and so on.

On this point, we have said on another occasion that the perfect will of God is that we love each other to the extent that we sacrifice ourselves, the one for the sake of the other. When we cannot do this, however, we ought at least to collaborate with each other. If it happens that we are unable to do even this, then at least we should not fight each other. But if we fail to achieve even this, at least we should observe the international rules of war, such as those relating to the protection of the unarmed, to the care of the wounded and captives, to respect for cultural monuments, and so on. Surely, similar classifications of the will of God exist in most cases in life. The religious leader ought constantly to try to raise the moral level of his people. And that all religious leaders of all religions, and especially those of Christianity and Islam, be invited to assist in raising the moral level of the people is one of the purposes of interreligious dialogue.

At this point, we ought to clarify—as well as to underscore for the purpose of removing any misunderstanding—that we do not wish to see the creation of a universal religion consisting of the common elements of all the existing religions. Also, we do not strive to promote a theological dialogue concerning the truth of each creed, each religion, or the superiority of one or another among them. We strive only to promote mutual understanding of the faithful, cultivation of tolerance, cooperation among them for peaceful activities, respect for the faith of each other, and the creation of a climate of reconciliation and peaceful dialogue on any subject bearing on peaceful relations among human beings.

The Goal of Interreligious Dialogue

On the basis of these general aims, we are able to mention some of the expected results of interreligious dialogue. And first of all we ought to mention the abolition of mistrust, between Christians and Muslims, that has been bequeathed to them to a considerable degree by their rich history. Unfortunately, this mistrust has not yet been extinguished but is rekindled from time to time by authors on both sides. Yet the projection of possible or impossible suspicions regarding the intentions or actions of the one or the other party and the cultivation of a climate of fear renders no benefit but rather inhibits normal life and progress, increases the energy spent unproductively on the anticipation of foreseeable dangers, and disturbs the psychological peace of the citizens. Through dialogue it becomes amply clear that it is not the difference of religion that causes tensions, and so the quest for the true cause or causes is directed to another area of life, where they can be more easily identified and treated.

Second, a better understanding of the way of thinking of the faithful of each religion is achieved through interaction of the faithful of other religions. This removes many misunderstandings and contributes to an appropriate adaptation of behavior of the one toward the other, to the willingness to respect his convictions, and to better collaboration.

And, third, it fosters the mutual acquaintance of the leading representatives of the religions and the development of personal bonds and relations between them—a fact that facilitates further enrichment and cultivation of peaceful relations, given that these leading agents play an important role in the formation of prevailing opinion among the faithful of the religion to which they belong.

Surely there are also other benefits resulting from a well-conducted interreligious dialogue, and, among them, the blessing of God is of no small consequence. Our experience so far gives us optimism and hope. But, of course, no one is ignorant of the fact that such great and important results take time to mature. Nevertheless, no well-intentioned effort remains totally unproductive. For this reason we do not lose our hope, but we struggle with faith and love to promote dialogue, which brings us closer to God, as it brings us closer to one another.

We thank you because you listened with interest and attention to the humble and informational address of our Modesty. We wish you all every blessing from God. We kindly ask that you allow us to close this speech with a few disparate verses from a poem of Jalal-ad-Din Rumi that bears the title "Religious Strife":

> The blind religious practitioners are in a dilemma.
> But the worthy practitioners from the one or the other side stand firm.
> Each side is happy with its way.
> Love alone can stop their strife.
> Love alone brings assistance when you ask for it against their arguments.
> Eloquence is dumbfounded before love:
> It does not dare start a controversy.
> It is like a beautiful bird that has perched on your shoulder and your soul is afraid in case it causes it to fall off:
> You do not dare either to move or to breathe.
> Love is like this bird: It makes you silent.
> It places the lid on the pan that is boiling.

Let us all wish that this love may direct the hearts of human beings. Let it be so.

Relations between Christians and Muslims: III

Message for the Dialogue between Muslims and Christians, Athens, December 10, 2008.

It is with feelings of great joy and love that we salute this seminar being held in the city of Athens to launch the Interreligious Training Partnership Initiative, which aims to provide joint training opportunities for young imams, priests, theologians, and students from their respective Muslim and Christian Orthodox communities of Europe, Central Asia, North Africa, and the Middle East.

This seminar is not only significant but also timely. The occasion of the commemoration of the sixtieth anniversary of the Universal Declaration of Human Rights is a unique opportunity for all members of the human family, the world at large, and religious and political leaders to remember this extraordinary accomplishment. This sixtieth anniversary is a time not only to remember that day in 1948 when nations came together in Paris to sign the Universal Declaration but also to remember the prominent authors of the powerful and relevant acknowledgment, enshrined in the Declaration, that all human beings have fundamental rights and freedom. It includes two important guarantees to the citizen: the democratic framework within which state authority and the civil rights of the individual should function, and the guarantee of religious freedom for all citizens.

As a purely spiritual institution, the Ecumenical Patriarchate of Constantinople embraces a truly global mission that strives to raise and broaden the consciousness of the human family—to foster the understanding that we are all dwelling in the same house. In its most basic sense, this is the meaning of the word *ecumenical*—for the *oikoumene* is the inhabited world, the earth understood as a house in which all peoples, races, tribes, and languages dwell.

This consciousness of the human person as a member of the human family goes well beyond the concepts of the *citizen* or the *individual* in society as a whole. It is deeply rooted in the term *human person*, which is founded on the divine principle that all persons are created in the image and likeness of God. The Christian faith, according to which mankind and the fullness of creation all have their origin in God, stresses the sacred, independent, and intrinsic value of the human person. This is at the very basis of today's dialogue on peace, social justice, and human rights. The principle of the universal value of these ideals, which constitutes the kernel of today's international dialogue, would be inconceivable without the aid of the Christian doctrine of the ontological unity of the human race.

Furthermore, mankind is endowed with the divine gift of freedom, through which the human person becomes self-aware and able to choose between good and evil (Gen. 2.16–17). This divine gift enables man to progress infinitely toward spiritual perfection, but at the same time it implies a danger of disobedience, the risk of independence from God and, therefore, of the Fall. Such is the terrifying role played by evil, present within man and in the world, in issues of peace and freedom. The consequences of this evil are the scourges and vices that have become predominant signs of our times: secularization, violence, the absence of moral standards, racism, the arms race, and wars.

As we have reaffirmed many times, violence committed in the name of religion is a crime against religion. We affirmed in the Brussels Declaration of 2001 that these acts of violence committed by members of religious communities "do not reflect the teaching of these religions and therefore religious beliefs are not responsible for the acts of adherents which are committed by transgression or by misinterpretation."[6] It is only through dialogue that heinous acts of violence will come to an end—that is, dialogue between faiths and dialogue within our faiths. All efforts toward promoting collaboration among the faithful of our respective religious traditions for the sake of peaceful coexistence are encouraged.

While we live in times of an exceedingly deep and multifaceted crisis in spiritual values, the faithful of our two religions are called to the higher level of spiritual development and life, to transcend human failings and the lapses into ways of life inconsistent with divine will. Our respective religious traditions have inexhaustible spiritual reserves, which can contribute to the actualization of the values of peace, social justice, and human rights in relations between individuals and peoples, irrespective of religious, national, racial, social or other differences. In our love of the one God and our love of neighbor, we are able to enhance dialogue and understanding for the sake of the peace of God in the world. For this reason, always believing in the possibility of peaceful coexistence and cooperation between believers and all citizens of goodwill, we must find practical ways to optimize mutual understanding and respect and cooperation.

We, both Christians and Muslims, children of the one and only God, have the unity of the human race as a fundamental belief. We are called to become better acquainted with one another and to draw closer together, to promote dialogue between us in every way, and especially during this age, which is preeminently one of communication. For this reason, it was always the practice to include young participants in our academic Christian–Muslim consultations. This form of participation contributed to what is being launched today for a more specific contribution to "capacity-building for interreligious dialogue." It is with the hope that you will acquire the necessary experience and skills in this seminar, an ongoing process, for you to return to your respective religious communities and call others to dialogue within the framework of your responsibilities, by working directly with young people in education, culture, or social-work settings.

---

6. For the full text, see Chapter 6, "Major Declarations: Public Proclamations."

With these thoughts in mind and with feelings of profound affection for the young religious leaders from the Christian tradition and the Muslim religion who are learning about communication, dialogue, and intercultural competence, we would like to express the hope that this seminar will serve as a fine example for other similar seminars to be organized elsewhere in the future—for the purpose of achieving "the peace that surpasses all understanding," for the common good of both religions taking part, and for humanity in general.

The Fast of Ramadan: I

Message for the commencement of Ramadan, 2008.

It is with feelings of great joy and love that we greet, from the Ecumenical Throne of Orthodoxy, all Muslims in the world on the occasion of the beginning of the month of Ramadan. We consider this a suitable moment to address a brief message, one appropriate to this period of fasting and prayer, for the faithful of Islam as we continue to promote the peaceful coexistence of the two religious traditions.

Furthermore, the beginning of Ramadan coincides with the first day of September, the Feast of Indiction,[7] which is the first day of the ecclesiastical year of the Orthodox Church and also the day of protection of the natural environment, a day marked by prayers and supplications for all creation and to be offered by this holy center of Orthodoxy. This day serves as an invitation to all to remain faithful to a natural use of all God's creation, "offering thanks to the God, who created the world and granted everything to us."

In light of the spiritual and moral dimension of the environmental problem and of these times marked by an exceedingly deep and multifaceted crisis in spiritual values, the faithful of our two religions are called to a higher level of spiritual development and life, to transcend human failings and the accompanying lapses into ways of life lower than the divine will. Our respective religious traditions have inexhaustible spiritual reserves that can contribute to the realization of the values of peace, social justice, and human rights in relations between individuals and peoples,

7. The beginning of the ecclesiastical calendar. The Ecumenical Patriarch issues such a message annually on the occasion of Ramadan.

irrespective of religious, national, racial, social or other differences. Common practices of our spiritual traditions include fasting, prayer, philanthropy, almsgiving, and charity. Furthermore, in our love of the one God and our love of neighbor, we are able to enhance dialogue and understanding for the sake of the peace of God in the world. For this reason, always believing in the possibility of peaceful coexistence and cooperation between believers and all citizens of goodwill, we must find practical ways to optimize mutual understanding, respect, and cooperation.

With these thoughts in mind and with feelings of profound affection for all the Muslim faithful, we would like to express the wish that Ramadan will help bring peoples and nations together to attain the true meaning of life, the hope of immortality, and the propagation of peace and goodwill on earth—especially in the regions suffering from war—and with the hope of salvation for all people.

The Fast of Ramadan: II

Message for the commencement of Ramadan, 2006.

Our Muslim brethren are preparing, during the month of Ramadan, to fulfill their obligation of fasting in order to gain the love of God. Fasting is a discipline found in all religions, and it is carried out for the sake of pleasing God. Our Lord Jesus Christ commands us to fast not for the sake of display before people but for our Father in heaven (Mt. 6.16–18).

In the Qur'an, too, it is said that the primary purpose of fasting is for us to control the passions, in order to appear worthy of divine love. It is also said that differences with respect to the time and manner of worshipping God will not prevent people from being united in divine love.

In the name of our Orthodox faithful, on the occasion of the month of Ramadan, we congratulate our Muslim brethren, with whom we have always enjoyed relations of mutual love and friendship. We pray that these cordial relations will continue to increase for the benefit of humanity.

Our prayer to God is that love, and the justice that results from love, may prevail throughout the world in order that expressions of hatred and violence may be forever erased by the light of love.

We beseech God to bless the month of Ramadan 2006 for the world of Islam, toward whom once again we convey our congratulations, love, and greetings.

Self-Love and Love of Others: Minorities in Muslim Nations

Address to the Orthodox and Ancient Eastern Christians of Bahrain, September 26, 2000.

Blessed is God, who has granted us the unexpected opportunity of the present meeting. We are full of joy and gratitude to God for this opportunity. Being deeply moved, we offer thanks to His Highness, the emir of Bahrain, Sheikh Hamad Bin Isa Al-Khalifa, for the honorable invitation offered to our humble person to visit this God-protected emirate. We also warmly thank Your Eminence, our dearly beloved brother in Christ, the metropolitan of the Arabian Gulf States, Constantine, for your great care and the toil that you have taken with eagerness and love for the preparation, organization, and realization of this present official visit to this country.

We bring to you the greetings of the Great Mother Church of Christ, the Church of Constantinople, as well as our own personal greetings. Our love embraces you, and we pray that the Almighty One send his grace on you in his own hidden way, which he alone knows, since the lack of a sacred church and a permanent priest deprives you of the grace of the regular celebration of and participation in the Divine Liturgy and the other holy sacraments. Desire the Lord in the way that the deer strongly desires water from springs, "and the Lord will give you living water, of which when you drink you will never spiritually thirst again" (John 4.3–42).

Your presence among our Muslim brothers, who have on many occasions endured painful experiences from their encounters with Christians, must create within you a desire to put forth your best self. Your current situation provides a very good opportunity for vigilance, care, and a more systematic exercise of virtue. Indeed, Jesus Christ gave us the commandment that our light must shine before all people so that they will see our good deeds and glorify our Father in heaven. This commandment applies all the more to Christians, such as yourselves, who live among people who follow another religious tradition—for it is more important that others who follow another religious tradition form a better impression about us as faithful Christians than it is for our own fellow Christians to form such impressions about us. In this way, they will glorify God, the one who transforms the faithful through his grace and who continuously sacrifices them until they perfect themselves on their path toward him.

If we do not show appropriate conduct, we are in danger of hearing God's painful words, that "His name is blasphemed among the nations because of us" (Rom. 2.24). This is a heavy reproach not only because we bear the responsibility for our bad actions but also because of the scandal created in the conscience of our fellow human beings as a result of these actions.

Our love for ourselves, for God, and for our neighbor must be activated, however, so that we will not be allowed to harm ourselves or others. We must stress that the commandment to love our neighbor demands that we love God as ourselves. Therefore, the love we offer to ourselves is lawful and is permitted by God. But here, something paradoxical happens. While we think that we love ourselves, we often behave in a manner detrimental to ourselves, especially when we have the conviction that we are acting in a way that benefits ourselves. Frequently, we protest against someone who shows us what is good for us, telling this person that he is limiting our freedom and self-expression. If, for example, we have acquired a bad habit, such as overeating, love for self, health, and life ought to impose a limit on the amount of food we eat. Whenever we exceed that limit, we behave as enemies of ourselves, as if we hate ourselves—something quite unprecedented, since it is probably only the human being and the devil who become self-destructive as a result of a perverted love for themselves.

In the language of the Church, this spiritual disease is known as *self-love*, which differs from a healthy love for ourselves. Self-love differs from this other healthy type of love in the sense that, whereas true love encompasses the entire human being, both body and soul, and aims at the prosperity and bliss of the entire human existence, self-love turns exclusively toward the physical and psychological passions, loving not the entire existence of the human being and the attainment of bliss—which results in absolute joy and peace—but only the temporary and pain-causing pleasures of the soul and body. Self-love, therefore, is the trunk of the tree from which sprout the branches of hedonism, avarice, and unbridled ambition, the three great passions that bring misery to humanity.

Through his grace, Christ calls us to free ourselves from this self-love and to live in peace, self-sufficiency, temperance, and self-knowledge, as virtuous people who appropriately and prudently use all the goods of the earth, which his generosity offers to us. With his blessing and gratitude, God has enjoined to us whatever good he has in store for the enjoyment of humanity as well as for the relaxation of the human body and spirit.

All these goods "are obtained through toil," for that is why he who truly loves himself is a lover of work, a lover of toil, a lover of learning, a lover of truth, a lover of hospitality, a lover of progress, a lover of humanity, a lover of honor and is not a lover of hedonism, avarice, and unbridled ambition. You know from the experiences of your life that what we are saying to you is true, repeating the words of the Lord. Love for ourselves demands that we be virtuous.

Continuity and Renewal: Jewish–Christian Relations: I

Message to the Third Academic Meeting of the Dialogue between Judaism and Orthodox Christianity, Athens, March 21, 1993.

From the holy center of Orthodoxy, we address all the participants with this paternal greeting, the biblical greeting par excellence: Peace be among you! This greeting reminds us of the multitude of common elements and characteristics between Christians and Jews and, above all, that these living traditions of faith have their roots in the same biblical ground.

This common spiritual origin of Christians and Jews seems today, more than ever, to offer a fruitful ground for rejection of the consequences of the mutual hostility that prevailed in the past and for the establishment of a new relationship between them, genuine and authentic, rooted in the willingness to work toward mutual understanding and improved knowledge of each other.

Today's favorable circumstances for easier communication and mutual rapprochement, as well as for the success of this task, are even more favorable in the special context of Eastern Orthodoxy, which has always believed and confessed the irreplaceable value of the human person and the equality of all human beings created by God. Eastern Orthodoxy has never encouraged racist ideas and theories and has never, in practical terms, experienced those historical maladies that can be observed elsewhere, such as racial discrimination, social marginalization and isolation, proselytism, persecution, and genocide of people who belong to a different culture or worship God in a different manner.

Quite the contrary, the reciprocated moving expressions of solidarity and support, shown in the past and also recently, toward the Jews living in this geographical area and suffering diverse persecutions, rather reinforce the hope that this God-pleasing task will bear fruit in the framework of a new and constructive rapprochement of Orthodox Christians and Jews living together under the same sky and in the same world.

And so, approaching each other in this positive fashion, free of any inherited negativity, Orthodox Christians and Jews can in a brotherly way exchange their rich experiences, particularly in the area of biblical studies, the teaching concerning tradition, the theology of the person, spirituality, et cetera and further define the boundaries and the limits of their possible collaboration in this world where faith in God is more and more threatened.

Today more than ever, those who believe in God, especially those who are members of the same spiritual family, are called to offer together, and in dialogue, the rich witness of their traditions in the urgent and necessary quest for better solutions to the great and serious problems that we face—the collapse of moral and spiritual values in general and, in particular, the violation of the value of the human person, the unique and incomparable image of God.

With these thoughts on the occasion of this present meeting, we wholeheartedly wish from the Ecumenical Patriarchate that the work of the Third Academic Meeting between Orthodoxy and Judaism be crowned with complete success, become the beginning of a series of fruitful encounters reinforcing and consolidating the establishment of the dialogue between Orthodox Christians and Jews, and so respond more effectively to the anguished aspirations of contemporary humanity, which impatiently awaits a life-giving breath from a renewed contemporary religious discourse.

Faithfulness to the Sources: Jewish–Christian Relations: II

Opening address at the Fifth Academic Meeting of the Dialogue between Judaism and Orthodox Christianity, Thessaloniki, May 27, 2003.

We regard as most fortunate the synchronicity involved in our visit to this city for the present meeting that is taking place within the framework of the Fifth Academic Meeting in the Dialogue between Judaism and Christianity. That is why we have come here. With pleasure we address to you a cordial greeting of love and honor, and with pleasure we hope for a fruitful outcome of this dialogue and for conclusions to be drawn that will promote greater understanding and peaceful coexistence among people.

Unfortunately, we are living in a world that has not yet overcome its religious confrontations—not, of course, that our wish is for a homogeneity of faith, a utopian outcome in the context of the contemporary world, but rather for a mitigation of religious acrimony between the adherents of various religions. This is a vision that slowly, but hopefully, is beginning to appear achievable. It is true that the past we carry with us is full of painful experiences. Supporters of one religion often raise impenetrable walls between themselves and the supporters of another religion. The need to protect the unity of the believing multitudes and to retain them as members of a particular religious group leads to overemphasizing differences and, not infrequently, to slandering the members of another religious group, and sometimes even to taking adverse measures against them, actions that unfortunately have not ceased to be taken even today.

Academic discussions such as the present one are not of a proselytizing nature. Even when issues of faith are being discussed, the purpose is not to convince the interlocutor to change from one faith to the other. The purpose is solely to promote understanding of the thinking of the interlocutor who belongs to another religion and so, with full scholarly awareness, to communicate calmly with him in order to eliminate the fanaticism that still appears sometimes among the less enlightened adherents of one religion or the other. For, regrettably, the phenomenon of religious fanaticism has not disappeared.

The elimination of fanaticism is accompanied by the removal of fear and in any event presupposes its removal. As the fanatic is basically a fearful and insecure person, he worries about the very existence of a difference of faith between himself and the other, and he worries about whether this difference jeopardizes his own faith and his own being. This means that the fanatic, in his innermost being, is not absolutely convinced of the truth of his faith and seeks to reassure himself, not through the metaphysical means appropriate to religious faith, or even through reasoned arguments as befits a modern intelligent human being, but by eliminating or exorcising everyone with a different faith. The more insecure he feels about his own faith, the more fanatic he is, overcompensating in some way for his lack of conviction by deeds that are meant to declare his great faith. In this sense, fanatics are not the select members of a religion but rather its weakest members.

People who are firmly convinced and who live the truth of their faith in practice are peaceful and imperturbable and friendly to all. Their faith is not endangered in their innermost being. Therefore they can, with a feeling of complete security, encounter any other faith and converse with advocates of any other faith. They listen, examine, and investigate everything. They set out honestly their own experience of the otherworldly and the supernatural and understand other people's comparable experiences, for they are in a position to compare these with their own experience without confusion, without doubt, without danger, and without fear, not because of a lack of comprehensiveness or receptivity but because of a greater knowledge, by virtue of which they can discern the truth dispassionately—that is, without their judgment's being influenced by personal or group interests, by notions about the possible repercussions that a given different religious tradition might have on their own existence and worldview.

In this regard, it will be useful for us to recall Aristotle's[8] sound epigrammatic observation about the influence that judges' own interests exert on their decisions. The great sage of antiquity said, "With regard to

8. 384–322 B.C.

judges, frequently their own vested interest becomes involved, so that they are unable to see the truth clearly, and their judgment is clouded by what they perceive as being sweet or bitter for themselves." What happens in a court judgment can certainly happen in any other area of judgment. All people, whether Christians or Jews, are susceptible to the danger of having their judgment clouded by what they perceive as being in their own interest. And herein lies the usefulness of academic discussions such as this one: being academic, by definition they presuppose the objectivity and composure of scholarly investigation and carry research forward unaffected by "the sweet or the bitter" and by any emotion other than the quest for truth.

Commitment to Peace and Justice

The phenomenon of religious faith, when the study of it goes beyond the limits of sociological or psychological investigation and penetrates into the innermost being, is for the most part as inaccessible and profoundly personal as is the love between two people and the loving relationship between them. The personal existence of God and the personal existence of man merge in a mystical and ineffable relationship of love and communication, and what takes place in it is shrouded in silence. Therefore academic discussions about the phenomenon of religion usually revolve around the visible manifestations of a given religiosity because it is impossible to touch the unapproachable and inconceivable depth of a personal relationship between man and God.

Most people maintain a superficial, shallow relationship with God or, even more frequently, with the image of God that they have created. They are completely indifferent to the relationship in question, even though they declare themselves members of a religious community. They are more interested in the progress of the community in question from the human viewpoint—that is, in promoting it, an interest that reflects their own ambition and desire to gain distinction, and they consider the existing personal relationship between them and God only in a very offhand way. This is why the will of human beings is frequently put forward as being the will of God and why there occur between religious communities confrontations and conflicts that reflect the conflicts between the ambitions of their members and not, of course, the nonexistent confrontations of God in the person of the members of religious communities.

Judaism and Christianity have been living in a state of dialogue for two thousand years. Because Christianity is known to have sprung forth from the birthplace and from the people of Judaism, though it has a different worldview and a different concept of God, and consequently it developed differently. At the center of the differing viewpoints lies the controversial person of Jesus Christ and the fact of the Cross, which the Apostle Paul, a Jew, described epigrammatically as being "to the Jews a stumbling block and to the Greeks foolishness" (1 Cor. 1.23).

Carrying on discussion in this fashion, in an academic context, we do not seek to change the faith of our interlocutor on these crucial points or on other points of lesser importance. We are seeking to change the dispositions of our interlocutors toward others and to be led to dialogue in good faith, full of love and mutual respect. Beyond this, it is a matter of free choice for each person, that choice being respected and accepted by all as a possibility.

The stubborn insistence on one faith certainly differs from fanaticism. The believer who is not a fanatic insists on his faith but at the same time accepts with a friendly disposition any person who does not belong to it, even though he considers his own convictions to be correct. On the contrary, the fanatic does not tolerate the existence of either a different faith or of a person belonging to a different faith. He does not want to see the reality of the existence on earth of different religious faiths. We, who are taking part in this discussion academically, have of course evolved beyond that point and are able to listen to others dispassionately and to converse peacefully.

The anticipated result will not, in all likelihood, be a concurrence of faith, but it will be an increase of love and mutual understanding. This is the great profit, both metaphysical and worldly, for both sides of the dialogue, as the grace of God watches over the mild-tempered, humble, and peaceful man and directs his heart onto the straight road.

The theme of this conference—"Faithfulness to our Sources: Our Common Commitment to Peace and Justice"—has many facets, which will surely be analyzed by the distinguished speakers. No one will have failed to remark that both the religions in today's dialogue have a common point of departure in what our Old Testament calls the self-revelation of God as a personal being. Nevertheless, after the appearance of the person and teaching of Jesus Christ, those who believed in him established an independent faith, a superstructure that does not abolish the Mosaic and in general the Old Testament revelation of God but rather supplements it by teaching that is more ecumenical and sacrificial—which, however, is not always satisfactorily applied by his followers.

It is a fact that *peace* and *justice* in their various senses are fundamental concepts in both religions. In the present dialogue, the anticipated deeper investigation of the content of these terms in the teachings of each religion will contribute to the fuller understanding of them and to the identification of possible historic errors in their practical application.

The Imperative of Interreligious Dialogue: I

Address to the Plenary of the Parliamentary Assembly of the Council of Europe, Strasbourg, January 22, 2007.

We convey to you greetings of love and honor from the Church of Constantinople, based for centuries in the Istanbul of today. We extend to all of you with sincere joy the blessings and warmest wishes for personal as well as collective happiness and longevity. Furthermore, we would like to express our gratitude for the honor of this invitation to demonstrate in your presence our concerns and thoughts on this very timely and extremely interesting topic, namely "The Necessity and Goals of Interreligious Dialogue."

We are well aware of, and we commend, your zeal for human rights, for rapprochement and mutual acceptance of cultures, and for peaceful cooperation among peoples. We are fully aware that you know more than what we are about to tell you. We take courage to address you and to state as loudly and as clearly as we can that, as the first bishop of the Orthodox Church, we congratulate you on your work and your principles. We work with our limited powers to ensure that respect of human rights will prevail on a universal level, especially where religious traditions oppose one another on this issue.

It is indeed a great honor to address the continent's oldest political organization, here in the historical city of Strasbourg. Among the aims of this council, according to its regulations, is to achieve a greater unity between its members, defend human rights and the rule of law, and promote awareness of a European identity based on shared values, while cutting across different cultures. It is in this light that we are addressing this plenary, for our mission has many goals in common with yours. We stand in front of you as an ancient European institution that has been present for almost seventeen centuries and that may even be the second oldest institution in Europe. Those of us who serve this institution would be very unhappy indeed if our service consisted only of a role equivalent to that of a museum guard. We strongly believe that the value of your welcome to us here today, as representative of the aforementioned institution, has its roots not only in the recognition and appreciation of the historicity of the Ecumenical Patriarchate of Constantinople and New Rome but mostly in your interest for the living tradition of the ecumenicity of its message.

In welcoming us here, you bear witness to the ministry and message of the Ecumenical Patriarchate through the ages. Our historical mission has been truly ecumenical—in other words, international and universal, because we serve commonly accepted and always valid principles and values. And, as you know, the Eastern Roman Empire, the so-called Byzantine, in which the institution of the Ecumenical Patriarchate developed, was a political system that was totally different from the modern national, or civic, state. Its political pattern was multinational and multiracial; it aspired to ensure the peaceful coexistence of peoples and traditions, the so-called *Pax Romana*, which later developed into *Pax Christiana*, after the rise of Christianity.[9]

Roman Law and Byzantium

Deeply experienced Christian faith; Roman law, which was constantly being developed owing to Christian influence; and widespread Greek education—these constituted the basic agents of Byzantine civilization. These unifying elements did not in any way nullify the particularities and individuality of different cultural traditions. A characteristic example of the respect for these particularities and individuality is the fact that there was no attempt to nationally assimilate the Christianized peoples—that is, no attempt to Hellenize them. On the contrary, they were given the opportunity to develop their national and cultural identity, as is indicated by the

9. See John Meyendorff, *The Byzantine Legacy in the Orthodox Church* (Crestwood, N.Y.: St. Vladimir's Seminary Press, 1982).

very offering of a special alphabet to the Slavic world and by many other similar examples.

The Patriarchate of Constantinople and New Rome, which was given the title *Ecumenical* in the sixth century, was given the right, by a decision of the Fourth Ecumenical Council in 451, to have under its authority all territory outside the boundaries of the Byzantine Empire that were not under the jurisdiction of any other patriarchate. This expanded and increased the communication of the Patriarchate with the multitude of peoples and traditions, both within and outside the legal boundaries of the empire, in such a way that dialogue with both the peoples of wholly different religions as well as with heterodox Christians became an integral part of its existence.

Therefore, for the Ecumenical Patriarchate, dialogue is neither something unprecedented nor a modern effort but rather an experience and a practice of millennia. Indeed, after the Schism between the Eastern and Western churches in 1054 was official, the Ecumenical Patriarchate became the expression and mouthpiece of the unity of all Orthodox.[10] It is under this virtue that the Ecumenical Patriarchate holds discussions with the churches that came about after the Schism and the Reformation. It does so with a sense of responsibility for service to the truth and for the restoration of the original unity of all Christians.

In 1453, after the succession of the Byzantine Empire by the Ottoman Empire, the Ecumenical Patriarchate became the representative, to the sultan, of all Orthodox Christians who lived within the boundaries of the new empire.[11] We can see that the Ecumenical Patriarchate was in constant dialogue with the Muslim world, though not always on an equal basis. During these almost six centuries, the Patriarchate has lived together with Muslims and discussed with them on various levels and concerning various goals. As we used to say, we in Turkey have with our

10. See Philip Sherrard, *Church, Papacy, and Schism: A Theological Enquiry* (London: SPCK, 1976; Limni, Greece: Denise Harvey, 1996); Steven Runciman, *The Eastern Schism: A Study of the Papacy and the Eastern Churches in the XIth and XIIth Centuries* (Oxford, U.K.: Clarendon Press, 1955); John Meyendorff, *Byzantine Theology: Historical Trends and Doctrinal Themes* (New York: Fordham University Press, 1983).

11. See Steven Runciman, *The Fall of Constantinople, 1453* (Cambridge, U.K.: Cambridge University Press, 1965; Canto Edition: 1990).

Muslim brothers not only an academic dialogue but one of practical coexistence, one that comes from our living together side by side.

Furthermore, during the last few decades, there has been a particular effort made for the development of interreligious dialogues, especially among the three great monotheistic religions. Many academic meetings of leading representatives of the three monotheistic religions have taken place, either on our initiative or with our participation; many important and interesting decisions have been made, and many important declarations have been signed—for example, the Bosphorus Declaration, the Brussels Declaration, and so on.[12] Moreover, with the purpose of promoting the mutual opportunity to know each other better and to cultivate friendship, we, having been officially invited, have personally visited many countries with Muslim-majority populations, such as Bahrain, Qatar, Iran, Libya, Azerbaijan, and Kazakhstan.

Dialogue: Part of the Territory of Being Human and Free

The necessity and the usefulness of interreligious dialogue have become part and parcel of what it means to be human in today's world. It is well known that the inhabitants of our planet confess many religions and that on many occasions a variety of tendencies and denominations have developed within each religion, many times even with contradictory beliefs. It is also known from history that many times in the past, and on certain occasions even in our time, religious reasons were advanced to lead individuals or even entire peoples to warfare or to invigorate the militancy of those involved. There are even some analysts of the future of humanity who consider a bloody clash of religions and of religious populations to be inevitable. There are even some who believe that God needs their power to enforce his will on the world.

We, however, the people of the so-called Western civilization, have been convinced that pure religious faith in itself does not find any pleasure in involving its followers in warfare and conflicts with the faithful of other religions, for the truth does not walk with militant power or with numerical superiority—or with any other superiority, for that matter. The conviction that divine truth is vindicated by victory in war has been

12. For the full texts of these declarations, see Chapter 6, "Major Declarations: Public Proclamations."

abandoned today as inaccurate. The truth is known through the Word (*logos*) and the personal experience of it, in a pure and selfless heart. According to the prophet Elijah, the Lord revealed himself in a light murmuring sound and not in earthquakes and fire.

Therefore, if we desire to move toward the knowledge of truth, which liberates the person from the chains of prejudice and of every kind of deception, we ought to use the God-given gift of the Word (*logos*) with a pure and selfless intention. The word, as an expression and as a justification of our convictions, when exchanged with our interlocutors, becomes a dialogue (*dialogos*). And it is absolutely necessary, for it marks the very existence of a human being as a personal being. There are in nature many creatures that have been endowed with the ability to receive messages from their environment and to react to these messages, but, of all earthly creatures, only the human being can converse with his or her fellow human beings in words.

Dialogue is necessary first and foremost not because of all the benefits and advantages that can possibly derive from it but because it is inherent in the nature of the human person. The truth of this is such that the person who declines to participate in dialogue denies, indirectly, this very human quality. Indeed, not only does one deny this human quality to those whom he or she does not accept in dialogue, but one also, as is self-evident, abolishes one's very own humanity, for by not showing any respect for the dignity of the other, one acts as if one lacks the most salient human characteristic, respect for a human person, both one's self and any other person. In Christian teaching, as it has been expressed by a contemporary person of some experience, God engraved the human being with his mark, the deep, embossed, and unchangeable creative seal, and he does not revoke it. The seal of God is the freedom of the human being.

The fact that those culturally more advanced than the ancient peoples established dialogue between judges and those who were judged, or those who were in litigation, as a necessary precondition for the validity and legitimacy of the judicial verdict is very relevant. These fundamental principles of a fair trial continue to apply even for our contemporary world. The person who will judge at a trial must listen to both sides that are involved in the litigation. All of this is based on the principle of dialogue. The two parties constitute, together with the resultant supreme rule of dialogue, the sublime expression of respect for the human person. Pope

Benedict XVI in his message for January 1 of this year referred to this very point. It is this respect that constitutes the fundamental criterion for spiritual growth and comprises simultaneously the fundamental rule and the unshakable pedestal of all human rights.

According to our predecessor St. John Chrysostom, the most sublime of all personal beings, God, is in constant dialogue with us, that being a token of the utmost honor with which humanity is engulfed. God does not refuse dialogue, not even to those who honestly deny his existence. However, he cannot enter into dialogue with those who are furtive, surreptitious, perverse, and not pure in their hearts. For dialogue presupposes honesty and becomes objectively impossible when there is deceit, secrecy, or any other kind of expediency.

It is well known that nowadays the dynamics of our world involve a mixture of contests of power and every kind of dialogue. Many try to force their opinions and convictions onto others through various types of power, whether cultural, moral, economic, terrorist, or even military. At the same time, many other people discuss innumerable issues, trying to convince their counterparts of the validity and accuracy of their positions. Out of these two ways, the one that is, as a matter of fact, in harmony with respect for the human person for the human rights, is the way of dialogue, for it rejects the inhumanity and violence of coercion.

The Dynamics of Interreligious Dialogue

The interreligious dialogue, in the context of religion, is one of the most difficult dialogues, for the so-called religions of revelation accept that they express the divine truth through the revelation of God himself. Nevertheless, the existing dispersion of the religious groups and the opposing convictions that they confess prove that some of them are wrong by definition, for one rules out the other, and of course it is neither possible nor thinkable that God can be the cause of such discrepancy or division. Therefore, it must be unquestionably accepted that one of the controverted teachings derives not from God but from people and from their misinterpretation of the divine revelation.

And so there is a broad area for questioning what the truth can be whenever something that is offered as truth contradicts itself. Through calm and dispassionate discussion and sincere dialogue, people can identify their differences and the human interventions that have altered the divine truth and led to the support of teachings that, while claiming to express the divine truth, refute one another and result in a logical impossibility.

Of course we do not consider the relinquishment of religious convictions to be the goal of interreligious dialogue; neither do we consider interreligious dialogue an easy task, especially in times such as ours, when we face many wars and conflicts all across our planet. And that is because nowadays on many occasions people use their religious differences, or their religious convictions, to help define their particularity and individuality, and this particularity they consider to be the cornerstone of their national hypostasis, or of what constitutes them as different.

And so, to the extent to which national consciousness and hypostasis is an inevitable element of the particularity and individuality of peoples and of nations, people will legitimately defend their indefeasible right to define themselves by their religion, although to our mind the subjection of religion to the service of national purposes is not correct.

In any case, we will for many centuries to come have many religions and even more religious convictions, all of which will differ from one another. This fact, in view of economic and informational globalization, brings the faithful of the various religions into frequent communication and renders their unofficial dialogue an everyday phenomenon. Even the official dialogue among religious leadership is being promoted in a sense, since religious leaders cannot ignore reality, nor can they sequester themselves in a selfish isolation.

In any case, the religions that consider themselves possessors and carriers of the divine truth feel that they have an obligation to spread their faith, and by definition they cannot isolate themselves. Existing predicaments for the realization of interreligious dialogue on a theological level do not hinder but on the contrary promote opportunity for the mutual acquaintance of persons and ideas, the cultivation of religious tolerance and coexistence, and the elimination of fanaticism and of other fixed prejudices. These goals are of great importance, for, they serve peace, which is the cornerstone of all cultural progress.

In particular, it has been observed that there is a dearth of religious education, especially in the case of religions that are not predominant in a given country. This dearth has been observed even among those who have received higher education. This results in the easy circulation of a variety of deceptive perceptions and prejudices, which obstruct peaceful cooperation among people. Through systematic dialogue, it is possible to gradually improve the level of mutual understanding and awareness of the religious dimensions of all peoples and civilizations so that that longstanding prejudices will be put aside. We must not overlook that, for many peoples and civilizations, religious faith and the religious element at large play an important role in private, social, and national life—much more so than in the societies of contemporary Western civilization.

The Goal of Interreligious Dialogue

Of course, we expect not only an improvement of the perceptions that the Christian world has of the non-Christian world but also a proportionate improvement of the perceptions that the non-Christian world has of Christianity. Unfortunately, numerous un-Christian actions and behaviors of the Christian peoples have created the widespread impression that these actions and behaviors are somehow sanctioned by Christianity. Similarly, the actions of the adherents of other religions are often associated with those religions, which, however do not embrace those actions. It is therefore necessary to clarify the context of each religion, discerning the selfish actions of their adherents in question, not their religion, responsible for their actions. This separation of responsibilities, which is one of the goals of interreligious dialogue, protects from phobias that reach out from the past and obstruct present-day peaceful and well-intended cooperation.

Another important goal of interreligious dialogue is to approach the extremely important issue of human rights. It is a known fact that Western civilization, under the influence of the evangelical principles of the equality of human beings, of freedom of conscience, of the protection of the weak, of justice and of love, and of many more, but also under the influence of the ideas of humanism, has, especially since the Enlightenment, gradually raised the institution of human rights to a high level. This runs counter to other civilizations, some of which either occupy themselves very little with human rights or even have legislation whereby they discriminate against certain categories of people, such as minorities, women, children, slaves, and so on.

They have even developed metaphysical teachings through which the existing situation is interpreted as being in agreement with the heaven-mandated will in human affairs! As is readily realized, such views, whereby some people endow the violation of fundamental human rights with a moral investment of religious and metaphysical beliefs and thereby legitimize those beliefs, cannot be easily abandoned. If, however, we declare for the improvement of living standards for all people in our declarations, then we ought to include that issue as an item in the agenda of our interreligious dialogues.

We believe that the moral force of respect for the human person regardless of gender, age, race, religion, or economic, educational, or any other kind of status is so great that it will overcome the longstanding spiritual infirmities that allow those in power to ignore or, even worse, to legally violate human rights. Serious effort is needed in order to allow the discussion of these issues among those who have not respected human rights. Nevertheless, it is very promising that in every society there are always advanced minds that realize the importance of human rights and work hard for their wider acceptance, even in civilizations that are not familiar with these concepts.

At this point, we must mention that the Ecumenical Patriarchate and the surrounding Greek Orthodox minority in Turkey feel that they still do not enjoy full rights. Examples of this deprivation include the refusal to acknowledge and recognize legal status for the Ecumenical Patriarchate, the prohibition of the operation of the theological school of Halki,[13] property issues, and many more. We do recognize, however, that many reforms

---

13. The Patriarchate's international theological school at Halki (Heybeliada, on the Princes' Islands in the Sea of Marmara) has been closed since 1971, pursuant to a Turkish law forbidding private universities to function. The closure would appear to be in breach of Article 40 of the Treaty of Lausanne and Article 9 of the European Convention on Human Rights. Yet Halki served as the formative and theological center for numerous leaders of the (especially, but not only) Greek-speaking Orthodox world. The function of Halki had been diminished both as a secondary school and graduate seminary since the late 1950s. The magnificent nineteenth-century building contains a library of forty thousand books and historical manuscripts as well as classrooms filled with old wooden desks and spacious reception and dormitory rooms. It is Patriarch Bartholomew's dream and desire to reopen the theological school.

have been made and some remarkable steps have been taken for the development of the domestic law on the model of the European standard. We have always supported the European perspective of Turkey, as we anticipate the remaining steps to be taken according to the standards of the European Union.

What is accomplished fluently through interreligious dialogue is the cultivation of a spirit of tolerance, reconciliation, and peaceful coexistence of the faithful of the various religions, free from fanaticism and phobias. Contrary to political positions that often foster a spirit of conflict and confrontation, catching within it victims and victimizers alike, we try to sow the spirit of equal rights and responsibilities for all and for their peaceful cooperation, regardless of their religion, for only through the opening of hearts and minds and the acceptance of those who are different as equal to ourselves—only through that is it possible to build peace in this world.

There is one more goal of the interreligious dialogues, and it is not any less important. This is the enrichment of each believer's mind through his consideration of things seen from the perspective of somebody else's religion. This enrichment releases us from partiality; it allows us to have a higher and wider understanding of beliefs; it fortifies the intellect, and very often it leads us to a deeper experience of the truth and to a very advanced level of our growth, in the presence of the divine revelation.

For example, love, as a selfless feeling and experience of sacrifice toward the beloved, is an utmost challenge of a conscience, but it was not required by all simultaneously, for many, because of their obduracy, were not yet ready to accept such a high and self-sacrificial demand. However, this love, which in the beginning was achieved only by a few, has reached the point that it is the motivation for actions and programs and institutions, such as the Council of Europe, devoted to the relief of poverty, to the assistance of those who are affected by natural disasters, to the acknowledgment and protection of human rights at large, to religious freedom, and of many more good ends, which would have been considered impossible or utopian a few centuries ago, or even a few years ago.

In many religions we can find, if we are willing, ground for doing good. A common search for this ground through dialogue will prove to be very fruitful. The sacred books and sources of each religion allow many interpretations and approaches. It is in our hands to choose every time what is most appropriate and most peaceful, what is most consistent with respect for the human being and what increases peace, solidarity, altruism, love. We are obliged to ascend the degrees of the scale of good and not to descend. Let us work for the ascension to the next degree for the benefit of all.

As the first bishop of the Orthodox Church, we are obliged to serve the ideals of peace and human caring in the Christian gospel. It is with the courage of this service that we dare to address a heartfelt plea to the Parliamentary Assembly of the Council of Europe, to persons who are responsible, in their decision-making roles in European societies, for world order and peace. Therefore, exert your influence, your political art and science, in order to restore freedom of life and the free expression of religious traditions in our world today so that citizens of contemporary states will not be persecuted, will not be cast aside and marginalized, will not be required to forfeit their churches and their properties just because their religious convictions are different.

We are certain that the Council of Europe is interested not only in various advantages to the European countries but also in the preservation and promotion of the accomplishments of the civilization, which constitute the very identity of Europe. Religious freedom and human rights in general are such accomplishments. Each and every offense against religious freedom and human rights mutilates human civilization. It is a sign of regression and of the frustration of human hope. We have the certain and undoubted hope that things will improve through the contribution of all of you, our beloved and honorable members of the Council of Europe. And "hope will not let us down," as St. Paul states.

The Imperative of Interreligious Dialogue: II

Lecture at the Islamic College in Libya, September 11, 2003.

It was with great joy that we accepted the invitation by your historic country to visit you and speak within the framework of interreligious dialogue between the religions of Christianity and Islam. We come with two identities. We come as a simple fellow human being and also as the first in order among equal bishops of the Orthodox Christian Church, presiding hierarch of the Orthodox Church of Constantinople.

We bring you the wholehearted and friendly greetings both of our Modesty personally and also on behalf of the Church to which we belong and that we represent. We also express from this podium our warm thanks to the World Islamic Call Society and its general secretary, the Reverend Dr. Mohammad Ahmed Al-Sherif, and to all the honorable members of the executive council of this society for the invitation to speak before you about the timely and important subject of interreligious dialogue.

This is not the first time that we have dealt with this issue; and of course neither is this the first time that you have heard about it. The World Islamic Call Society, from the time of its very foundation, included in its constitutional goals the realization of interreligious dialogue, and it has conducted at least one official dialogue with the Vatican as the representative of the Roman Catholic Christian Church. This resulted in such remarkable mutually agreed-on pronouncements as "no compulsion should be used on persons or societies in the name of religion." That dialogue also came to the remarkable conclusion that, as a subject of preaching, antagonism should be replaced with cooperation. At the same time, the Ecumenical Patriarchate, which we head, has cooperated with others to organize numerous international academic interreligious meetings and conferences with the participation of representatives of the major religions. During these conferences, specific subjects have been examined, and mutually accepted decisions have been made. Some of them have already become universally recognized by the global community, such as the Bosphorus Declaration, according to which "every crime in the name of religion is a crime against religion."[14]

Humanity currently finds itself in a situation where the necessity of dialogue as a method of solving conflicts and problems in every area of human life has become clear. The coexistence of members of different religions is increasing, and they interact now in a uniquely direct way, owing to recent advances in the mass media and means of transportation and to the immigration of followers of one religion to countries where another religion predominates.

Moreover, the establishment of numerous international organizations, the first of which was the United Nations, has led representatives of different peoples with different religions and civilizations into the halls of international conferences and to the tables of bilateral or multilateral

14. For the full text, see Chapter 6, "Major Declarations: Public Proclamations."

negotiations, to find solutions to several problems. This has resulted in increased familiarity between peoples and a greater tolerance for their respective religious and cultural preferences and peculiarities.

And so both the unofficial dialogue that has been conducted on a personal level between followers of both of these two great religions (as well as of others) and frequent high-level international meetings have prepared hearts and minds for a more official dialogue involving spiritual leaders and scholars of religion. Such a dialogue would aim to clarify the many centuries-old misunderstandings about the true content of the world's religions. It would also aim to preserve, and not to block for religious reasons, the possibility of peaceful cooperation between peoples of different religions.

Coexistence of Christians and Muslims, especially in the Mediterranean region, has been the rule for centuries and has made these groups of people familiar with each other, created friendships and cooperation, and facilitated discussions and exchanges of views, and it has given rise to mutual understanding. In particular, Arabic- and non–Arabic-speaking Christians alike have lived in the Arabic world together with Muslims, and the literature of both religions has greatly benefited as a result.

Moreover, in the countries of Syria (which hosts the Orthodox Patriarchate of Antioch in Damascus), Lebanon, Jordan, Palestine (which is the ancient see of the Orthodox Patriarchate of Jerusalem), and others, the percentage of Christians compared to the Muslim majority is not negligible. This centuries-long daily interaction, cohabitation, and cooperation between both the simplest and the most erudite members of the communities and the elevation of individuals from both religions to high positions in government has made people spiritually interested in a more responsible and substantial dialogue.

Absoluteness and Apologetics

To be sure, exchanges of information about the teachings and spiritual experiences of both religions have taken place throughout the centuries, and indeed still take place within communities. But it is also true that the nature of faith, and especially of Christian and Muslim faith, involves a high degree of absoluteness, which sometimes becomes intensified so as to prevent followers of one religion from converting to another.

This has resulted in an increase in apologetic works, works whereby the superiority of one religion's claim to truth is set over and against another's. In cases like these, the discussion highlights oppositions and differences and does not lead to peaceful mutual understanding but rather to mere logical argumentation. However, there also exist progressive minds that consider faith in God as a strong connection between these two religions. These people, without equating the religion with the other person, are more interested in discovering the deeper message of God that both religions contain within themselves than in focusing on the differences that exist between them. This does not imply indifference to the faith or minimalism regarding its substantial elements or syncretism; it implies only a friendly attitude toward the person who believes and worships in a way different from ours, because this person on his spiritual path is in God's sight. The depth of the soul, where this journey takes place, is a holy and inviolate place, where no coercion can exist, for God himself grants us the time for the protracted and barely discernible inner workings of faith.

The call for a more profound investigation and for a friendly attitude that leads to an end to conflict is not recent. Many centuries ago, Jalal ad-Din Rumi wrote in his poem "The Religious Conflict":

> The blind face a dilemma when they worship,
> While the powerful on the one and on the other side stand established:
> Every place is happy with its way.
> Only love can make their conflict stop.
> Only love comes to help when you call for help against their arguments.

Accordingly, we have come not to set our arguments against yours in the framework of conflict. We have come in a spirit of love, in response to your kind invitation, to get to know you and to offer you our desire for interreligious dialogue—for dialogue is born of speech, equality, and mutual respect of those who engage in it. When equality is absent, the speech of a superior to his subordinate becomes a commandment, and that of a subordinate to his superior becomes beggary, praise, or cajolery. When a relationship of hostility persists between those who communicate, speech becomes contradiction. Cases such as these are spiritual disputes where a mere logical victory of the one over the other is the goal; surely this cannot be called dialogue.

When one party in a discussion is not interested in receiving something from the other and instead wants only to give, it is not dialogue that results but rather monologue. What a tragedy it is that many people engage in mere monologue, while thinking that they conduct a dialogue! This is a common phenomenon and from the spiritual point of view is more repugnant than contradiction; in arguments between people who openly disagree, there exists at least a kind of communication. The one who responds to what he is told tries to understand his interlocutor and to present his objection to the other's views. However, the person who conducts a monologue, even if he has heard the other, has not thought about what he has heard. Neither does he truly respond but instead says whatever he initially intended to say, indifferent to what he has been told. Some describe this as the dialogue of the deaf, behavior that does not deserve the name of dialogue.

Dialogue: A Divine Gift

True dialogue is a gift from God to humankind. According to St. John Chrysostom, archbishop of Constantinople in the fourth century A.D., God himself is always in dialogue with humans. God speaks through the prophets and the Apostles, and he also speaks through his creation. "The heavens declare the glory of God" (Ps. 19.1), exclaims the holy Psalmist, and whoever is able to listen with understanding to the silent words of created beings is blessed.

Dialogue is most necessary and useful for the interaction of men! It is so useful that God himself uses it when he speaks in various ways to man and when he listens to man's prayers. Life would be impossible without dialogue. It is through dialogue that a mother communicates with her children, teaches them, participates in their joy and pain, comforts them, encourages them, listens to their difficulties, and eases their way to maturity. It is through dialogue that a teacher cultivates knowledge, that a preacher of the faith catechizes, solves enquiries, bears burdens, and serves the believer. Dialogue promotes science, broadens horizons, communicates feelings, changes emotions, reveals truths, dissolves illusions, abolishes prejudice, cultivates relationships, forges bonds, and makes the human person what he is. Speech is justified only when it is truly responded to, and true response to speech is dialogue.

The speech of God, reflected in the speech of humans, constitutes a fitting example of dialogue, for there is no place for coercion in religion, and ultimately faith cannot be obtained through threats but is rather encouraged through gentle persuasion. The person who refuses to engage in dialogue will always remain spiritually poor. He suffers from the illusion of self-sufficiency and the horror of insecurity. He sees only by the light of his own eyes and refuses to enrich himself with what the eyes of others have seen; he listens only through his own ears and refuses to hear what the ears of others have heard. If he starts down a wrong way, he is unable to change direction, for he does not speak with any who can show him the right way.

Dialogue is safe and beneficial because it does not eliminate the responsibility, of each member of the conversation, to form a considered opinion. Whatever subject arises in the course of a conversation, the participant listens carefully, examines and evaluates it, and then either accepts or rejects what he has heard. Consequently, dialogue does not upset the convictions of the one who engages in it; it does not alter his convictions against his will but only when he himself decides to refine them. Dialogue between followers of our two religions is indeed both necessary and beneficial.

Let us now make a small attempt to engage in theological interreligious dialogue. The Christian faith teaches that Jesus Christ is the son of God. The Qur'an states that God does not have a son. There appears to be a clear contradiction between these two teachings. But is this really so? Christian doctrine affirms, that no matter what we positively say about God, it is in the end never possible to define God, because God is beyond every definition. God is unknowable and incomprehensible to our weak human mental powers.

Therefore, concepts of God are but anthropomorphic icons of him. They aid us in our limited ability to fully understand him, but we must always bear in mind that every human conception of God is inferior to what he really is. We know only a part, as the Apostle Paul says. Consequently, the identity of Jesus Christ as the son of God expresses a reality, though not as understood by the simple person, who associates this reality with his relationship with his son. Because of this simplification, Christian teaching also uses another expression to describe Jesus Christ. It calls him the Incarnate Word of God, the One-who-became-flesh. The Gospel of John begins by declaring, "In the beginning was the Word, and the Word was with God, and the Word was God" (Jn. 1.1). It adds that "the Word became flesh and dwelt among us" (Jn. 1.14)—that is, became human and lived among us.

It is easier for human logic to accept that God "possesses Word"—that is, that he is able to express Himself; a god without the capacity for self-expression is not an acceptable god. However, the use of the term "Word of God," and especially "incarnated," together with the term "Son of God," enlightens more lucidly the reality of "Jesus Christ." However, none of these terms, separately or in combination, could ever define this reality exactly. This is why holy scripture and the writings of the great ecclesiastical thinkers use many other terms for the Word of God, such as "Wisdom of God," "Light of Light," "Son of Man," and others. With these, they try to express different angles, or rays of a reality that exists above human understanding and logic.

The Word of God and the Words of Man

The ideal is always superior to the expressive ability of the human mind. That an expression is understood to be incapable of conveying a given reality in its entirety is not a cause for scandal for the sincere Christian, for he knows the *apophatic* (or negative) character of *kataphatic* (or positive) theology. In every positive expression about divine realities, there necessarily exists an apophatic element, one that affirms that human logic is insufficient to define them and that something inexpressible must lie beyond expressions.[15]

From everything we have said, it is clear that, for the thinking man, Christian or Muslim, the belief that God does not have a son, on the one hand, and, on the other, the belief that Jesus Christ is both the Incarnate Word and son of God, may not be as essentially opposed as they seem. For Christians do not accept that Jesus Christ was born of God in the

15. See the anonymous writings of Dionysius the Areopagite in the early fifth century; and Andrew Louth, *Denys the Areopagite* (London: G. Chapman; Wilton, Conn.: Morehouse-Barlow, 1989).

same way that the sons of human men are born. And so they can respond in agreement to the Muslim who refuses to believe something so crude and can affirm that the issue goes deeper, to the true relationship of the Word of God with God and to the Incarnation of the Word.

Mehmet the conqueror of Constantinople asked the patriarch of the time, Gennadios (or Georgios) Scholarios,[16] about this issue. The patriarch replied that for us Christians it is out of the question that the Word of God does not possess substance. So we Christians believe in a Word of God who is substantial, and from this point of view we call him son of God, without of course implying a father–son relationship comparable to the human one.

From this short but representative analysis, we see that dialogue, when engaged in with goodwill and deep knowledge of the issues leads, if not to agreement, then at least to mutual understanding and rapprochement, to the removal of misunderstandings that have sometimes prevailed for centuries, and to the realization that those who seem opposed to us are not always necessarily so. Therefore, before we say that we disagree on a specific issue, we must investigate it more deeply. This is so we might realize with surprise that we agree, even if it does not seem so, or that we are very close to agreeing.

Something else that causes disagreement and conflict, not only between different religions but also within the same religion, is to treat a part of the truth as if it were the whole truth. It is has been shown that human logic cannot express everything. There are thoughts and experiences and objects for which no specific words or expressions exist. Consequently, human beings are driven to use images or comparisons. For example, it is said that, at the time of Christ's transfiguration, his clothes became "white as the light," although light is not exactly white.[17] During the ascension of St. Paul to a world totally unlike our earthly one, he ascended "unto the third heaven" and heard "unspeakable words," and none of his readers, except perhaps a rare few, have any experience of what the third heaven or the unspeakable words are like. Consequently,

---

16. First Patriarch of Constantinople under Ottoman rule, Gennadios (1400–72) was a learned philosopher and theologian.

17. See Andreas Andreopoulos, *Metamorphosis: The Transfiguration in Byzantine Theology and Iconography* (Crestwood, N.Y: St. Vladimir's Seminary Press, 2005).

each member of his audience, or each one of his readers, though he might have an inkling of what he who expressed himself in this way wanted to communicate. Nevertheless, this reader does not understand everything.

In cases like these, if we consider the small piece of the truth that we can understand as comprising the whole truth, we will be led into serious misunderstandings and disagreements. Moreover, when we unhesitatingly insist that we possess the right and correct understanding, we are led into those conflicts and divisions that every religion experiences. We of the Orthodox Church accept that the Church correctly interprets Christian teaching as expressed through the holy synods, made up primarily of its hierarchs and other erudite and righteous believers. The Roman Catholic Church accepts that the pope infallibly expresses the truth when he speaks *ex cathedra.* The majority of Protestant churches believe that the truth is expressed through each congregation or even through each individual believer separately.[18] This may lead to ambiguity in the faith, to the relativization of everything.

The correct path is not of course the relativization of everything but rather the acknowledgment that the abilities of the human mind are limited. The person who understands his and other men's mental insufficiency is peaceful and humble and conciliatory toward his fellow human beings who might understand a particular truth in a different way. He chooses what he considers the most correct view according to his best judgment, or according to the judgment of the Church or the religion to which he belongs, but he does not condemn those who with good intentions have chosen another view. And he always prays to God that the deeper meanings of the holy texts might be revealed to everyone, because in many cases they are not disclosed at the first reading.

Social and Personal Conditions of Dialogue

This brings us to a third point, which is concerned with the interpretation of the word of God within the context of the conditions in which it was expressed, of the people to whom it was addressed, and of the spiritual situation of today's believer. We all know that many commandments of

---

18. See John Meyendorff, *The Primacy of Peter*, 2nd edition (Leighton Buzzard, U.K.: Faith Press, 1973).

God are provisional, concerned with a specific place and time—advisable actions within the context of the conditions of a specific people. If we attempt to enforce today commandments that were handed down long ago but we do not make the necessary distinction, we will act against the will of God—for, though it is written in the Old Testament that God commanded the extermination of a certain person or nation, this does not allow us today to exterminate a person or nation, believing that we thereby fulfill the will of God. Unfortunately, many people, citing verses from scripture written long ago for other people in other circumstances, attempt to justify their misguided actions or lead astray their fellow human beings who might not have knowledge enough to resist them.[19]

Special attention must be paid to the level of spiritual progress of the believer for whom the commandment has been given. It is evident that what has been commanded of the faithful solitary ascetic, who is completely dedicated to God, is not always similarly valid for the householder, who lives within society. There certainly exist commandments that are equally valid for all people, but there also exist commandments given to the beginners on the road to virtue, as there exist pediatric nurses who are suited only for infants.

Similarly there exist infant words and childish words and words for spiritual maturity. It is the duty of every era to investigate which of the earlier commandments remain valid. For we must distinguish the universal will of God that is valid for all people of every era—the will that covers such virtues as charity, faith, and the like—from the provisional commandments of God, such as specifically how acts of charity are to be performed. This does not mean that the essential will of God changes but that, since we humans are changeable, our approaches to the will of God change according to our spiritual situation. That is another reason for humility and peace—for, although some followers of one religion interpret the will of God in one way while other followers of the same or of another religion interpret it in a different way, this does not mean that one of them must be wrong or that everyone is equally wrong. Someone spiritually more advanced than someone else may understand God's will

19. See John Breck, *The Power of the Word* (Crestwood, N.Y.: St. Vladimir's Seminary Press, 1986); and John Breck, *Scripture in Tradition: The Bible and Its Interpretation in the Orthodox Church* (Crestwood, N.Y.: St. Vladimir's Seminary Press, 2001).

differently. And as we have no other judge besides our own often untrustworthy self to determine who is right, we ultimately are held responsibility for our choice.

Of course there are religious leaders who lead the faithful, but each person himself chooses the religious leader he wants to follow, and he is responsible for his own choice. All this means that we need discretion, that it is a mistake to be fanatical and to condemn our fellow human beings who might think or believe in a way different from ours. It means that dialogue is necessary for mutual understanding and for peaceful coexistence and cooperation. Despite the absoluteness that provides the foundation for every religious faith, interreligious dialogue is also necessary, because, as our knowledge of other religions increases, so too does our understanding of our own religion. Finally, a better understanding of our own religion and of one or several other religions helps us to better understand what God expects from humankind and to better discern the weaknesses or inaccuracies that may lie beneath our beliefs.

Certainly not every believer is able to undertake such comparisons, for he might not have the knowledge or the necessary wisdom. Specialized spiritual knowledge and experience are called for, and this is why the leading representatives of each religion conduct interreligious dialogues today. In this way, suspicions of proselytizing are avoided, a high level of discussion is maintained, and fears of compromising elements of one's faith and of one's affection for one's fellow speaker, who belongs to a different religion, prove unjustified. We say this because unfortunately the less educated of believers are not only unqualified to participate in interreligious dialogue but they also hold those who participate in them in suspicion, doubting their religious honesty and integrity.

This is why we explicitly declare that interreligious dialogue does not take place either for participants to enter into alliances with members of other religions or for them to badger the other into acceding to their beliefs. They take place rather for the cessation of religious intolerance, for the triumph of mutual understanding, and for the establishment of certainty of the good intentions of both sides and are characterized by respect for each person's cultural background and freedom of religious choice. During the fourteenth century, a dialogue was conducted between the great Christian theologian and saint Archbishop Gregory Palamas of

Thessaloniki[20] and distinguished representatives of Islam. Of course they did not entirely agree, but one of the representatives of Islam stated that for him the time should come when mutual understanding between followers of the two religions would exist. St. Gregory agreed to this statement and wished that time would come soon. Today we are able to wish, and we do wish wholeheartedly, for this to be fulfilled in our days.

Freedom and Religion

Message to the Sixth Academic Meeting of the Dialogue between Judaism and Orthodox Christianity, Jerusalem, March 14, 2007.

We offer you our most sincere blessings and profound thanks for your efforts and determination in addressing what may indeed be the most pressing issue facing the world community. That is the issue of "Religious Liberty, and the Relationship between Freedom and Religion." How do we, assembled in this convocation, advance the cause of tolerance and respect for religious difference? How do we form a consensus about what is the proper and just role of our respective governments in protecting religious freedom? How do we provide leadership and guidance for a world that all too often sees religious difference as a threat to a sense of religious orthodoxy that is misguided and fanatical? These are the questions that you will be addressing over the next few days.

Please allow us to offer you some thoughts about this critical endeavor. We sit today on the throne of a long and illustrious line of predecessors: the Apostle Andrew foremost, and patriarchs and archbishops, who have constantly been confronted with the forces of governmental power and its ability to do good and, frequently, to do evil. These venerable spiritual forebears, who have held our sacred see's responsibilities before us, have realized that a difficult balance must be struck between the interests of state and those of religion. Political forces can often be destructive and corrosive of the eternal truths of religion. Often a misguided sense of homogeneity has dominated the impulses of those who held control, no matter how temporary and fleeting, of government power.

20. St. Gregory (1296–1359) is the preeminent theologian and defender of Hesychasm. See John Meyendorff, *St. Gregory Palamas and Orthodox Spirituality* (Crestwood, N.Y.: St. Vladimir's Seminary Press, 1974).

The dangers of this quest for homogeneity are chronicled in the darkest annals of history. Ultimately, the mechanics of this devastating force are always the same—we objectify those who hold different religious views, we stop considering as human, as our brothers and sisters, those who hold differing religious beliefs, and we think of them as "a Jew," as "a Christian," as "a Muslim," as "a Hindu," or as "a Buddhist." They are no longer our neighbors—no longer "Moisha," "Giorgos," or "Ahmed." Their essential humanity is obscured. They become obstacles to our political aspirations. They become nothing more than targets of full-force governmental power.

Ultimately, the love of God demands that we have an existential sense of *agapē*, a love that involves a personal and intimate exploration of our love for God and neighbor. We emphasize here *personal and intimate*, because we cannot truly love humanity in general. We can only love another person. And, as we read in Deuteronomy, we must learn to love God with all our heart, mind, and soul, and our neighbor as ourselves. Love is our personal response to the love of God, which is extended, by grace, to an intimate expression of *agapē* to another person—and that person is our neighbor. Hate, in turn, deludes us into thinking that there is such a thing as "a Jew," "a Christian," or "a Muslim." Evil deceives us into thinking that some person or group is what we label them.

Therefore, as you discuss and examine this critical topic of religious freedom, we challenge you all to reflect on the events of your lives. Personalize what respect and tolerance mean to you. Do not engage in some exercise in abstraction, but talk about how you want to treat your neighbors and how you want your neighbors to treat you. After all, as believers and servants of God, we know that it is impossible to say both that we love God, whom we have not seen, and that we hate our neighbor, whom we see every day of our lives on God's inhabited earth.

Concepts of Creation in the Abrahamic Faiths

Address to the Summit on Religions and Conservation, Atami, Japan, April 5, 1995.

Combining the environmental issues of our day with theological presuppositions can be likened to a paradoxical and even eccentric enterprise.

To our awareness, ecology is representative of the pursuits of practical and convenient strategies. Contrariwise, theology or even theological cosmology, if used only as terms of expression, are to many people self-evidently related to abstract theoretical research. They refer to dogmas and ideologies and have little or no bearing on the practical aspects of life and or on practical theological problems.

Contemporary ecology, as thematic scientific research, but also under the guise of crusading movements for the salvation of the earth's ecosystem, is an expression of the various characteristics focusing on the human interest in what is practical. The logic behind the protection of the environment is projected purely as a logic of convenience. If we do not protect the natural environment, our own survival will be jeopardized and become problematic. Very soon the presence of humankind itself on our planet will be threatened. Day by day, the danger of the degeneration and even the extinction of the human race grows increasingly marked and appears increasingly imminent. . . .

Stemming from this logic of convenience, the ecological movements of today demand that rules be set down for how man should use nature. Ecology aspires to be a practical ethic of human behavior toward the natural environment. But, as does every other ethic, ecology too raises the question "Who determines the rules of human behavior, and by what authority? What logic makes these rules compulsory, and what is the source of their validity?"

The Logic and Ethic of Ecology

The correctness of ecological ethics is borne witness to by its evident usefulness. It is logical and obvious that, in order for humankind to survive on earth, contracts with the natural environment must be demanded, contracts that permit human survival. However, the rationale behind intentionally using what is convenient and advantageous has led to the destruction of the natural environment. Man destroys the environment not because he is motivated by irrational self-gratification; rather, he destroys it by trying to take advantage of nature in order to secure more conveniences and comforts in daily life.

The logic of the destruction of the environment is precisely the same as that of the protection of the environment. Both "logics" confront nature as an exclusively useful given. In this way, the difference that exists between the two "logics" (that of the destruction and that of the protection of the ecosystem) is only quantitative. Ecologists demand limited and controlled exploitation of the natural environment—that is, a quantitative reduction—which would also permit its further, long-term exploitation. They ask for the rational limitation of nonrational usage—in other words, for a kind of consumer rationalism, which is "more correct" than the consumer rationalism that characterizes today's exploitation of nature. They ask for consumer "temperance" or "moderation" in consumerism.

Yet, who will determine or define the "more correct" way of applying such temperance or moderation? And by what means? The request, even though it appears to be extremely rational, is, by definition and in practice, irrational. By definition it is contradictory because consumerism cannot come into conflict with consumerism. And it is irrational in practice because most of the earth's population does not accept being deprived of conveniences and comforts that the destruction of the environment has secured for a small minority who live in "civilized" societies.

In order for the request of ecologists to be maintained, another logic is required, one capable of substituting the logic of convenience. The request should be founded in an entirely different intentionality. One example of this would be in the altruism of someone who cares about the destiny of future generations. Another would be the embrace of a "quality" of life not judged by the criteria of consumer ease and abundance—in other words, universally accepted intentions that are based on something other than making use of what is convenient must be demanded. And in defining these intentions it is, from all accounts, impossible for everyone to agree only on rational criteria. People must therefore come up with different needs and another hierarchy of needs. And different needs come only when, in the consciousness of the people, nature (or the world) acquires another meaning, one that is not tied exclusively to the convenience of those who would exploit it.

The monotheistic religious traditions preserve the attitude that natural reality is not exclusively convenient. In these traditions, the world is a creation of God. The use of the world by humans constitutes a practical relation between man and God, since God gives and man receives the natural goods as an offering of God's divine love for the sake of the world.

In Islam, the Qur'an teaches that all animals live in community and that they are known and accountable before God (sura 6, verse 38). It also denounces the arrogance of those who treat the rest of creation without respect:

> Do you not see that it is God whose praises are celebrated by all beings in the heavens and on earth, even by the birds in their flocks? Each creature knows its prayer and psalm; and so does God know what they are doing. And yet, you understand not how they declare His Glory. (Sura 24, verse 41)

Humanity and the Environment

Within this picture of all creation arising from a loving creator God, the question has to be asked, "What of humanity?" What role do the Abrahamic faiths ascribe to human beings? The answer is clear, the consequences immense.

Psalm 8 addresses this question directly:

> I look up at your heavens, made by your fingers,
> at the moon and the stars you set in place—
> ah, what is man that you should spare a thought for him,
> the son of man that you should care for him?
> Yet you have made him little less than an angel.
> You have crowned him with glory and splendor,
> made him lord over the work of your hands,
> set all things under his feet,
> sheep and oxen, all these,
> yes, wild animals too,
> birds in the air, fish in the sea
> traveling the paths of the ocean. (Ps. 8.3–8)

Christianity inherited this tradition, as Jesus shows when he compares the value of human beings to sparrows both loved and cared for by God, though human beings are a hundred times more important (Lk. 12.6–7). It is also the case that the sense of human beings being part of a bigger picture, a part of God's greater purpose, is to be found in equal strength within both Jewish and Christian texts. For example, in the Torah, in Genesis 9, the covenant with Noah after the flood is not just with Noah and his descendants—the human race—it is with all life on earth. Similarly, the purpose of life, death, and the Resurrection of Christ as St. Paul speaks of it in Romans 8 and in Colossians 1 is not just for human beings but for the sake of all life on earth.

Ultimately, for Judaism, Christianity, and Islam, humanity is the most important, the most significant species, and with this comes responsibilities. Islam expresses this in the notion of humans being khalifas. A khalifa is a vice-regent, someone appointed by the supreme ruler to have responsibility over a given area in an empire. The Qur'an (in sura 2, verse 30) uses this phrase as a description of the role of humanity. We have been given great authority by God, but it is to be used only on God's behalf, not for our own ends and ambitions. The Qur'an makes it clear that any abuse of this power, any wanton or wasteful use of the world's natural resources, is repugnant to God and therefore to Islam.

Two fundamental consequences emerge from attitudes such as this: The first consequence is the understanding that the world is meant to be used by humans not for their own purpose but as the means whereby they come into relationship with God. If humans change this use into egocentric, greedy exploitation, into oppression and the destruction of nature, then man's own vital relationship with God is denied and refuted, a relationship predestined to continue into eternity.

The second consequence is the understanding that the world as a creation of God ceases to be a neutral object for man's use. The world incarnates the word of the Creator, just as every work of art incarnates the word of the artist. The objects of natural reality bear the seal of the wisdom and love of their Creator. They are the word of God calling man to come into dialogue with him. Nevertheless, it is a given historical fact that the attitude that the world today is a neutral object to be used—over which man exercises dominion for his own egocentric pleasure—constitutes an attitude that was born and shaped in the bosom of Christian Europe.

The analysis of the historical conditions and theoretical presuppositions would require special study, as they lead Christian Europe to supplant the relationship between man and the world with the perception of man's unlimited domination over the world. The reasons for this differentiation are not unrelated to the reasons that incited the painful Schism of the eleventh century. It remains a fact today that man's necessary change in position with regard to the natural environment has foreshadowed a change in the meaning that man gives to matter and the world. Ecology cannot inspire respect for nature if it does not express a different cosmology from what prevails in our culture today, and one liberated from naïve materialism to the same extent that it is liberated from naïve idealism.

Principles of a Christian Worldview

We will try to underscore in epigrammatic fashion the possibility of Christian cosmology as it contributes to this extremely timely quest. Our tenuous impressions rely mainly on the works of St. Gregory of Nyssa, St. Maximus the Confessor,[21] and St. Gregory Palamas. This does not mean, however, that there do not exist other ecclesiastical authors dealing substantially with this problem.

The epicenter of this patristic contribution is the introduction of a third ontological category for interpreting the fact of existence and the cause of its beginning: It is the category of "energies," to which is added the relation between "essence" (*ousia*) and "hypostasis," which ranks highest in the ontological categories of philosophy. Although the beginning of the problem for ecclesiastical thought was mainly theological, we will borrow adequate analogies from anthropological experience to make these ontological categories clearer for us who live in the contemporary world.

When we are talking about the essence of man, we are referring to a common means by which every human participates in what exists, in his being. We say that man is a being who walks upright; is humorous, logical, and poetical-creative; and has an imagination, judgment, will, the ability to love, and so on. All these are indications of means by which every human exists—indications of the same essence, or nature, of man. Certainly, the essence of man, the universal means of human existence, does not exist detached from specific individual existences. Each human setting realizes one existential fact—the common essence. Each "hypostasizes" the common "essence"; each is the hypostasis of the essence. The essence of human nature exists only in a hypostatic, or personal, state.

---

21. One of the formative theologians of the Orthodox Church, Maximus the Confessor (580–662) was a monk who suffered for upholding the fullness of Christ's human nature and will. See Andrew Louth, *Maximus the Confessor* (New York: Routledge, 1960).

But the common indications of essence, those that the individual existence also hypostasizes, are real existential possibilities; they are indications of the means by which every human existence is realized. And so we are speaking about the energies of either essence or nature, while referring to the fact of the existential possibilities of either essence or nature. Every human existence is potentially realized; each individual is a realized actuality of bodily and psychical functions with possibilities for reason, will, imagination, and judgment.

Every human individual being "hypostasizes" the common energies of human nature in a singular, disparate, and unrepeatable way. Each human being has reason, will, imagination, and judgment, but each individual person speaks, understands, wills, imagines, and judges in a singular, disparate, and unrepeatable way. Consequently, the energies of human nature constitute an ontological fact, which characterizes the common way of existence for human beings, but those energies make this way hypostatic. The energies hold back and reveal the absolute existential otherness of the subject.

We know the human subject, the otherness of human existence, because of the energies by which its subjectivity is realized and manifested. We know the composer Johann Sebastian Bach when listening to his music. We know the artist Rembrandt through his paintings. The sounds of Bach's music or the materials and the colors on the canvases of Rembrandt are of a different nature from the human nature of both artists. Nevertheless, the poetic, creative energy of the artist, what reveals his hypostatic otherness, is realized through heterogeneous natures. Music, colors, writing, marble, clay—all these activate the word of the musician, the painter, the writer, the sculptor. They reveal the person of the artist, his existential identity and otherness.

The ontological content of this category of "energies" implies that we ascribe the ontological "beginning" of matter and of the world to a personal God—not to the essence of God, but to the energies of God. The divine energies reveal the word of the personal otherness of God, a word realized through matter, an essence totally different from that of God.

Fifteen centuries before the theory of quanta in contemporary physics, ecclesiastical thought confirmed that matter is energy, "a subscription of logical qualities," a created result of the uncreated divine energy. The difference in the "essence" between the created and the uncreated does not exclude, nor does it hinder, the created from acting as "word" of the uncreated or from revealing the created energy and the hypostatic otherness of the personal God-Logos.[22] In the same manner, the sounds and the colors, even though they are heterogeneous natures of the human person, activate the "word" of the creative energy and the hypostatic otherness of Bach or Rembrandt.

Only when human beings confront matter and all of nature as the work of a personal Creator does the use of matter and all of nature in turn establish a true relationship between man and natural reality rather than the domination by man over it. Only then will it be possible to speak about an "ecological ethic" that does not borrow its regulatory character from conventional rational rules but rather from the need for a person to love and be loved within the context of a personal relationship. The reason there is beauty in creation, therefore, is amorous love; it is a call from God to man; it is a call into a personal relationship and to communion of life with him, a relation that is vital and life-giving. Contemporary ecology could then be the practical response of human beings to God's call, the practical participation in our relationship with him.

Is the ontological clarification of the meaning of matter and of the world enough to prompt a different relationship between contemporary man and matter and the world? Of course not! In order for man to confront nature with the respect and fear with which he confronts a personal artistic creation, the theoretical clarification must become a powerful source of knowledge and socially validated. At this point the role of social dynamics as referred to in ecclesiastical tradition and community can be determined as long as the ecclesiastical conscience is purged of its liberation from an ideological structure and from its inert retirement in the restoration of institutional formalisms. . . .

The great challenge to which the Abrahamic faiths of the monotheistic traditions are called today is found in the unexpected givens of contemporary physical science, the captivating new cosmology that comes out of the study of quantum mechanics—the energetic quality of matter, the relativity of place and time as dimensions of matter, the constantly increasing anthropocentric intentionality of the universe. The language of physical science today shows us universal reality as an active word that is

22. See John Meyendorff, *A Study of Gregory Palamas* (London: Faith Press, 1964).

not hypostatically localized except in its contact with the word of the human person.

If there is a future for the ecological demands of our contemporary times, this future is based, we believe, in the free encounter of the historical experience of the living God with the empirical confirmation of his active word in nature.

The Peace of God in the World: I

Inaugural address at the World Conference, Brussels, December 19, 2001.

We address to you a wholehearted greeting and welcome you all fraternally on this notable day on which God has gathered us here, so that together we may make one more effort toward peaceful coexistence and cooperation among the three monotheistic religions and also among all peoples.

The well-known tragic events of September 11 of this year ending demand that we reveal to all peoples the peaceful and peace-loving person of God and to dispel the impression that God blesses human bloodshed. We have always declared that war in the name of religion is war against religion and that we must separate political from religious activism, so that what is done by political dictates is not confused with what is taught by our three monotheistic religions.

Your presence in this hall reveals your eager response to the invitation to a common discussion and consideration of the subject of "the peace of God in the world" and allows us to hope for the success of this meeting, which we wholeheartedly desire. The great erudition and the high and acknowledged moral standard and authority of all of you who participate in the present event guarantee that the search for the truth will be sober and objective and that your peace-loving disposition and fraternal collaboration with one another will be sincere.

We thank you for your attendance and for your contributions, which we have been eagerly waiting to hear with much interest. We also thank all those who honor this meeting with their presence, and we address to them too our heartfelt salutation. Permit, therefore, our Modesty, to expound briefly and in an introductory manner our concerns, which prompted us, together with His Excellency the president of the Commission of the European Union, to invite you to participate in this meeting.

We, the representatives of our religions, and through us these religions themselves, are accused of being responsible for destructive and bloody clashes among human beings. We are accused of directing civilizations to bloody confrontations and competitions for dominance, of being behind the slaughter that history has already recorded with horror and also the forthcoming one that is expected to be revealed, according to the predictions of those who think that they can foretell the future.

Often we hear the followers of one religion casting blame, for all inhuman deeds that occur to them, on the followers of another religion. We read in books, both old and new, accusations against any one of the three religions that are represented here, or against all of them—that they are responsible for horrific deeds and inhuman behavior toward those of other faiths or toward those who stray from their traditional faith. Some of our critics, especially certain humanist philosophers, arrive at the point of suggesting that contemporary man should either abandon all religion or construct a new one, one of human origin and comprising all that the human spirit accepts concerning God.

Indeed, our accusers submit to the universal court of humanity an infinite series of homicidal acts of religious bigotry and religious fanaticism. They make a most severe case against us, the representatives of the religions, and against these religions themselves, by recalling a whole series of events: the condemnation of Socrates to death by the democratic court of the ancient Athenians (through a slight majority of votes) on the charge "that he does not worship the gods whom the city worships" and introduces, instead, new deities; or the terrible persecutions of the Roman emperors against the early Christians; or the persecutions of Jews by certain Christians in medieval times; or the murderous conclusions of crusades and conquests; or the inter-Christian and inter-Muslim wars that produced victims by the hundreds; or finally, the contemporary racial holocausts, which are not unaffected by religious prejudices.

We ought, then, to offer a word of self-defense to those who put such devastating questions to us. Are we really happy with the shedding of human blood? Do we bless slaughter? Do we approve of homicide? Do we believe that God is pleased with the taking of human life or that he is satisfied with the sight and the smell of human blood?

Do we also believe that the terrible words of Krishna, which we read in the "inspired song"—namely, the Bhagavad-Gita—and are addressed to Arjuna, are lawful in our present times as well? We mean the words "Rise up, then, and acquire fame, through victory over the enemies; enjoy a rich kingdom; since your enemies have been already murdered by me and no one else, you alone should become the instrument" (chapter 11, verse 33).

Peaceful Coexistence among Monotheistic Religions

Do we believe that God approves of murders and is in need of us to serve as his instruments of these executions? Truly, we find impossible to accept—on the basis of the faith of all of us present here in this hall, the representatives of the three monotheistic religions—that the compassionate, merciful, and long-suffering God, who does not desire the death of the sinner but rather his repentance, conversion, and salvation, approves of all the abhorrent events that history has recorded with grief and that our hearts behold with pain.

We then, as responsible representatives and distinguished scholars of these religions, are obliged to differentiate between the true, compassionate teaching and faith of each of them and the various heterodox teachings that pose as expressions of the will of God in accordance with the teaching of each religion but are in fact mere expressions of human notions concerning his will.

For human beings always seek a justification of their deeds and do not hesitate to claim that their actions, and especially those that increase their power and domination over their fellows, take place in conformity with the will of God. The fact, however, that there are so many rival views of the will of God bears witness to the logical necessity that not all of them can be correct.

Consequently, there is need of critical investigation of all that appears as, or is claimed to be, the will of God—investigation on the basis, first, of the generally accepted divine properties of love for humanity and merciful disposition and, second, of the selfish or unselfish disposition of the speaker. Beyond these, we may also consider the historical and all other conditions that prevailed at the time when the will of God was expressed, since God often tolerates, on account of the hardness of heart of the people, certain actions as being better than others that are worse, the tolerated actions being still not perfect or fully pleasing to him.

If, on the other hand, it is true, as we believe, that human beings ought to strive constantly toward improvement of their morals and their social relations, then surely we must today reject certain manners of behavior—for example, slavery and piracy—that in the past were deemed lawful and permissible. War, too, as a means of dominating others or imposing a religious faith, ought to be included among those practices that need to be kept under strict moral control.

In the New Testament, the sacred scripture of the Christians, very little is said about material war, either casually or negatively. Much is said, however, about the spiritual struggle that is undertaken for our sanctification and the purpose of uprooting the evil that exists within us. In addition, much is said about peace, both internal and social. Peacemakers are declared blessed and are called sons of God (Mt. 5.9). Christians are admonished to maintain peace with all human beings as much as possible (Rom. 12.18). God is characterized as the God of peace. The word *peace* is used as a blessing and as salutation. The peace of God is given to human beings as a perfect gift, and the incarnation of the Word of God is generally announced as the cause of peace on earth.

Likewise, in the Old Testament and in the Qur'an, the sacred books of Jews and Muslims, although much is said about various wars, peace is most clearly placed on a much higher moral level than war. The hundreds of references to peace in the Old Testament lead to the conclusion that peace is granted as a gift from God, that it is regarded as desirable by all people, that it is recommended as something to be sought after and pursued, that it accompanies those who love the law of God, and, finally, that it constitutes a divine blessing.

In the Qur'an, peace is characterized as the supreme good (chapter 4, verse 127), and it is explicitly stated that God invites all to the way of peace (chapter 9, verse 26). It is said that he who murders one who did not commit murder is a murderer of the human race (chapter 5, verse 35)—and this, of course, constitutes a clear condemnation of acts of terrorism that are committed against unsuspecting innocents. The Qur'an also makes explicit that religion is not to be imposed. On this point, of course, others who are more informed scholars of the Qur'an than we are will speak more fully.

In our view, however, external peace is based on a peaceful relation with God and on a personal relation with fellow human beings. "If one does not conquer one's spiritual enemies [evil dispositions], one cannot be at peace," says Abba Isaac the Syrian.[23] "For nothing is as able to produce peace, as the knowledge of God and the acquisition of virtue," adds St. John Chrysostom.[24] In addition, St. James writes that wars and battles proceed from desires and especially from avarice, which leads to theft of human goods (Jm. 4.1–2).

In conclusion, we would say that social peace presupposes inner peace, which, in turn, presupposes a peaceful relation with God and respect for fellow human beings. The latter presuppose conformity to God's manner of life as lover of humanity, goodness, and peace. We know that there are different religious views among us. We do not consider it necessary to have these differences extinguished in order to achieve social peace. We respect our fellow human beings and their convictions, and it is exactly on this basis that we engage in dialogue and peaceful cooperation with them.

History presents to us many wise leaders who were able to rule many nations peacefully, by showing respect for the religious and cultural particularities of their subjects, as we will hear in the special communications of this meeting. The example of these leaders ought to be an inspiration to us. There is room today for us too to develop a sincere respect for each other as well as a peaceful collaboration for the promotion of the peace of God in the world. The coexistence of believers of the various religions, which existed in the past and continues to exist today in many countries, especially in the Middle East, constitutes a model to be imitated and adopted throughout the world.

We, the religious leaders, are obliged to lead the peacemaking process and not to follow behind the politicians. More important still, it is not fitting for us to create obstacles to peace through the preaching of fanaticism and bigotry. We are certain that no one among the distinguished

---

23. *Ascetical Treatise* 68. Isaac the Syrian, or Isaac of Nineveh (d. ca. 700), is a renowned and influential mystic.

24. PG55.57–58.

representatives and believers of the various religions who participate in the present meeting is deprived of a good disposition toward the peace of God and the peaceful coexistence and cooperation among the members of the monotheistic religions. This is because we do not speak of a syncretistic combination of faiths but of a cooperation among human beings while the faiths are preserved.

The Peace of God in the World: II

Concluding address at the World Conference in Brussels, December 20, 2001.

We have been filled with joy, having heard during these days various views being expressed concerning the peace of God in the world. They agree with each other, although they originate in many and different religious traditions.

The common point, which conjoins all of our views and us, is that we place the person of God as the starting point of our existence and the will of God as the foundation of the moral evaluation of human behavior. For us the world has a purpose; human existence has a purpose; history is moving toward an end, and spiritual laws govern its path, just as natural laws regulate the harmonious operation of the universe. It is the good Creator that instituted all these purposes and laws and the harmonization of our life with them as a guide to our eternal bliss.

There are two other positions that stand against this common faith. The first one dominates a great number of human beings of so-called Western civilization and has its foundation in a kind of autonomous humanity that has been cut off from any relation with God. The second ignores the unique person of God and tries to approach natural life and supernatural reality by means of a multitude of spiritual beings, which, under various names and characteristics, control the freedom of humanity. Both of these positions lead to a hopeless emptiness, because they do not supply either a satisfactory answer to the panhuman quest concerning the meaning of existence or a possibility of personal relation with the other person, a relation that is constantly being sought.

To fill this emptiness, the autonomous human beings of the West keep inventing life theories and ideologies, which, as abstract intellectual constructions, do not supply any experience of relatedness, nor do they abolish loneliness. The human beings that seek to communicate with the spirits, either in the East or in the West, discover that no warmth and no love grows between them but rather a relation of servile dependence.

We who believe in a personal God have received the experience of his love and peace, which come to dwell in our soul, fulfilling it and giving it rest, as the communion of personal human beings with the great God is restored. There is a multitude of lovers of God throughout the centuries who have expressed this love for God with superb poetic constructions.

"Let my meditation be sweet to Him," sings David, the prophet-king (Ps. 103.34). "Who shall separate us from the love of God?" asks the Apostle Paul (Rom. 8.35). "Beginning and end You are to me in all the treasure of my life," sings the contemporary Muslim mystic.[25]

There is, then, one and essentially common point among all of us, and this is the love for God and the personal relation with him. The most delicate and sensitive spirits of these three religions, the more they approach God and are refined, the more they advance toward an understanding of the faith and religious experience of the other. One may differ in many respects as far as the traditional faith of the other is concerned, and yet he may also sense that both he and the other seek the same person of the Most High, the God of All-goodness.

What is regarded by some as an extreme viewpoint—namely, the statement of a contemporary Muslim theologian that, if the scandal of the Cross did not exist, then Islam and Christianity not only would have been drawn closer together but would have been fused to form one religion—is rather typical.[26] Equally characteristic is what the Greek Jewish poet Yosef Eliyia[27] wrote:

> You are not the first, nor the last to be Crucified,
> O sweet Jesus, in this world of bitterness and envy;
> and yet, your glory is immaculate within the race of the mortals.
> You may or may not be the Son of God, yet you are a God of pain!

25. Ishmael Emre, in his *Breathings*.

26. See Hasan Hanefi, *Le monde islamique entre revolutionaires et reactionaires, Verse et controverse* (Paris: Les Musulmans, 1971), 55.

27. Noted Greek Jewish poet of the early to mid–twentieth century, from Ioannina, Greece.

Mysticism and Love, Not Fundamentalism and Hatred

Those who wrote these texts were certainly sensitive recipients of the love of God and in some way bridge-makers of communication among the believers of the three religions. If we stand with befitting awe before the personal search of each soul, who, born in a certain religious tradition, opens her wings in order to fly into her search for the beloved, we realize that it is our human duty to show absolute respect for the personal journey of every human being toward the supreme love. Then we are able to embrace that soul in peace and to follow her journey in utter silence and prayer, whether she walks along with us or follows another path, because God, her beloved Lord, expects her and will show her the way. No push and no pressure are needed from our side, only affection and peace. There are also, of course, the less sensitive souls, those who have little interest in the love of God. If we wish to lead them to it, we also need peace, because the turmoil created by conflicts can hide the voice of love.

Finally, there are also the nihilists, who, in a spirit of egocentrism, are happy with the mere enjoyment of this fleeting life. To them, peace is a useful means of achieving their worldly objectives, which can be replaced at any moment by another condition that serves them better.

As religious ministers, we cannot endorse the abolition of peace, which they use as a means for their egocentric aims. Neither can we endorse the irregular condition that such nihilists create again in order to facilitate their aspirations. We firmly insist on the peace of God as the godliest of all conditions. But we are not satisfied simply with a moralistic condemnation of violence, on the mere basis of humanist principles, which cover up the emptiness of the life of religious nihilism and secularism.

The obvious and vital operation of religious faith is what enlightens the meaning of existence and of the coexistence of human beings as a personal relation between man and the personal God and, consequently, a personal relation among human beings. We do not take up the role of a moralist pedagogue, who sanctions regulations and takes care for their observance. We propose a manner of life in communion with God and with our fellow human beings, a manner that is imbued with faith—that is, with confidence, without which no personal relation can develop.

Our present proposal is the fruit of our life experience and renders redundant the condemnation of violence, of bigotry, of fanaticism, because the development of the proposed personal relation renders impossible the exercise of violence and fanatical or hateful actions against the beloved person with whom we are in a communion characterized by love and confidence.

Fanaticism and fundamentalism render null and void religious faith understood as confidence and personal relation. This is because, in place of the personal call of God for a personal relation in love and for spiritual relation with human beings, they substitute the objectified truth, which is like a road roller that flattens persons for the sake of achieving an ideological twist. Personal relation is always a relation of absolute and personal freedom, and hence the religious faith as personal relation is always an offspring of freedom.

The ego refuses to take risks with respect to personal authority. It is satisfied with the relation to authority. It refuses the insecurity of the acceptance of the "thou" as of equal value with itself and prefers the security of the personal ideological twist, which justifies all its personal choices. Faith in God and confidence in his Word demands the opening up of the *I* to the *Thou*[28] of the fellow human being. This opening up is the foundation of religion, and when it is achieved it is accompanied by peace, in the ancient Semitic and comprehensive meaning of that word—fullness, blessing, repose, life, prosperity, harmony with nature and with fellow human beings and with God, and, generally, salvation and glory.

This peace, which is the real offering of religion, passes all understanding and is certainly incomparably higher than any conventional social order and harmony that is achieved through respect for human rights, through dialogue, through collaboration and reconciliation. This is because all these social goods, which are truly worthy of attention and pursuit, and which are indeed met within any contemporary pluralistic society, do not involve the personal communion of her members or compensation for the deepest feeling of loneliness and isolation, which the members of contemporary societies that consist of a great multitude of individuals who never communicate with each other do experience. This lack of personal communion in love constitutes the basic ground on

28. From the title of a book (*I–Thou*) by Austrian-born Jewish philosopher Martin Buber (1878–1965), known for his religious existentialism.

which every kind of painless attack against fellow human beings is developed, whether this finds its expression as economic exploitation, violence, hedonism, or any other form of objectification.

As religious leaders, acquainted with human imperfection, we speak the language of the truth adapted to the spiritual level of each individual. We condemn terrorism as socially harmful. We recommend, as socially advantageous, peace and cooperation among citizens, regardless of religious faith and of every other distinction. Above all these, however, we place the personal relation of love for God and one's fellow human beings. This relation is the perfect model toward which we must strive, and when this is accomplished, and to the extent that it is, violence and war are abolished and peace is established, because "love does not think of evil" about any fellow human being (1 Cor. 13.5).

With this feeling of love for all fellow human beings—those who share the same faith, those who differ in faith, those who agree with us, and those who disagree—we conclude our present discourse. We thank you for your attention and your patience in listening to us as well as for your effective contribution to the achievement of our peaceful cooperation for the establishment of the peace of God in the world, and we address to you our wholehearted farewell.

6

Major Declarations: Public Proclamations

Religion and the Environment: I

Common Declaration signed by HH Pope John Paul II and HAH Ecumenical Patriarch Bartholomew at the Vatican on June 29, 1995.[1]

Blessed be the God and Father of our Lord Jesus Christ, who has blessed us in Christ with every spiritual blessing. (Eph. 1.3)

1. We thank God also for this fraternal meeting of ours, which took place in his name and with the firm intention of obeying his will that his disciples be one (Jn. 17.21). Our meeting has followed other important events, which have seen our Churches declare their desire to relegate to oblivion the excommunications of the past and to set out on the way to reestablishing full communion. Our venerable predecessors Athenagoras I and Paul VI became pilgrims to Jerusalem in order to meet in the Lord's name, precisely where the Lord, by his death and Resurrection, brought humanity forgiveness and salvation. Subsequently, their meetings at the Phanar and in Rome have initiated this new tradition of fraternal visits in order to foster a true dialogue of charity and truth. This exchange of visits

1. On the evening of Thursday, June 29, 1995, Pope John Paul II and Ecumenical Patriarch Bartholomew I signed a common declaration in the Vatican at their last meeting before the Patriarch's departure from Rome. The following is a translation of the declaration, which was written in Italian.

was repeated during the ministry of Patriarch Dimitrios, when, among other things, the theological dialogue was formally opened. Our new-found brotherhood in the name of the one Lord has led us to frank discussion, a dialogue that seeks understanding and unity.

2. This dialogue—through the Joint International Commission—has proved fruitful and has made substantial progress. A common sacramental conception of the Church has emerged, sustained and passed on in time by apostolic succession. In our Churches, the apostolic succession is fundamental to the sanctification and unity of the people of God. Considering that in every local church the mystery of divine love is realized and that this is how the church of Christ shows forth its active presence in each one of them, the Joint Commission has been able to declare that our Churches recognize one another as sister churches, responsible together for safeguarding the one Church of God, in fidelity to the divine plan and in an altogether special way with regard to unity.

We thank the Lord of the Church from the bottom of our hearts, because these affirmations we have made together not only hasten the way to solving existing difficulties but henceforth enable Catholics and Orthodox to give a common witness of faith.

3. This is particularly appropriate on the eve of the third millennium, when, two thousand years after the birth of Christ, all Christians are preparing to make an examination of conscience on the reality of his proclamation of salvation in history and among men.

We will celebrate this great jubilee on our pilgrimage toward full unity and toward that blessed day, which we pray is not far off, when we will be able to share the same bread and the same cup, in the one Eucharist of the Lord.

Let us invite our faithful to make this spiritual pilgrimage together toward the jubilee. Reflection, prayer, dialogue, reciprocal forgiveness, and mutual fraternal love will bring us closer to the Lord and will help us to better understand his will for the Church and for humanity.

4. From this perspective we urge our faithful, Catholics and Orthodox, to reinforce the spirit of brotherhood, which stems from the one baptism and from participation in the sacramental life. In the course of history and in the more recent past, there have been attacks and acts of oppression on both sides. As we prepare on this occasion to ask the Lord for his great mercy, we invite all to forgive one another and to express a

firm will that a new relationship of brotherhood and active collaboration will be established.

Such a spirit should encourage both Catholics and Orthodox, especially where they live side by side, to a more intense collaboration in the cultural, spiritual, pastoral, educational, and social fields and avoid any temptation to indulge in undue zeal for their own community to the disadvantage of the other. May the good of Christ's Church always prevail! Mutual support and the exchange of gifts can only make pastoral activity itself more effective and our witness to the gospel, which we desire to proclaim, more transparent.

5. We maintain that a more active and concerted collaboration will also facilitate the Church's influence in promoting peace and justice in situations of political or ethnic conflict. The Christian faith has unprecedented possibilities for solving humanity's tensions and enmity.

6. In meeting one another, the Pope of Rome and the Ecumenical Patriarch have prayed for the unity of all Christians. In their prayers, they have included all the baptized who are incorporated into Christ, and they have asked for an even deeper fidelity to his gospel for the various communities.

7. They bear in their heart a concern for all humanity, without any discrimination according to race, color, language, ideology or religion.

They therefore encourage dialogue, not only between the Christian churches but also with the various religions and, above all, with those that are monotheistic.

All this doubtless represents a contribution to and a presupposition of the strengthening of peace in the world, for which our Churches pray constantly. In this spirit, we declare, without hesitation, that we are in favor of harmony among peoples and their collaboration, especially in what concerns us most directly: we pray for the full realization of the European Union, without delay, and we hope that its borders will be extended to the East.

At the same time, we make an appeal that everyone will make a determined effort to solve the current burning problem relating to ecology, in order to avoid the great risk threatening the world today due to the abuse of resources that are God's gift.

May the Lord heal the wounds tormenting humanity today and hear our prayers and those of our faithful for peace in our Churches and in the whole world.

Religion and the Environment: II

The Venice Declaration, signed on June 10, 2002, by HAH Ecumenical Patriarch Bartholomew and HH Pope John Paul II.

We are gathered here today in the spirit of peace for the good of all human beings and for the care of creation. At this moment in history, at the beginning of the third millennium, we are saddened to see the daily suffering of a great number of people from violence, starvation, poverty, and disease. We are also concerned about the ills for humanity and for all creation resulting from the degradation of some basic natural resources such as water, air, and land—degradation brought about by an economic and technological progress that does not recognize and take into account its limits.

Almighty God envisioned a world of beauty and harmony, and he created it, making every part an expression of his freedom, wisdom, and love (see Gen 1.1–25). At the center of the whole of creation, he placed us, human beings, with our inalienable human dignity. Although we share many features with the rest of the living beings, Almighty God went further with us and gave us an immortal soul, the source of self-awareness and freedom, endowments that make us creatures in his image and likeness (see Gen. 1.26–31, 2.7). Marked with that resemblance, we have been placed by God in the world in order to cooperate with him in realizing more and more fully the divine purpose for creation.

At the beginning of history, man and woman sinned by disobeying God and rejecting his design for creation. Among the results of this first sin was the destruction of the original harmony of creation. If we examine carefully the social and environmental crisis that the world community is facing, we must conclude that we are still betraying the mandate God has given us: to be stewards called to collaborate with God in watching over creation in holiness and wisdom.

God has not abandoned the world. It is his will that his design and our hope for it will be realized through our cooperation in restoring its original harmony. In our own time we are witnessing the growth of an *ecological awareness,* which needs to be encouraged, so that it will lead to practical programs and initiatives. An awareness of the relationship between God and humankind brings a fuller sense of the importance of the relationship between human beings and the natural environment, which is God's creation and which God entrusted to us to guard with wisdom and love (see Gen. 1.28). Respect for creation stems from respect for human life and dignity. It is on the basis of our recognition that the world is created by God that we can discern an objective moral order within which to articulate a code of environmental ethics. Seen from this perspective, Christians and all other believers have a specific role to play in proclaiming moral values and in educating people in *ecological awareness*, which is none other than responsibility toward self, toward others, toward creation. What is required is an act of repentance on our part and a renewed attempt to view ourselves, one another, and the world around us within the perspective of the divine design for creation. The problem is not simply economic and technological; it is moral and spiritual. A solution at the economic and technological level can be found only if we undergo, in the most radical way, an inner change of heart, which can lead to a change in lifestyle and of unsustainable patterns of consumption and production. A genuine *conversion* in Christ will enable us to change the way we think and act.

First, we must regain humility and recognize the limits of our powers and, most important, the limits of our knowledge and judgment. We have been making decisions, taking actions, and assigning values that are leading us away from the world as it should be, away from the design of God for creation, away from all that is essential for a healthy planet and a healthy commonwealth of people. A new approach and a new culture are needed, based on the centrality of the human person within creation and inspired by environmentally ethical behavior stemming from our triple relationship to God, to self, and to creation. Such an ethics fosters interdependence and stresses the principles of universal solidarity, social justice, and responsibility, in order to promote a true culture of life.

Second, we must frankly admit that humankind is entitled to something better than what we see around us. We and, much more, our children and future generations are entitled to a better world, a world free from degradation, violence, and bloodshed, a world of generosity and love.

Third, aware of the value of prayer, we must implore God the Creator to enlighten people everywhere regarding the duty to respect and carefully guard creation.

We therefore invite all men and women of goodwill to ponder the importance of the following ethical goals:

1. To think of the world's children when we reflect on and evaluate our options for action.

2. To be open to study the true values based on the natural law that sustains every human culture.

3. To use science and technology in a full and constructive way, while recognizing that the findings of science have always to be evaluated in the light of the centrality of the human person, of the common good, and of the inner purpose of creation. Science may help us to correct the mistakes of the past, in order to enhance the spiritual and material well-being of the present and future generations. It is love for our children that will show us the path that we must follow into the future.

4. To be humble regarding the idea of ownership and to be open to the demands of solidarity. Our mortality and our weakness of judgment together warn us not to take irreversible actions with respect to what we choose to regard as our property during our brief stay on this earth. We have not been entrusted with unlimited power over creation; we are only stewards of the common heritage.

5. To acknowledge the diversity of situations and responsibilities in the work for a better world environment. We do not expect every person and every institution to assume the same burden. Everyone has a part to play, but, for the demands of justice and charity to be respected, the most affluent societies must carry the greater burden, and from them is demanded a sacrifice greater than can be offered by the poor. Religions, governments, and institutions are faced by many different situations, but on the basis of the principle of subsidiarity all of them can take on some tasks, some part of the shared effort.

6. To promote a peaceful approach to disagreement about how to live on this earth, about how to share it and use it, about what to change and what to leave unchanged. It is not our desire to evade controversy about the environment, for we trust in the capacity of human reason and the path of dialogue to reach agreement. We commit ourselves to respect the views of all who disagree with us, seeking solutions through open exchange, without resorting to oppression and domination.

It is not too late. God's world has incredible healing powers. Within a single generation, we could steer the earth toward our children's future. Let that generation start now, with God's help and blessing.

Common Declaration: A Pastoral Message

Common Declaration signed by HAH Ecumenical Patriarch Bartholomew I and HH Pope Benedict XVI on the occasion of the formal visit by the latter to the Phanar, Istanbul, on November 30, 2006.

This is the day that the Lord has made, let us rejoice and be glad in it! (Ps. 117.24)

This fraternal encounter that brings us together, Pope Benedict XVI of Rome and Ecumenical Patriarch Bartholomew I, is God's work and, in a certain sense, his gift. We give thanks to the Author of all that is good, who allows us once again, in prayer and in dialogue, to express the joy we feel as brothers and to renew our commitment to move toward full communion. This commitment comes from the Lord's will and from our responsibility as pastors in the Church of Christ. May our meeting be a sign and an encouragement to us to share the same sentiments and the same attitudes of fraternity, cooperation, and communion in charity and truth. The Holy Spirit will help us to prepare the great day of the reestablishment of full unity, whenever and however God wills it. Then we shall truly be able to rejoice and be glad.

1. We have recalled with thankfulness the meetings of our venerable predecessors, blessed by the Lord, who showed the world the urgent need for unity and traced sure paths for attaining it, through dialogue, prayer, and the daily life of the Church. Pope Paul VI and Patriarch Athenagoras I went as pilgrims to Jerusalem, to the very place where Jesus Christ died and rose again for the salvation of the world, and they also met again, here in the Phanar and in Rome. They left us a common declaration which retains all its value; it emphasizes that true dialogue in charity must sustain and inspire all relations between individuals and between churches, that it "must be rooted in a total fidelity to the one Lord Jesus Christ and in mutual respect for their own traditions" (*Tomos Agapis*, 195).[2] Nor have we forgotten the reciprocal visits of His Holiness Pope John Paul II and His All Holiness Dimitrios I. It was during the visit of Pope John Paul II, his first ecumenical visit, that the creation of the Mixed Commission for theological dialogue between the Roman Catholic

2. *Tomos Agapis: Vatican—Phanar* (1958–1970), ed. D. Papandreou, B. Archondonis, P. Duprey, and C. Dumont (Rome–Istanbul, 1971).

Church and the Orthodox Church was announced. This has brought together our Churches in the declared aim of reestablishing full communion.

As far as relations between the Church of Rome and the Church of Constantinople are concerned, we cannot fail to recall the solemn ecclesial act effacing the memory of the ancient anathemas, which for centuries had a negative effect on our Churches. We have not yet drawn from this act all the positive consequences that can flow from it in our progress toward full unity, to which the mixed Commission is called to make an important contribution. We exhort our faithful to take an active part in this process, through prayer and through significant gestures.

2. At the time of the plenary session of the Mixed Commission for theological dialogue, which was recently held in Belgrade through the generous hospitality of the Serbian Orthodox Church, we expressed our profound joy at the resumption of the theological dialogue. This had been interrupted for several years because of various difficulties, but now the Commission was able to work afresh in a spirit of friendship and cooperation. In treating the topic "Conciliarity and Authority in the Church" at local, regional, and universal levels, the Commission undertook a phase of study on the ecclesiological and canonical consequences of the sacramental nature of the Church. This will permit us to address some of the principal questions that are still unresolved. We are committed to offer unceasing support, as in the past, to the work entrusted to this Commission, and we accompany its members with our prayers.

3. As pastors, we have first of all reflected on the mission to proclaim the gospel in today's world. This mission, "Go, make disciples of all nations" (Mt 28.19), is today more timely and necessary than ever, even in traditionally Christian countries. Moreover, we cannot ignore the increase of secularization, relativism, even nihilism, especially in the Western world. All this calls for a renewed and powerful proclamation of the gospel, adapted to the cultures of our time. Our traditions represent for us a patrimony, which must be continually shared, proposed, and interpreted anew. This is why we must strengthen our cooperation and our common witness before the world.

4. We have viewed positively the process that has led to the formation of the European Union. Those engaged in this great project should not fail to take into consideration all aspects affecting the inalienable rights of the human person, especially religious freedom, a witness and guarantor

of respect for all other freedoms. In every step toward unification, minorities must be protected, together with their cultural traditions and the distinguishing features of their religion. In Europe, while remaining open to other religions and to their cultural contributions, we must unite our efforts to preserve Christian roots, traditions, and values, to ensure respect for history, and so to contribute to the European culture of the future and to the quality of human relations at every level. In this context, how could we not evoke the very ancient witnesses and the illustrious Christian heritage of the land in which our meeting is taking place, beginning with what the Acts of the Apostles tells us concerning the figure of Saint Paul, Apostle of the Gentiles? In this land, the gospel message and the ancient cultural tradition met. This link, which has contributed so much to the Christian heritage that we share, remains timely and will bear more fruit in the future for evangelization and for our unity.

5. Our concern extends to those parts of today's world where Christians live and to the difficulties they have to face, particularly poverty, wars, and terrorism, but equally to various forms of exploitation of the poor, of migrants, women, and children. We are called to work together to promote respect for the rights of every human being, created in the image and likeness of God, and to foster economic, social, and cultural development. Our theological and ethical traditions can offer a solid basis for a united approach in preaching and action. Above all, we wish to affirm that killing innocent people in God's name is an offense against him and against human dignity. We must all commit ourselves to the renewed service of humanity and the defense of human life, every human life.

We take profoundly to heart the cause of peace in the Middle East, where our Lord lived, suffered, died, and rose again, and where a great multitude of our Christian brethren have lived for centuries. We fervently hope that peace will be reestablished in that region, that respectful coexistence will be strengthened between the different peoples that live there, between the Churches, and between the different religions found there. To this end, we encourage the establishment of closer relationships between Christians and of an authentic and honest interreligious dialogue, with a view to combating every form of violence and discrimination.

6. At present, in the face of the great threats to the natural environment, we want to express our concern at the negative consequences, for

humanity and for the whole of creation, that can result from economic and technological progress that does not know its limits. As religious leaders, we consider it one of our duties to encourage and to support all efforts made to protect God's creation and to bequeath to future generations a world in which they will be able to live.

7. Finally, our thoughts turn toward all of you, the faithful of our two Churches throughout the world—bishops, priests, deacons, men, and women religious, laymen and laywomen engaged in ecclesial service, and all the baptized. In Christ we greet other Christians, assuring them of our prayers and our openness to dialogue and cooperation. In the words of the Apostle of the Gentiles, we greet all of you: "Grace to you and peace from God our Father and the Lord Jesus Christ" (2 Cor 1.2).

Peace and Tolerance: I

The Bosphorus Declaration, signed in Istanbul on February 9, 1994, during the International Peace and Tolerance Conference, cosponsored by the Ecumenical Patriarchate and the Appeal of Conscience Foundation.

I. The participants in the Conference of Peace and Tolerance wish to thank the government of Turkey for the courteous hospitality it has extended to us and for giving us an opportunity to pursue our deliberations on the vital issues of peace and tolerance.

The conference wishes to recognize the contributions of President Clinton, President Demirel, Secretary-General Boutros Boutros-Ghali, and all the other religious and political leaders who have sent messages of support.

In this declaration we wish specifically to refer to the Berne Declaration of November 26, 1992, which has given us a foundation on which to build. That declaration specifically states that "a crime committed in the name of religion is a crime against religion."

Since November 26, 1992, we have seen many crimes committed in the name of religion and we, the conference participants, wish to speak out vigorously against them. As recent events have shown, the crimes against humanity continue in Bosnia, Armenia/Azerbaijan, Georgia, and Tajikistan. The cruelties have continued unchecked, and we demand an end to this brutality.

We, the undersigned, reject any attempt to corrupt the basic tenets of our faith by means of false interpretation and unchecked nationalism. We stand firmly against those who violate the sanctity of human life and pursue policies in defiance of moral values. We reject the concept that it is possible to justify ones actions in any armed conflict in the name of God.

We wish to emphatically remind all the faithful that the scriptures of all three monotheistic religions specifically speak of peace as a supreme value. "Blessed are the peacemakers, for they will be called children of God." "Allah summoneth to the abode of peace." "His ways are the ways of peace."

II. We reiterate that the war in former Yugoslavia is not a religious war and that appeals and exploitations of religious symbols to further the cause of aggressive nationalism are a betrayal of the universality of religious faith. We emphasize the imperative of freedom of conscience and freedom of religion of every minority. We call for an end to the confiscation, desecration, and destruction of houses of worship and of holy and sacred places of whatever religious tradition. We totally abhor and condemn ethnic cleansing and the rape and murder of women and children. We demand the removal of obstacles that prevent humanitarian assistance from reaching those who are suffering.

We condemn the use of force in countries of the former Soviet Union. The conflicts in Georgia, Armenia/Azerbaijan, and Tajikistan must be concluded immediately, and solutions for the outstanding issues must be found by other means.

We recognize that all who are suffering are victims, but we single out specifically the most tragic and innocent victims, who are the children.

III. We ask our religious communities to embrace in God's love those children from the areas of conflict and to extend all possible assistance to the suffering children, to help them find spiritual, psychological, and physical healing. We cannot emphasize enough that spiritual nourishment is a paramount requirement; religious communities must be supported. We also recognize that all the countries suffering from conflict have had a long, dark period of communism during which there was little or no spiritual education. We urge all faiths to redouble their efforts for spiritual guidance for those who were deprived.

We wish to recognize also that tension exists within faiths and urge the leaderships of those faiths to bring about peaceful resolutions to the issues that divide them.

IV. The conference participants, like all others who have followed these tragic conflicts, observe with horror the forced migration of refugees. Millions have experienced or are threatened by forcible displacement. Therefore, we call on all religious faiths to speak out clearly and consistently against these actions. We condemn those who uproot families from their homes, tear children from their parents, divide husband and wife in the name of false nationalism. We expect all religious leaders to stand fast in the protection of all those threatened by involuntary migration, whatever their religious beliefs or ethnic backgrounds. We demand that all refugees who have left their home involuntarily be permitted to return with dignity and honor; that the religious communities strengthen their institutions to receive, assist, and protect refugees of whatever faith; that religious and lay relief agencies develop procedures to coordinate their efforts. As long as the conflicts continue, we urge all countries to extend temporary asylum to victims while granting opportunity for refugee status to those who truly seek it, to increase resources for relief, and to work with all who are of good faith for the cessation of hostilities.

V. The participants in the Conference on Peace and Tolerance have agreed unanimously to utterly condemn war and armed conflict, to demand that no hostile acts be perpetrated on any peaceful group or region in the name of a religious faith, to demand the initiation of constructive dialogues to solve outstanding issues between those of different faiths, and to demand the right to practice one's religion in freedom and with dignity.

VI. We have deliberated carefully and are in agreement that the wanton killing must stop, that those who continue to perpetrate such heinous acts are criminals, and that, although we have no weapons of war and no armies for combat, we have a greater strength—the strength of spiritual might. We totally condemn those who commit the brutalities, killing, rape, mutilation, forcible displacement, and inhuman beating.

VII. We, the conference participants, have decided to establish an Appeal of Conscience Conflict Resolution Commission to deal with ethnic conflicts. This commission will be made up of representatives from all of the faiths and from all of the countries represented at this conference. The

Appeal of Conscience Conflict Resolution Commission will be responsible for informing commission members and recommending ways and means to deal with the scourge of extreme nationalism and ethnic conflict.

Peace and Tolerance: II

Second Declaration signed in Istanbul on November 9, 2005, during the International Peace and Tolerance Conference, cosponsored by the Ecumenical Patriarchate and the Appeal of Conscience Foundation.

I. We, the participants in the Conference on Peace and Tolerance II: Dialogue and Understanding in South East Europe, the Caucasus and Central Asia, cosponsored by the Ecumenical Patriarchate and the Appeal of Conscience Foundation, wish to thank the government of Turkey and the president of the Office of Religious Affairs, Professor Dr. Ali Bardakoğlu, for their courteous assistance and cooperation, as we have assembled to focus on the vital message of peace and tolerance that we wish to bring to the countries of those three regions.

The conference wishes to take into account the important concerns conveyed by President George W. Bush; Secretary-General of the United Nations Kofi Annan; His Holiness Pope Benedict XVI; the president of the European Union Commission, José Manuel Barroso; the secretary general of the World Islamic Call Society, Dr. Mohamed Ahmed Sherif; the director general of UNESCO, Koishuro Matsura; Her Excellency Mrs. Marietta Giannakou, minister of Education and Religious Affairs of the Hellenic Republic, and by the many other religious and political leaders who have sent messages of support.

We applaud the recent initiative taken by the secretary-general of the U.N. on the establishment of the Alliance of Civilization. We recommend that the alliance be enhanced through interreligious dialogue, that it consult and cooperate with national political and religious leaders to investigate and recommend to the secretary-general remedial measures concerning acts of religious and ethnic violence.

II. This conference continued the deliberations on peace and tolerance that began in Berne in 1992 and continued here in 1994. While most of the deadly conflicts that raged then have ceased, unfortunately there is still distrust, suspicion, and the threat of harm as well as intermittent violence in the regions represented. It is our aim, as religious leaders of our countries, to militate against those dangerous paths, heal painful memories, and encourage all to exhibit in their actions the spirit of "live and let live."

As spiritual leaders of the children of Abraham, we are obligated to diminish ethnic and religious tensions. In that spirit we call on all leaders of faith to preach, teach, and practice love, tolerance, and understanding of one another and other faiths and ethnic communities in their mosques, churches, and synagogues, in their families, schools, and seminaries. We must also accept responsibility for promoting education, nurture, and encouragement among all members of our communities, women and men, young and old, exhorting them to engage in committed efforts to ensure that the injuries and conflicts of our past will not be repeated.

Recently Southeastern Europe has witnessed significant positive developments toward mutual dialogue, reconciliation, and cooperation. We recognize the important, continuing, and intensifying activities by the United Nations and the OSCE in Southeastern Europe and welcome the progress they are making. However, serious problems still exist with respect to protection of religious and ethnic rights and tolerance. Crimes continue to be committed in the name of religion. We reiterate, in our most vigorous voice, that such actions must stop. As stated in the Appeal of Conscience Declaration signed in Berne, Switzerland, in 1992: "A crime committed in the name of religion is a crime against religion."

We deplore those who preach violence toward other faiths and ethnic communities. Believing in the sanctity of human life, we firmly stand against those who violate and defy basic human values. We reject all actions that corrupt the basic tenets of our faiths by means of false interpretation and unchecked nationalism. And we vigorously reject the assertion that justification of an action in any armed conflict can be attributed to God. Such justification will not lead to peace. We demand the firm establishment of the rule of law with respect to fundamental human rights in all countries represented at this conference and urgently seek to encourage all to ensure proper care of refugees and internally displaced peoples and active protection of minorities.

The scourge of international terrorism that defiles the tenets of morality of our monotheistic religions has intensified since 1994. We condemn as lawless murderers those who engage in such heinous crimes and call on all religious leaders to speak out forcefully against them.

It is vital to remember, and we remind all the faithful emphatically, that the scriptures of all monotheistic religions consider peace a supreme value and vocation. As we said in 1994, "His ways are the ways of peace," "Blessed are the peacemakers, for they will be called children of God," "Allah summoneth to the abode of Peace."

III. We call on religious leaders in Southeastern Europe, the Caucasus, and Central Asia to support without reservation all interreligious dialogues for peace, justice, and human rights and strongly encourage them to become partners in sincere and open dialogue with each other.

We reject violence and totally and unconditionally condemn the use of force, ethnic cleansing, and brutality. We demand that all hold safe and protect the religious edifices and monuments of all religions, in keeping with United Nations Resolution A/RES/55/254 for the Protection of Religious Sites, which was adopted unanimously by the General Assembly. We ask for the appointment of a special representative to monitor compliance with that resolution.

IV. We understand and lament the inhuman suffering of innocents that results from the consequences of violent conflict, and we recognize the tragedy of those peace-loving peoples of faith who are victimized because of their faith, but we most especially recognize the plight of innocent children, the elderly, and the infirm, who are the most helpless victims of conflict. Therefore, we ask the religious communities to nurture and assist the suffering children, the sick, and aged, no matter what faith they profess, to help them find spiritual, psychological, and physical healing.

V. We, the conference participants, recognize that much has been accomplished since 1994. Although wars have diminished in number, tensions still exist, fueled by intemperate rhetoric, and have flared into brutal acts. We resolutely reject the use of language that incites people to violence. We encourage religious leaders to work with the political leadership in their respective countries to promote peace, justice, and human and religious rights.

VI. The participants in the Conference on Peace and Tolerance have unanimously reaffirmed the previous agreement made at the first Peace and Tolerance Conference in 1994, condemning wanton killing and calling for it to stop. We believe that those who engage in such heinous acts are criminals; we abhor those who commit or threaten brutality, killing, rape, and mutilation; we deplore those who engage in the destruction of religious edifices, shrines, and monuments; we reject war and armed conflict, praying for reconciliation, coexistence, and peace; we demand that no hostile acts be perpetrated against any peaceful group or region in the name of religious faith; we pray that constructive dialogues be continued, to resolve outstanding issues between those of different faiths; we affirm the right to practice one's religion in freedom and with dignity.

VII. We humbly express our gratitude to God for the opportunity he has granted us to reaffirm our commitment to deliberate together in order to promote peace, justice, and human dignity.

The Brussels Declaration

"The Peace of God in the World: Toward Peaceful Coexistence and Collaboration among the Three Monotheistic Religions." Signed in Brussels on December 20, 2001.

Grateful to God for this opportunity to come together, we, the participants of this interreligious meeting, have gathered at the invitation of His All Holiness Bartholomew, the Ecumenical Patriarch, and His Excellency Romano Prodi, president of the European Commission, in Brussels, Belgium, on December 19–20, 2001. Mindful of the horrific terrorist attacks of September 11 in the United States of America, and equally mindful of the existing conflicts in various regions of the world, we have considered in a spirit of goodwill and sincere disposition the positive contributions of Judaism, Christianity, and Islam to the present condition of humanity. It is precisely on the basis of our respect for the diversity of our religions that we engage in this dialogue. Based on these discussions, we, therefore, strive to fulfill our common responsibility to proclaim together "The Peace of God in the World" as embodied within the teachings of our respective religions.

1. The will of God is for the peace of heaven to reign on earth. The peace of God is not the mere absence of war; it is the gift of abundant life. There is indeed an immediate and inseparable connection between

peace and justice. Therefore we pray constantly for peace to prevail in the world and for peaceful coexistence among the faithful of all religions in our modern, multicultural, and multiethnic global society.

2. Recognizing that, in the history of humankind, members of religious communities have committed crimes, we express our regret and repentance. We nevertheless affirm that extremists do not reflect the teachings of these religions, and therefore religious beliefs are not responsible for the acts of adherents that are committed either by transgression or by misinterpretation. This is why we reaffirm the statement, of the 1992 Berne Declaration and the 1994 Bosphorus Declaration, that "a crime committed in the name of religion is a crime against religion."

3. One major role of religion is to bring the peace of God into the world on a local and global level. It is the responsibility of religious leaders to prevent religious fervor from being used for purposes that are alien to its role.

4. A fundamental common element of our monotheistic religions is faith and confidence in the good, human-loving, compassionate, and merciful God. The offer of God's love is open to all human beings for free acceptance and without constraint, regardless of race, ethnicity, culture, or gender.

5. The response to God's invitation by the believer is achieved through faith, which is expressed through prayer, love, good works, respect for the other, and in contributing to a just society and social order. Indeed, the essence of each religion is manifested best by those who are pure of heart.

6. All of our religions consider justice and peace as gifts and blessings from God and as duties of every human being to one another. None of them approves of violence, terrorism, or ill treatment of human beings. All of them disapprove of religious justification of violent and inhuman actions, which do not conform to the spirit of peace and justice, of peaceful cooperation, and of respect for the dignity of the human person.

In view of these truths:

7. We emphasize the need to address causes of local and regional tensions, especially in the developing world. Injustices do exist, and we respect the efforts of those who strive to redress them. Nevertheless, this is not a justification for evil that would destroy innocent human life. Hence the call, in all of our religions, is to bring peace with freedom, justice, and human rights.

8. We unanimously reject the assumption that religion contributes to an inevitable clash of civilizations. On the contrary, we affirm the constructive and instructive role of religion in the dialogue among civilizations.

9. We urge those who shape public opinion to avoid putting at risk the good relations and peaceful cooperation of all people through the projection of extremist religious views as representative of authentic religious belief.

10. Rejecting all forms of discrimination, we support the principles of mutual respect, reciprocity, human rights, religious freedom, peaceful coexistence, and multireligious cooperation.

11. We appeal to all of the leaders of the peoples of the world to make every effort toward the peaceful resolution of conflicts. In the spirit of peaceful coexistence, we call for an end to the violence in the Middle East and for a return to the peace process. We therefore pray that, wherever there are clashes, people will come to enjoy peace with justice. Our conviction is that all moral, political, and financial resources should be used to improve the integral development of all human beings and nations.

12. In solidarity, and sustained by our respective spiritual resources, we commit ourselves to cooperate in efforts that lead to peace in the world. To this end, we address a joint appeal to all men and women of goodwill in all walks of life—and particularly to those whose religious and political positions carry the responsibility to work for the benefit of the common good—to be convinced of this call to peaceful collaboration.

13. In unity, solidarity, and love, with the prayer that our efforts will lead to "The Peace of God in the World," we commit ourselves and call on our respective religious communities:

> a. To engage educators, members of the media, policymakers, and other individuals as well as institutions in civil society, in order to enhance understanding of religious communities and their beliefs and to familiarize them with these communities' respective historical, cultural, and religious heritages worldwide. With regard specifically to education, this calls for the elimination from textbooks of prejudicial and discriminatory statements or references concerning religions, cultures, and ethnic groups.
>
> b. To support ongoing and new interreligious and cross-cultural initiatives, including youth initiatives, in as many regions as possible throughout

the world. Mindful that discriminatory behavior is learned rather than innate, we commit ourselves to educating our spiritual leaders and faithful in the ways of peace, mutual respect, and trust.

c. To continue our dialogue and encourage all efforts to promote collaboration among our three religions, as demonstrated by the participants of this meeting.

d. To foster communication networks that promote the exchange of views and ideas on a regular basis.

The Bahrain Declaration

The conclusion to the Tenth Session of the Muslim–Christian Dialogue, held in Manama, capital of the kingdom of Bahrain, October 30, 2002.

In accordance with the directives of His Majesty Sheikh Hamad Bin Issa Al-Khalifah, king of the kingdom of Bahrain, and in response to a proposal by His All Holiness the Ecumenical Patriarch Bartholomew I, and to enhance cooperation between Muslims and Christians on the road to reinforcing peaceful coexistence and international cooperation between them, to exchange views on contemporary issues of mutual importance, to establish a mutual basis of understanding between believers from both religions, to achieve peaceful coexistence on three levels—local, regional, and international—and to lay the foundations of world peace that are based on the common basis embodied in the values matrix that combines the divine message of Islam and Christianity.

By hosting the Tenth Session of the Muslim–Christian Dialogue Conference in accordance with its rooted belief in the importance of dialogue on all levels, Bahrain calls all peoples and nations, in search of peaceful coexistence and the negation of violence, to work on reinforcing the dialogue methodology; it also calls for the exchange of views on contemporary issues in the service of humanity, for achieving security and happiness for mankind, for sparing mankind the dangers of conflict (reminding all peoples and nations at the same time of the noble principles embodied in the messages both of Islam and of Christianity), for the achievement of mutual coexistence, and for the respect of religious and national specificities; Bahrain encourages constructive cooperation and supports the efforts of Muslim and Christian scholars and intellectuals in efforts to consolidate bases of peaceful coexistence and in respect for the other, in accordance with the teachings of Islam and Christianity.

And building on the aims of this conference in which Muslims and Christians have assembled for constructive, purposeful dialogue, the participants urge the following:

1. Continue with dialogue and encourage efforts aimed at cooperation for achieving peaceful coexistence.
2. Cooperate, after the interreligious dialogue, in healing the traumatic experiences of the historic past, by taking concrete initiatives addressed to the local society, so as to remove negative prejudices and to foster respect among their faithful for the particularity of other religious traditions.
3. Work together in an international perspective on modern interreligious dialogue to promote the idea of peace with freedom and social justice and to extend protection for human rights to relations between peoples and nations on a global scale.
4. Realize that violence breeds violence and that suppression breeds animosity and hatred, so that concerned authorities should stand up to tackle violence through constructive dialogue rather than repression.
5. Highlight religion's principles—tolerance and mercy toward mankind—and give the real reason for its purposes, which are to achieve happiness for mankind and establish security, safety, and peaceful coexistence on earth.
6. Respect the national, religious, and cultural specificities of each society.
7. Remove impediments to people's proper and correct understanding of their religion.
8. Encourage civil-society organizations in every community to assume their role in protecting individuals from confused intellectual invasion and in protecting individuals mentally, psychologically, and ethically from any ensuing harm.
9. Care for the rights of the human being and work toward realizing his security and safety by ensuring that concerned authorities are doing what they are entrusted with in this regard.

10. Spread to all concerned individuals, through education and mass media, the right understanding of Islam and Christianity—a correct method that, for information on each religion, returns to that religion's authentic accepted sources.

The participants and organizers of the conference are delighted to convey their heartfelt feelings of gratitude and appreciation to His Majesty Sheikh Hamad Bin Issa Al-Khalifah, the king of Bahrain, for his support of the conference, despite conflicting engagements, in accordance with His Majesty's belief in the necessity of supporting the spirit of cooperation, understanding, and love among nations and peoples.

The participants also highly commended the spirit of fraternity, mutual harmony, love, and objectivity that characterized their conference, expressing their appreciation to the people and government of Bahrain for the hospitality extended to them. The participants and organizers also expressed their gratitude to His Excellency Sheikh Abdullah Bin Khaled Al-Khalifah, minister of Justice and Islamic Affairs in the kingdom of Bahrain, who patronized the conference, representing His Majesty Sheikh Hamad Bin Issa Al-Khalifah, king of the kingdom of Bahrain; to His Grace Bishop Emmanuel of Reghion, director of the Office of Interreligious and Intercultural Relations of the Ecumenical Patriarchate; to all Muslim and Christian scholars and intellectuals for their papers, commentaries, and discussions during the conference; and to all chairpersons and members of the committees working in preparation for this conference.

May God Almighty grant success to mankind on the road to righteousness and wisdom.

The Amaroussion Declaration

"Religion, Peace, and the Olympic Ideal," an interreligious conference held in Athens, August 11, 2004, on the occasion of the Olympic Games.

The convocation of the international Interreligious Conference by His All Holiness Ecumenical Patriarch Bartholomew and by Mayor Panayotis Tzannikos of the Olympic Municipality of Amaroussion, under the auspices of His Excellency President Constantine Stephanopoulos of the

Hellenic Republic, with the participation of eminent representatives of Judaism, Christianity, Islam, and Buddhism is one of the events taking place in Athens on the occasion of the opening of the Olympic Games. The conference seeks to reflect religion's special mission in achieving peaceful coexistence among all human beings and all peoples of the world.

The Olympic ideal manifests the lofty spiritual and moral values of the great cultural heritage of Greek classical antiquity, which have influenced all major cultural traditions of the world to a greater or lesser extent, because in those values human beings were conceived of in reference to the *physical* and *metaphysical* reality of the world. Thus, in those values the human position of supremacy was interpreted without human beings' being cut off from the divine or from the worldly, and without their being identified with any specific religious tradition, philosophical theory, or system of ideology. Consequently, they assumed an enduring significance for all humanity. The heritage of the Olympic Games is an important aspect of this effulgence, which grows still brighter on account of the Games' homecoming.

We, the participants in the Interreligious Conference of Athens, as representatives of the major religions of the world, are fully aware both of the profound relationship between the religions and the cultural traditions of all peoples and of the special responsibility of religions to advocate established moral values. Therefore, on this momentous occasion we jointly declare our hope that our message, as it reaches out far and wide from this forum, will reverberate within the hearts of the adherents of all religions and especially within the hearts of their youth and within the hearts of those who have responsibility for leadership in our world.

1. It is our common understanding that the *divine* and the *human* converge in all religions upholding the sanctity of human life, and that therefore each in its own special way emphasizes the values of liberty, justice, brotherhood, solidarity, and love, with a view toward peaceful coexistence among all human beings and all peoples, particularly in our modern multicultural global community.

2. We acknowledge that religions have occasionally been abused in the past to serve national, political, religious, and other expedients that are extraneous to their spiritual mission and that, in their name, and in deviation from their teachings, crimes and atrocities have been perpetrated against innocent people. Given that, we expressly and categorically repudiate all

violence, terrorism, or criminal action carried out ostensibly in the name of religion, thereby reasserting our interreligious declaration that all crimes perpetrated in the name of religion are crimes against religion itself.

3. We repudiate all forms of nationalist, racist, religious, social, and other discrimination, by means of which morbid religious intolerance and fanaticism are harbored; we repudiate these together with the seeking of justification for bellicose conflicts and organized terrorism, a proclivity that is to the obvious immense detriment of the peaceful coexistence of all human beings and all people. Therefore, we launch an appeal to the spiritual leaders of all religions to undertake the work that is necessary and to cooperate in efforts to defuse these perilous confusions, in order thereby to achieve the truly credible furtherance of God's will that peace, social justice, and respect for fundamental human rights will prevail.

4. We also launch an appeal to political and intellectual leaders of all peoples and international bodies to avail themselves of the opportunity to make use of the institutional role of religion in a positive manner, in order to achieve the peaceful resolution of local, regional, and more general conflicts and to realize an ambitious plan for *education toward peace*, in order to remedy the prepossessions and painful experiences of the past. We urge that the cooperation of all contemporary mass media be secured for this plan, in order that the widest possible outreach be achieved.

5. We reassert our unwavering resolve to continue with our constructive interreligious dialogues both to achieve a spirit of mutual understanding and sincere cooperation and to promote such a spirit in the practical affairs of our contemporary multicultural society. Accordingly, we give our full support to all interreligious and intercultural initiatives that are guided by such a spirit.

6. From this forum so kindly given to us by the Olympic Municipality of Amaroussion, we extend a special invitation to the youth of all religious and cultural traditions to join us in embracing the vision of peace through personally striving as *peacemakers*, since this hallowed endeavor seeks to preserve the sanctity of life, to restore the integrity of divine creation, and to attain social justice in the relations of all human beings and all peoples, wherefore the crown of victory of such peacemakers is recognized by all of humanity as the loftiest of all crowns.

Index

www.ingramcontent.com/pod-product-compliance
Lightning Source LLC
Chambersburg PA
CBHW030641150426
42811CB00076B/2003/J
* 9 7 8 0 8 2 3 2 3 1 7 1 3 *